Promoting Academic Success with English Language Learners

The Guilford Practical Intervention in the Schools Series

Kenneth W. Merrell, Founding Editor
T. Chris Riley-Tillman, Series Editor

www.guilford.com/practical

This series presents the most reader-friendly resources available in key areas of evidence-based practice in school settings. Practitioners will find trustworthy guides on effective behavioral, mental health, and academic interventions, and assessment and measurement approaches. Covering all aspects of planning, implementing, and evaluating high-quality services for students, books in the series are carefully crafted for everyday utility. Features include ready-to-use reproducibles, lay-flat binding to facilitate photocopying, appealing visual elements, and an oversized format. Recent titles have Web pages where purchasers can download and print the reproducible materials.

Recent Volumes

RTI Applications, Volume 2: Assessment, Analysis, and Decision Making
T. Chris Riley-Tillman, Matthew K. Burns, and Kimberly Gibbons

Daily Behavior Report Cards: An Evidence-Based System of Assessment and Intervention
Robert J. Volpe and Gregory A. Fabiano

Assessing Intelligence in Children and Adolescents:
A Practical Guide
John H. Kranzler and Randy G. Floyd

The RTI Approach to Evaluating Learning Disabilities
Joseph F. Kovaleski, Amanda M. VanDerHayden, and Edward S. Shapiro

Resilient Classrooms, Second Edition: Creating Healthy Environments for Learning
Beth Doll, Katherine Brehm, and Steven Zucker

The ABCs of Curriculum-Based Evaluation:
A Practical Guide to Effective Decision Making
John L. Hosp, Michelle K. Hosp, Kenneth W. Howell, and Randy Allison

Curriculum-Based Assessment for Instructional Design:
Using Data to Individualize Instruction
Matthew K. Burns and David C. Parker

Dropout Prevention
C. Lee Goss and Kristina J. Andren

Stress Management for Teachers: A Proactive Guide
Keith C. Herman and Wendy M. Reinke

Interventions for Reading Problems, Second Edition:
Designing and Evaluating Effective Strategies
*Edward J. Daly III, Sabina Neugebauer, Sandra Chafouleas,
and Christopher H. Skinner*

Classwide Positive Behavior Interventions and Supports:
A Guide to Proactive Classroom Management
Brandi Simonsen and Diane Myers

Promoting Academic Success with English Language Learners: Best Practices for RTI
Craig A. Albers and Rebecca S. Martinez

Promoting Academic Success with English Language Learners

Best Practices for RTI

CRAIG A. ALBERS
REBECCA S. MARTINEZ

THE GUILFORD PRESS
New York   London

© 2015 The Guilford Press
A Division of Guilford Publications, Inc.
370 Seventh Avenue, Suite 1200, New York, NY 10001
www.guilford.com

Printed in Canada

This book is printed on acid-free paper.

Last digit is print number: 9 8 7 6 5 4 3 2 1

Library of Congress Cataloging-in-Publication Data

Albers, Craig A., 1971–
     Promoting academic success with English language learners : best practices for RTI / Craig A.
Albers, Rebecca S. Martinez.
     pages cm.—(Guilford practical intervention in the schools series)
     Includes bibliographical references and index.
     ISBN 978-1-4625-2126-5 (paperback : acid-free paper)
     1. English language—Study and teaching (Elementary)—United States—Foreign speakers.
2. Limited English proficient students—United States. 3. Response to intervention (Learning
disabled children)—United States. 4. Academic achievement—United States. I. Martinez,
Rebecca S. II. Title.
     PE1128.A2A347 2015
     372.652'1044—dc23

                                                                        2015009920

About the Authors

Craig A. Albers, PhD, is Associate Professor of Educational Psychology in the School Psychology Program at the University of Wisconsin–Madison, where he also serves as Chair of the interdisciplinary Prevention and Intervention Sciences Program. Prior to joining the University of Wisconsin in 2004, Dr. Albers worked as a school psychologist in the Kyrene School District in Phoenix, Arizona. His research focuses on universal screening, prevention, and early intervention services; the provision of school psychological services to English language learners (ELLs); and the measurement and resulting intervention implications of English language proficiency assessment. Dr. Albers is the author of Alternate ACCESS for ELLs, an English language proficiency measure designed for use with ELLs with significant disabilities, which is currently administered in 34 states. He is also Associate Editor of the *Journal of School Psychology*.

Rebecca S. Martinez, PhD, is Associate Professor in the School Psychology Program at Indiana University. A native Spanish speaker, Dr. Martinez was raised in Mexico City, Mexico, where she attended elementary school through the third grade. After obtaining her bachelor's degree, she joined Teach for America and became a bilingual education teacher on the Texas–Mexico border. Her research and practice focus on the prevention of and intervention for children's academic failure, particularly for ELLs. Dr. Martinez has published multiple book chapters and peer-reviewed empirical articles.

Contents

List of Tables, Figures, and Appendices

TABLES

FIGURES

APPENDICES

CHAPTER 1

Introduction

The statistics are clear: The student population in U.S. schools has become and is increasingly growing more heterogeneous in terms of linguistic, cultural, and racial diversity. The statistics also clearly indicate that a significant number of schools are failing to meet the needs of many students; these students include those considered to be "traditional" in the sense that they are classified as white and native English speakers, and also those who are considered to be linguistically, culturally, or racially diverse. The fundamental argument is that those of us working in the educational system need to reconsider how we go about providing an exceptional education to *all* of these students. In years past, we believed that *students* needed to be ready for school. This deficits-based approach is outdated, and the challenge is now to ensure that *schools* become ready—and willing—to meet the needs of *all* students, irrespective of what characteristics students bring with them to the school setting. Thus, the education system has reached a crossroads in which our fundamental assumptions about how best to educate our children are undergoing significant and (in some cases) radical change. Although these burgeoning educational changes and implicit educational mandates apply to all students, they particularly apply to students classified as English language learners (ELLs[1]), who are the focus of this book. These changes are perhaps best represented by the widespread adoption of a service delivery model that has been referred to variously as response to instruction, response to intervention (RTI), or response to instruction *and* intervention (RTI[2]). For all intents and purposes, however, the terms are identical. In this book we adopt the term *response to intervention* (RTI) because this appears to be the most commonly utilized description we have come across in our collective experience

---

[1]Numerous terms have been proposed to refer to non-native English-speaking students, including English learner (EL), limited English proficient (LEP), English as a second language (ESL) learner, and English language learner (ELL). We use the term ELL, consistent with terminology used by the federal government and many professional organizations. Additionally, others (e.g., Francis, Rivera, Lesaux, Kieffer, & Rivera, 2006a, 2006b) suggest that ELL is the preferable term, because it emphasizes accomplishments rather than deficits (e.g., LEP).

teaching, writing, and utilizing RTI at our respective universities and across the country. In this book, we also consider RTI to be a schoolwide framework for academic instruction, and as such, RTI cannot optimally operate without each of the components being implemented in a comprehensive and integrated manner. Inherent in the definition of *response to intervention* is the notion that *instruction* and *intervention* are simply interchangeable terms describing the act of teaching, which involves transferring learning from one person (i.e., teacher) to another person or group (i.e., learner/s). Within this book, we specifically address how to transfer this learning to ELLs. Although we are advocating the use of RTI models with ELLs, much of what we discuss and propose is applicable to all students, as there is increasing evidence that *all* students are ELLs to some degree (in the sense that all students need to acquire English *academic* language proficiency, or the language used in school settings for academic gain). Our focus in this book is on ways that schools can effectively incorporate teaching of ELLs into their existing RTI models. RTI has great potential to influence ELLs' educational trajectories positively. Most notably, the successful implementation of RTI models potentially can reduce the overidentification of ELL students in special education (where they are not always ideally serviced) and simultaneously identify ELLs who have true disabilities and for whom special education is ideally suited.

THE PHILOSOPHY GUIDING THIS BOOK

To be successful in the prototypical U.S., English-dominant public school, ELLs must not only learn communicative (i.e., social) English but they must also become proficient in English *academic* language, which experts estimate can take 7 years (or more!) to develop and is dependent on a wide number of mediating and moderating variables (Dixon et al., 2012; Thomas & Collier, 1997). We assert that academic success in the United States requires a command of basic *English language,* as well as mastery of *academic language* and tasks in English. Indeed, ELLs who are educated in the United States are expected by federal law to be taught to read at grade level by the third grade (No Child Left Behind Act of 2001 [NCLB], 2002). Identifying best instructional practices for promoting language proficiency and academic success in English in the ELL population is an urgent educational priority; indeed, we consider it a cultural imperative. Ensuring that ELLs have an opportunity to benefit academically likely is not possible without providing educators with first-rate professional development, in vivo instructional coaching opportunities, and time during the instructional day to collaborate with other educators on planning and instruction. Equipping teachers to provide outstanding educational opportunities for ELLs is urgent in light of the exponential and sustained increase of ELL students in American schools. Consequently, our purpose in this book is to provide a wide audience of preservice and inservice educators (e.g., teachers, classroom aides or paraprofessionals, administrators, school psychologists, speech–language pathologists, and other staff members who work with ELL students) a pragmatic, go-to manual that will help them integrate the core principles of RTI in their daily work with ELLs. Although the practices and principles we describe in the chapters of this book do not guarantee successful outcomes, they certainly increase the likelihood that all students, including ELLs, can achieve acceptable—even exceptional—rates of academic progress in U.S. schools.

In 1974, the Supreme Court ruled in *Lau v. Nichols* that teaching ELLs in a language they do not understand—and failing to provide them with appropriate supplemental instruction—is a violation of ELLs' civil rights. No specific guidance about how to address this educational directive was offered by the Court, so it was up to each state to determine how best to meet the academic needs of its ELLs. Consequently, wide-ranging philosophies about how best to teach ELLs have proliferated in the literature and in the field for almost four decades, with resulting evidence that is rarely definitive and sometimes even contradicts prior research results. As authors of this text, we want the reader, prior to reading this book, to be aware of our personal stance regarding the controversial topic of teaching ELLs. In our collective professional work and activism efforts on behalf of immigrant, migrant, and later generation ELLs over the past two decades, we have been unwavering in promoting maintenance of ELLs' native language and culture. Indeed, promoting and furthering the native language actually *bolsters* academic achievement in English (Goldenberg, 2010)! Moreover, one of us (R. S. M.) is a native of Mexico who, despite being educated in the United States for the last 30 years, has very proudly maintained her bicultural heritage and native language. Nonetheless, as two successful working professionals who have the careers we have *because* of our education in U.S. schools, we also consider *mastery of Academic English language in school as the foundation for personal, academic, and vocational success in the United States.* We recognize, and accept the fact, that our stance may be met with opposition. Nevertheless, we have both an ethical obligation to present information that will empower our readers and the ELLs with whom they work and a legal obligation to deliver information that is based on what works. Both of us are providers of professional development and consider this text to be a means of providing such training. The law is very clear that as *eligible* professional development providers, we are responsible for delivering training and knowledge that is rooted in science (Individuals With Disabilities Education Act, Section 1208 [2]). Thus, in this book, to ensure the academic success of all ELLs in U.S. schools, we cannot and will not present gimmicky solutions to a serious issue. We will, however, share with our readers the latest research, coupled with knowledge of best practices for increasing the likelihood that all students, including ELLs, will experience academic school success.

Our beliefs partially are driven by the reality of the current political and economic conditions within the United States, which often dictate educational pedagogy. Nevertheless, we do not intend to address these political issues and mandates, nor do we want to use these pages to rehash the same arguments that are addressed in other resources. Rather, our hope is to provide direction to educators throughout the country who are working on a daily basis with ELLs, and who are counted on to provide a high-quality education to *all* students. In short, we believe that safeguarding the academic success in *English* for *all* students—including ELLs—is the unrivaled responsibility of each and every educator in each and every school across the United States. For too many years we have heard the debate about whether schools should use a bilingual approach or an English-only approach when teaching ELLs. However, this debate overlooks a more important question: *How can educators promote ELLs' levels of academic success as compared to only facilitating acquisition of basic English?* In the following chapters, we aim to convey our position with respect (for student, family, and teacher), and an underlying sense of urgency for the work that must happen in schools *now* to ensure the academic, language, and personal success of ELL students.

THIS IS NOT AN RTI "HOW-TO" BOOK

When writing *Promoting Academic Success with English Language Learners*, we did not intend it to be a recipe book for "how to do RTI" or "how to do RTI with ELLs"; rather, it is a book about how schools that engage in RTI can successfully incorporate ELLs within their RTI model. Although we aim to introduce (or reinforce) the core principles of RTI, there are numerous books and websites that cover these concepts in greater detail. Thus, what we do intend this book to be is a clear demonstration of how RTI concepts (e.g., universal screening, data-driven instruction, core instruction, supplemental interventions) logically and necessarily *integrate* with one another—and with other fundamental principles of best practices in education—in a holistic model that prepares ELLs for success in U.S. schools.

We hope our readers recognize that they may already be implementing some, many, or even all of the best practices we describe in this book. Furthermore, we unequivocally believe that our readers do not need to buy costly programs or curricula to be successful in efforts with ELL students; they can apply the principles and strategies we outline in this book to existing curricular and instructional practices without delay, in whatever capacity they work in schools and with ELL students. Our hope is that our readers will take what they learn in each chapter and either strengthen their existing schoolwide RTI framework, if currently doing RTI, or begin to implement this instructional framework if they are not doing so already. Although RTI is a model intended to benefit *all* students, there are unique considerations and variations that must be taken into account if RTI is going to benefit ELLs. We attend to these issues in the following chapters, which we describe next.

CHAPTER CONTENT

In Chapter 2, "Who Are These ELLs?: Foundations, Demographics, and Outcomes," we examine the national trend of increased enrollment of ELLs, particularly in regions across the United States in which they have not significantly matriculated previously (e.g., the Midwest, rural schools, small towns, and villages). When examining these data, it should become apparent that educators throughout the country are encountering similar issues and likely are struggling to identify how to provide necessary and appropriate services to ELLs. We hope that the reader who is uneasy about providing services to ELLs—perhaps for the first time in his or her career—will find some comfort in knowing that many educators throughout the country have similar reservations about their ability to provide quality instruction to ELLs. Our hope is that the same reader will be reassured in the instructional and intervention strategies that we examine in the remainder of the book and will realize that many of these strategies hinge on basic, high-quality teaching practices that excellent teachers have applied for years.

In Chapter 3, "Understanding RTI and How It Will Help Your ELLs Succeed," we introduce the general RTI framework and the associated components within this paradigm. We realize that there are many texts, websites, and other resources on the topic; thus, our primary goal is to provide a brief overview of RTI and the problem-solving model (PSM) in the context of how these paradigms help educators optimally serve the academic, behavioral, and psychosocial needs of their ELLs. In particular, we emphasize that a PSM is highly appropriate for use with ELLs given the unique academic and language needs displayed by students who are learning to speak English as a second language. We feel it is necessary to reiterate what we stated previously, in that this text is not intended to be a recipe book for "how to do RTI." Rather, our goal is to educate the reader about the core principles underlying RTI—and in particular how to implement RTI with ELLs via the PSM—so that the reader (1) realizes that he or she very well may already be implementing some—or perhaps even most—of these best practices and (2) understands that he or she does not necessarily need to buy a program or curriculum to implement what we discuss in this book; we hope our readers will apply the principles and strategies we present as soon as they step back into their classroom and as their school works toward implementing or enhancing their existing RTI model! In this chapter, we also emphasize the importance of accountability and documentation in the RTI process.

One unique feature of Chapter 3 is that we introduce *ecological factors worksheets*, which are designed to facilitate the consideration of multiple ecological factors that can impact a student's level of school participation and academic achievement. These worksheets will become even more significant when we get to Chapter 7, where we discuss their use as a way to document exclusionary factors, which are critical variables to rule out as the primary source of a student's difficulties when one considers special education eligibility.

In Chapter 4, "The Critical Variable: Academic Language Proficiency and Its Impact on Students Learning English as a Second Language," we introduce and examine a concept that we consider to be the single, most critical variable in helping ELLs achieve at a high level in school: *English academic language proficiency*. Because many general education teachers report receiving limited or no preservice or training in working with ELLs, our goal in this pivotal chapter is to discuss the general English language acquisition process. There are specific linguistic concepts that educators must understand, recognize, and be able to implement if they are going to provide educational best practices to ELLs. For one, we examine and define the language concepts of *basic interpersonal communicative skills* (BICS), *cognitive academic language proficiency* (CALP), and *academic language* (AL). Next, we examine English language proficiency (ELP) standards, the connection between these standards and classroom instruction, and the measurement of ELLs' progress—through mandated ELP assessment—toward meeting these ELP standards. We then provide an overview of the controversial topic of language instructional models; again, however, we emphasize that we do not address the issue of what model should be used, as this is something that must be determined at the local educational agency level where an informed decision can be made. We do, however, maintain that *whatever* language instructional model is implemented, the goal is English AL proficiency, and that the school or district must collect data on an ongoing basis to document the effectiveness of instruction toward students' AL proficiency. Throughout the chapter, we emphasize the role of English AL proficiency and the considerations for implementing RTI with ELLs; we have yet to see this area specifically addressed in other RTI/ELL books currently on the market.

In Chapter 5, "Best Practices in Instruction and Assessment for ELLs at Tier 1," we introduce our proposed framework regarding best practices in assessment, instruction, and intervention within Tier 1 of an RTI model. One primary goal in this chapter is to discuss universal screening, progress monitoring, and early identification of ELLs who are either not making anticipated gains in English language acquisition or grade-level academic skills, or both. Again, and as we explained earlier, although we deeply value maintenance of the student's native language, we are unapologetic in our position that in U.S. schools, *English must be the target for instruction and intervention.* Consequently, we emphasize universal screening and progress monitoring while considering specific levels of ELP, which also has not been addressed in other resources covering RTI and ELLs.

Data (e.g., assessment results) are meaningless unless they are used to assist educators in improving instruction and intervention. Furthermore, assessment must be consistent, ongoing, valid, and reliable, so that necessary instruction and intervention changes can be identified and implemented quickly and appropriately. Thus, in Chapter 5, we go beyond a simple discussion of how to collect data; instead, we examine how to integrate data collection within our discussion of providing universal, sound instruction at Tier 1. The reader will notice that in our book, most of the discussion regarding core instruction focuses on the teaching of reading. This emphasis on reading should by no means be interpreted as the minimization of other core academic skills, such as writing, mathematics, science, and other content areas. In this book, our emphasis on reading is due simply to overwhelming evidence indicating a strong relationship between reading and all other academic content areas. Reading is the gateway skill to all of the content areas. Besides, most of the strategies that we discuss in relation to reading are simply excellent standard teaching practices and may therefore be used across the content areas. In this chapter, we consider the roles of the learning environment, culturally responsive teaching practices, instructional principles, and sound pedagogy.

In Chapter 6, "Monitoring Progress, Determining Growth Rates, and Intensifying Instruction for ELLs at Tiers 2 and 3," we expand the concept of progress monitoring and introduce ways to determine anticipated growth rates and how to intensify instruction at Tier 2. We believe that nearly all ELLs—*because* they are learning English as a second language—require frequent progress monitoring and intensified instruction (i.e., Tier 2) (in addition to universal benchmark screening, exposure to sound core instruction, and when needed, intense small-group and individual instruction) if they are to succeed. We describe in detail how to monitor progress—from documenting what is implemented to graphing data, and using data to make instructional decisions to modify or intensify instruction and/ or intervention. We also describe how to determine growth rates, set goals, and establish local norms. We describe the principles of intensifying instruction (i.e., rate, dosage, frequency, and duration) and apply them to the principles described in Chapter 5. We also illustrate a variety of evidence-based interventions that are appropriate for use at Tier 2.

To facilitate data collection and documentation of instructional and intervention efforts with ELLs experiencing academic difficulties, we describe and offer a set of *RTI program participation worksheets*, designed to facilitate the often-burdensome RTI record-keeping process. The worksheets are simple and do not take an inordinate amount of time to complete, because nobody likes doing more paperwork than is absolutely necessary! These worksheets are intended to help the reader document critical quantitative and qualitative information, such as what interventions have been tried, for how long and how well a student has responded. The worksheets can be a lifeline for both parents and educators should a student participating in RTI eventually be referred for special education consideration. Although in theory only a few students who participate in an effective RTI program will continue to experience academic difficulties, in these cases the data that were collected using the RTI program participation worksheets provide a large portion of the documentation needed in an evaluation to make wise determinations about special education eligibility and services. We have used the RTI program participation worksheets with graduate students taking advanced RTI practica and with countless teachers who have been trained in the RTI model. In Chapter 6, we also present a case study of Susana, and provide her RTI program participation worksheets to illustrate Tier 2 activities and one way to document them.

In Chapter 7, "Special Education Referral and Evaluation Considerations for ELLs Who Have Not Responded to Instruction and Intervention," we explore the situation in which students do not progress at an adequate or acceptable rate even when teachers use core sound instruction (Tier 1) and implement more intensive interventions (Tiers 2 and 3). In this chapter, we continue building on the principles presented in earlier chapters and reassure teachers that many ELLs simply need more opportunities to learn (OTLs) in the general education classroom with native English speakers. The principles we discuss in this chapter include ongoing progress monitoring and the provision of increasingly intensive intervention options. Chapter 7 also examines legal and ethical considerations in evaluating ELL students for special education eligibility; we emphasize that the RTI and PSM processes (as we have outlined) provide much of the necessary information to help eligibility teams establish whether the presence of exclusionary factors explain an ELL student's learning difficulties. Because the consideration of exclusionary factors is often ambiguous and confusing, we aim to facilitate understanding of what the school psychologist, special education teachers, regular education teachers, and other members of the multidisciplinary team should look for *prior to* formally recommending a comprehensive and individualized special education evaluation.

Finally, Chapter 8, "Next Steps: Conclusions and Directions for the Future," summarizes what we know about RTI with ELLs—and also what we do not know—or what we would really like to learn more about in the coming years as research continues to inform our practices with ELLs. Our hope is that this summary will assist the reader in realizing that RTI for ELLs consists of a series of actions and activities—many of which they may do already—integrated with one another to facilitate best practices in educating ELL students and ensuring their academic success in U.S. schools.

Many of the materials that we reference throughout the chapters are available in the end-of-chapter appendices. Our experience in implementing RTI models—with any group of students—has illuminated that one key to the successful implementation of RTI models is the efficient use of resources. Thus, whenever possible, we try to help efficiently provide excellent RTI services for ELLs.

We hope you find the following chapters helpful in your efforts.

CHAPTER 2

Who Are These ELLs?

Foundations, Demographics, and Outcomes

ELL students comprise one student group consistently identified as displaying inadequate academic achievement. For example, in 2012, only 7% of fourth-grade ELLs and 3% of eighth-grade ELLs read at or above proficient level in English reading achievement (compared to 35% and 33%, respectively, for non-ELLs; Snyder & Dillow, 2013). This depressed academic performance makes it difficult for educators to differentiate inherent learning difficulties from the complex process of learning a second language (Keller-Allen, 2006), commonly resulting in the inappropriate referral and identification of ELLs for special education services (see Chapter 7 for more information regarding special education referral and evaluation considerations for ELLs who have not made adequate progress). Determining how to reduce academic risk *and* enhance educational outcomes in the ELL population is an urgent educational priority—as evidenced by federal legislation such as the NCLB of 2001—and particularly in light of the sustained increase of ELLs in U.S. schools in recent decades and the anticipated continued growth in future decades.

Many educational professionals (e.g., regular and special education classroom teachers, administrators, school psychologists, school social workers) report that they received little to no preservice or inservice training to equip them with the competencies, skills, and dispositions necessary to ensure that ELLs make desirable academic progress (Walker & Stone, 2011). Furthermore, teachers have reported being reluctant to work with ELLs, because they feel unprepared to teach ELLs adequately (Walker, Shafer, & Iams, 2004). Even when pre- or inservice training may have occurred, many practices that have been advocated for use with ELLs have not been supported by research; thus, there is the likelihood that the practices are not effective (e.g., failing to teach reading to struggling readers explicitly and systematically), or perhaps worse, that they actually are preventing academic progress. In years past, we may have been able to rely on ESL or bilingual education teachers to provide educational services to ELLs, usually in pullout programs or segregated ESL classrooms. However, a number of factors work against continuing this dated service delivery model in which the onus of providing core instruction to ELLs falls to a few educators who are bilingual themselves *and* have specific training in providing instruction in a student's native language. First, as we describe in this chapter, Spanish-speaking ELLs account for approximately 70–80% of all ELL students enrolled in U.S. schools (Federal Interagency Forum on Child and Family Statistics, 2013; Office of English Language Acquisition, Language Enhancement, and Academic Achievement for Limited English Proficient Students, 2013), which makes it difficult to ensure that there will be bilingual staff members who speak the primary language for those remaining 20–30% of ELLs whose native language is not Spanish. Second, the increasing enrollment of ELLs in regions of the country that have not previously had ELL enrollment (e.g., states in the Midwest, rural schools) now are likely to have schools with only one or a limited number of ELLs (U.S. Department of Education, 2009), making it challenging for schools and districts to hire bilingual staff or develop bilingual programs for only a few students. A lack of certified bilingual staff members within these areas further complicates the issue. For example, bilingual education and English language acquisition consistently are identified by the U.S. Department of Education (2013) as high-need certification areas. During the 2009–2010 academic year, over 50% of Title III districts indicated that they experienced significant difficulties in recruiting ESL teachers, and 73% of district administrators working in schools with ELLs reported that a lack of expertise among classroom teachers in addressing the needs of ELLs was a moderate or major challenge (U.S. Department of Education, 2012c). Third, even if bilingual staff members and ESL classes were widely available, the fact remains that ELLs spend the majority of their time in the regular education classroom, thus requiring the classroom teacher (and support staff) to continue providing them with high-quality educational services. Finally, all students—ELLs *and* non-ELLs—are English language learners in that all students need to learn English academic language; thus, all students benefit from having classroom teachers and educational support staff who know how to facilitate and foster English academic language and provide quality core instruction and supplemental intervention services.

Because of the likelihood that most classroom teachers will at some point in their careers have at least one ELL in their classroom, we believe all preservice and inservice teachers must be equipped with the knowledge, skills, and dispositions necessary to work effectively with ELLs. These requirements also are imperative for other student service professionals to possess, including school psychologists, speech–language pathologists, counselors, social workers, and support staff. We believe school psychologists are in a particularly unique position to influence multiple aspects of educational service delivery for students who are ELLs and to promote positive academic and social–emotional outcomes for these students. In their role as instructional consultants, for example, school psychologists can inform teachers about research-based instructional practices for facilitating English language development and academic achievement for ELLs. As assessment experts, school psychologists can make decisions regarding which assessments should be used with ELLs to ensure the appropriateness of the assessments and the purposes for which they are being used. As professionals who also are largely responsible for meeting students' social–

emotional needs and providing school-based mental health services, school psychologists can model and implement best practices that meet the academic, social, and emotional needs of linguistically diverse students.

Given how important it is to have the necessary knowledge and appropriate skills for working with ELLs effectively, one of our guiding principles in writing this book was to describe only those principles and strategies (1) that have been demonstrated to be effective through research and (2) that we have actually seen implemented—or that we ourselves have implemented. The latter principle ensures that we describe strategies that are feasible, realistic, and really do work in actual classrooms with real ELLs. We emphasize the latter in part because so many educational practices are or have been based on what educators think *should* work. Going with your "gut feeling" is not an acceptable practice if you want real results. If you want real results in the classroom, you must begin by testing practices in your classroom that science has identified as *actually* working (albeit in other locations in under different conditions). Moreover, accountability requirements (federal, state, and local) demand that in education we (1) use effective practices based on scientifically sound research and (2) gather effectiveness data (e.g., data-based decision making, documentation of efforts; see Chapter 5 for guidance and worksheets) about student achievement in support of current and future instructional decisions.

Two of our goals in this chapter are (1) to introduce broad concepts that are applicable for working with *all* students, but especially ELLs, and (2) to normalize the apprehension and concern that many classroom teachers and other educators frequently experience when they first begin working with ELLs. Whereas many of you may have extensive experiences working with ELLs and are only seeking to further your knowledge regarding the RTI process, some of you may not be as familiar with the definitions of ELL status, the language acquisition process, or the convoluted assessment and language-monitoring processes, among other topics. Please do not be intimidated! We start in this chapter by discussing the definition of ELL status, followed by a review of statistics illustrating the national trend of increasing enrollment of ELLs and the corresponding educational implications of this increased enrollment, particularly in regions where ELLs have not matriculated previously (e.g., the Midwest). To assist those readers who may have limited knowledge regarding ELL students, we also describe some of the more pertinent and, we believe, unacceptable educational outcomes that have been reported for ELLs as a group of students.

ELL FOUNDATIONAL CONCEPTS

A thorough understanding of the educational needs of ELLs and specific approaches for addressing these needs requires knowledge regarding various ELL-related concepts; additionally, familiarity with these issues facilitates communication among colleagues and other professionals. Thus, we introduce and examine concepts associated with (1) the definition of ELL status; (2) ELL demographics, including the number of ELLs enrolled in schools and the languages spoken by these students; and (3) educational outcomes associated with ELLs.

Definition of ELLs

The NCLB of 2001 (Public Law 107-110, Part A, Section 9101 (25)(A–D)) of 2001, defines ELLs (referred to as "limited English proficient") as

an individual—

(A) who is aged 3 through 21;

(B) who is enrolled or preparing to enroll in an elementary school or secondary school;

(C) (i) who was not born in the United States or whose native language is a language other than English;

   (ii) (I) who is a Native American or Alaska Native, or a native resident of the outlying areas;

    and

    (II) who comes from an environment where a language other than English has had a significant impact on the individual's level of English language proficiency; or

   (iii) who is migratory, whose native language is a language other than English, and who comes from an environment where a language other than English is dominant; and

(D) whose difficulties in speaking, reading, writing, or understanding the English language may be sufficient to deny the individual—

   (i) the ability to meet the State's proficient level of achievement on State assessments described in section 1111(b)(3);

   (ii) the ability to successfully achieve in classrooms where the language of instruction is English; or

   (iii) the opportunity to participate fully in society.

As you will see later in this chapter, a federal definition of ELLs does not ensure that limited English-speaking students are uniformly identified and provided the same level of services in the schools. Rather, identification of ELL students is accomplished using a variety of measures, procedures, and criteria by which a student *could* be identified as an ELL student in one state but not necessarily in another (U.S. Department of Education, 2012c). This phenomenon is similar to the frequently heard criticism regarding the federal definitions of varying disability categories and corresponding eligibility criteria. In some special education eligibility categories (e.g., specific learning disabilities), a student who might be determined to be eligible for special education services in one region of the country (or even within a state or city) might not be eligible in a different region, simply because of the wide interpretation of disability definitions and eligibility criteria. These definitional inconsistencies are believed to result in some students receiving special education services when they may not have an actual disability, and in other students who might actually have a disability being determined not to be eligible to receive services. By providing educational services within a comprehensive RTI model (as we explore in Chapter 3), all students are provided core instruction and supplemental services based on their *educational needs* rather than on an *eligibility label* (e.g., student with a disability, student classified as an ELL). Even if a student is determined not to be an ELL student, or if a student with significant academic difficulties is determined not to be a student with a disability, the RTI model dictates that appropriate levels of services be directed to the student to address his or her educational needs—*regardless of a label or identified disability.*

ELL Demographics

Enrollment

ELLs represent the fastest growing segment of the school population and are enrolling in public schools across all regions of the United States at such a high rate that education professionals are more likely than ever to work with at least one ELL student—directly or indirectly—at some point in their teaching career. Data provided by the U.S. Department of Education (2012a, 2012b) indicated that during the 2010–2011 academic year, approximately 4.4 million students within U.S. schools (not including Puerto Rico or other U.S. territories) were identified as being ELLs and were participating in school programming for ELLs, representing approximately 8.8% of all public school students (see Table 2.1 for ELL population data by individual states). However, this ELL student enrollment estimate does not include the additional 13% of students who speak a language other than English at home (Federal Interagency Forum on Child and Family Statistics, 2012). Thus, approximately 22% of all public school students in U.S. schools speak a language other than English within the home setting.

Although California schools enroll an estimated one-third of all ELL students (i.e., 1,442,387 ELLs) in the United States, ELLs are enrolled in each of the 50 states, with the percentages of ELL students ranging from a high of 23% in California to a low of 0.6% in West Virginia. The majority of states experienced double-digit percentage increases in the number of ELL students during the past decade, however, with states such as South Carolina, Indiana, and Arkansas reporting increases of 828, 409, and 287%, respectively, between 1997 and 2008 (Batalova & McHugh, 2010). Perhaps more astonishing, however, is the growth in individual districts, with some districts experiencing growth rates of more than 4,000% in the prior 5-year period (National Clearinghouse for English Language Acquisition, 2011). Additionally, data suggest that approximately 68% of all public schools within the United States have at least one ELL student enrolled within their school (U.S. Department of Education, 2009). Schools in all types of community settings report having ELL students enrolled, with cities, suburbs, towns, and rural areas indicating that 77, 80, 66, and 50% of their schools, respectively, had at least one ELL student enrolled. Consequently, the likelihood that classroom teachers will have one or more ELL students within their classroom is higher than ever—and that likelihood will likely continue to grow throughout the foreseeable future.

TABLE 2.1. Enrollment and Percentage of ELL Students by State, 2010–2011

State	Number of ELL students[a]	Percentage of students[b]	State	Number of ELL students[a]	Percentage of students[b]
Alabama	17,559	2.3	Montana	3,299	2.3
Alaska	14,894	11.3	Nebraska	20,062	6.7
Arizona	70,716	6.6	Nevada	83,351	19.1
Arkansas	31,457	6.5	New Hampshire	3,965	2.0
California	1,442,387[c]	23.0[d]	New Jersey	52,580	3.7
Colorado	98,809	11.7	New Mexico	52,029	15.4
Connecticut	29,671	5.3	New York	207,708	7.6
Delaware	6,766	5.2	North Carolina	102,397	6.9
District of Columbia	3,741	5.3	North Dakota	2,788	2.9
Florida	229,659	8.7	Ohio	35,170	2.0
Georgia	80,965	4.8	Oklahoma	41,431	6.3
Hawaii	19,092	10.6	Oregon	58,662	10.3
Idaho	15,361	5.6	Pennsylvania	44,729	2.5
Illinois	174,335	8.3	Rhode Island	7,161	5.0
Indiana	48,574	4.6	South Carolina	36,360	5.0
Iowa	21,733	4.4	South Dakota	4,383	3.5
Kansas	39,323	8.1	Tennessee	29,680	3.0
Kentucky	16,351	2.4	Texas	718,350	14.6
Louisiana	11,617	1.7	Utah	41,805	7.1
Maine	4,792	2.5	Vermont	1,672	1.7
Maryland	45,500	5.3	Virginia	87,752	7.0
Massachusetts	52,610	5.5	Washington	90,282	8.6
Michigan	50,773	3.2	West Virginia	1,786	0.6
Minnesota	40,778	4.9	Wisconsin	43,562	5.0
Mississippi	5,617	1.1	Wyoming	2,602	2.9
Missouri	20,411	2.2	United States	4,367,057	8.8[e]

[a]Number of ELL students participating in programs for ELLs. Data from U.S. Department of Education (2012a).

[b]Denominator based on U.S. Department of Education (2012b).

[c]California did not report numbers of ELL students to the U.S. Department of Education in 2010–2011. The number of California ELLs during the 2010—2011 academic year (n = 1,442,387) was obtained from the California Department of Education, Educational Demographics Office website (*www.cde.ca.gov/re/pn/fb/index.asp*).

[d]Denominator (n = 6,217,002) obtained from *www.cde.ca.gov/ds/sd/cb/cefenrollmentcomp.asp.*

[e]Denominator (total population = 49,484,181 students enrolled in U.S. schools during fall 2010) based on U.S. Department of Education (2012b).

Languages Spoken

Spanish is the most frequently spoken language by ELLs; data indicate that Spanish is the primary language of up to 80% of ELLs (Office of English Language Acquisition, Language Enhancement, and Academic Achievement for Limited English Proficient Students, 2013), followed by Vietnamese, Chinese, Arabic, and Hmong (see Table 2.2 for the number and percentage of students reported to speak each of these languages during the 2009–2010 academic year). However, more than 460 languages are reportedly spoken in schools throughout the United States, with Spanish *not* being the most commonly spoken language by ELLs in seven states (i.e., Alaska, Hawaii, Montana, North Dakota, South Dakota, Maine, and Vermont; see Table 2.3 for the 5 most commonly spoken non-English languages by ELLs in each state). The Chicago Public Schools (2012), for example, have more than 120 different primary languages represented among their ELLs.

ELL Educational Outcomes

Understanding the varying reports of ELL educational achievement outcomes is challenging because of a number of issues, including the various methods of identifying and assessing English language proficiency (ELP), the type of language instruction provided, and inconsistencies in the types of accommodations that ELLs are allowed to use on standardized achievement tests in English (Kopriva & Albers, 2013). Despite these limitations, the data consistently indicate lagging academic achievement scores for ELLs, resulting in a significant and ongoing achievement gap between ELLs and native English speakers.

NCLB includes multiple state Title III accountability requirements regarding ELL ELP and academic achievement outcomes. State educational agencies establish these requirements, and districts that receive Title III funds must meet the objectives on an annual basis; those districts that fail to meet these objectives for 2 years or more are subject

TABLE 2.2. Most Frequent Primary Spoken Language for ELLs, 2009–2010

Primary language	Number of students	Percentage of ELL students[a]
Spanish	3,544,713	76.3
Vietnamese	85,252	1.8
Chinese	68,743	1.5
Arabic	51,585	1.1
Hmong	46,311	0.9

Note. Data from Office of English Language Acquisition, Language Enhancement, and Academic Achievement for Limited English Proficient Students (2013).

[a]Based on an estimated total ELL student population of 4,647,016 from data source.

TABLE 2.3. Top Five Non-English Languages Spoken in Each State, 2007–2008

State	Top five languages spoken	State	Top five languages spoken
Alabama	Spanish, Korean, Arabic, Russian, Japanese	Montana	Blackfeet, Crow, Other American Indian, Cheyenne, German
Alaska	Yup'ik, Inupiac, Spanish, Filipino, Samoan	Nebraska	Spanish, Vietnamese, Arabic, Nuer, Somali
Arizona	Spanish, Navajo, Other Non-Indian, Vietnamese, Arabic	Nevada[a]	Spanish, Tagalog, Chinese
Arkansas	Spanish, Marshallese, Hmong, Laotian, Vietnamese	New Hampshire	Spanish, Portuguese, Bosnian, Arabic, Vietnamese
California	Spanish, Vietnamese, Filipino, Cantonese, Hmong	New Jersey	Spanish, Korean, Arabic, Portuguese, Gujarati
Colorado	Spanish, Vietnamese, Russian, Korean, Hmong	New Mexico	Spanish, Navajo, Zuni, Keres, Vietnamese
Connecticut	Spanish, Portuguese, Chinese, Polish, Creole-Haitian	New York	Spanish, Chinese, Arabic, Bengali, Haitian Creole
Delaware	Spanish, Creole, Chinese, Gujarati, Korean	North Carolina	Spanish, Hmong, Vietnamese, Arabic/Egyptian, Korean
District of Columbia	Spanish, Chinese, Vietnamese, Amharic, French	North Dakota	Ojibwa, Spanish, Dakota/Lakota, North American Indian, Bosnian
Florida	Spanish, Haitian-Creole, Portuguese, Arabic	Ohio	Spanish, Other, Somali, Arabic, German
Georgia	Spanish, Vietnamese, Korean, Other, Chinese	Oklahoma	Spanish, Cherokee, Vietnamese, Hmong, Korean
Hawaii	Ilokano, Tagalog, Marshallese, Chuukese, Spanish	Oregon	Spanish, Russian, Vietnamese, Fante or Fanti (Ghana), Chinese
Idaho	Spanish, Shoshone, Russian, Bosnian, Serbo-Croatian	Pennsylvania	Spanish, Vietnamese, Chinese, Russian, Arabic
Illinois	Spanish, Polish, Arabic, Chinese, Urdu	Rhode Island	Spanish, Portug., Creole/pidgins/other Portuguese, Chinese, Khmer
Indiana	Spanish, Amish German, Arabic, Mandarin, Punjabi		
Iowa	Spanish, Vietnamese, Bosnian, Lao, Undetermined	South Carolina	Spanish, Russian, Vietnamese, Portuguese, Arabic
Kansas	Spanish, Vietnamese, Arabic, German, Lao	South Dakota	Lakota, Spanish, Hutterite, Dakota, German
Kentucky	Spanish, Japanese, Bosnian, Vietnamese, Mandarin Chinese	Tennessee	Spanish, Arabic, Vietnamese, Kurdish, Chinese
Louisiana	Spanish, Vietnamese, Arabic, Chinese, French	Texas	Spanish, Vietnamese, Urdu, Arabic, Korean
Maine	Somali, Spanish, French, Khmer, Chinese	Utah	Spanish, Navajo, Tongan, Vietnamese, Samoal
Maryland	Spanish, French, Chinese, Korean, Vietnamese	Vermont	Serbo-Croatian, Spanish, Vietnamese, Maay, Chinese
Massachusetts	Spanish, Portuguese. Khmer/Khmai, Haitian Creole, Vietnamese	Virginia	Spanish, Korean, Vietnamese, Arabic, Urdu
Michigan	Spanish, Arabic, Chaldean, Albanian, Japanese	Washington	Spanish, Russian, Vietnamese, Ukrainian, Somali
Minnesota	Spanish, Hmong, Somali, Vietnamese, Russian	West Virginia	Spanish, Arabic, Mandarin Chinese, Vietnamese, Russian
Mississippi	Spanish, Vietnamese, Arabic, Cantonese, Chinese	Wisconsin	Spanish, Hmong, Russian, Mandarin Chinese, Standard Arabic
Missouri	Spanish, Bos/Croat/Serb, Vietnamese, Arabic/Sudanese, Somali	Wyoming	Spanish, Japanese, Hindi, Filipino, Mandarin Chinese

Note. Data from Office of English Language Acquisition, Language Enhancement, and Academic Achievement for Limited English Proficient Students (2013).

[a]Only the top three languages were provided.

to state sanctions. These objectives, known as Annual Measureable Achievement Objectives (AMAOs), include the following:

- AMAO 1: Annual increases in the number or percentage of ELLs making progress in learning English (i.e., Are ELLs *progressing* toward English proficiency?).
- AMAO 2: Annual increases in the number or percentage of ELLs attaining ELP (i.e., Are ELLs *attaining* English proficiency?).
- AMAO 3: Adequate yearly progress (AYP) for ELL subgroup in meeting grade-level academic standards in English language arts and mathematics (i.e., Are ELLs *making* AYP in academic content areas?).

The most recent available AMAO data (U.S. Department of Education, 2012c) demonstrate the clear need to improve educational services provided to ELLs, because only 10 states (i.e., Alabama, Delaware, Maine, Mississippi, Nebraska, New Jersey, South Carolina, Tennessee, Texas, Wisconsin) reported meeting their AMAOs in the 2008–2009 academic year. At the district level, 55% of Title III districts reported having met all three AMAOs, but these 55% of districts only enrolled 39% of the total ELL population. Furthermore, 30% of districts with large (i.e., > 1,000) numbers of ELLs missed their AMAOs for 2 years consecutively, whereas 24, 20, and 16% of medium (i.e., 301–1,000 ELLs), small (i.e., 151–300 ELLs), and very small (i.e., 1–150 ELLs) districts, respectively, missed their AMAOs for 2 consecutive years.

Student-level data also illustrate the lagging achievement levels of many ELLs. At the national level, the average 2011 National Assessment of Educational Progress (NAEP) reading scale score for fourth-grade ELL students enrolled in public schools was 188 (Below Basic achievement level), whereas for non-ELLs, the average scale score was 224 (Basic achievement level; see Table 2.4 for NAEP reading scale scores for each state). This achievement gap was present for each of the 46 states (plus the District of Columbia) that reported student scores. This same pattern of scores and corresponding reading achievement gaps were also present for eighth-grade ELLs as compared to non-ELLs (see Table 2.5).

Figures 2.1 and 2.2 illustrate the differences in distributions between ELLs and non-ELLs for fourth- and eighth-grade students on the NAEP reading assessment. Nationwide, approximately 70% of fourth-grade ELLs scored in the Below Basic achievement category on the reading portion of the 2011 NAEP, which is substantially higher than the 30% of non-ELLs who scored within this level. Similarly, only 7% of ELLs scored within the Proficient or Advanced achievement levels, whereas 35% of the non-ELLs performed at the Proficient or Advanced achievement levels. Figure 2.2 illustrates the similar distribution of performance scores for eighth-grade ELLs.

It is not uncommon to encounter educators, support staff, parents, and community members who assume that students' lack of ELP only impacts literacy domains; however, mathematics achievement also appears to be heavily impacted by language proficiency levels, particularly in more complex mathematics concepts and processes. Once again, the NAEP data demonstrate the existence of an achievement gap between ELLs and non-ELLs in mathematics, as seen in Figures 2.3 and 2.4. At the fourth-grade level, 86% of ELLs scored at the Basic or Below Basic levels on the mathematics portion of the NAEP, whereas

TABLE 2.4. NAEP Reading Scale Scores by State for ELL and Non-ELL Students, Fourth Grade, 2011

State	ELL students	Non-ELL students	State	ELL students	Non-ELL students
Alabama	189	221	Montana	174	226
Alaska	153	216	Nebraska	191	226
Arizona	171	218	Nevada	193	220
Arkansas	197	218	New Hampshire	203	231
California	186	223	New Jersey	—[a]	232
Colorado	184	231	New Mexico	171	214
Connecticut	178	230	New York	187	226
Delaware	187	226	North Carolina	189	224
District of Columbia	179	202	North Dakota	198	226
Florida	195	227	Ohio	206	224
Georgia	191	222	Oklahoma	186	217
Hawaii	180	217	Oregon	183	222
Idaho	166	223	Pennsylvania	183	228
Illinois	180	223	Rhode Island	180	225
Indiana	197	223	South Carolina	207	215
Iowa	189	223	South Dakota	175	222
Kansas	203	226	Tennessee	177	216
Kentucky	—[a]	225	Texas	197	223
Louisiana	197	211	Utah	167	224
Maine	186	223	Vermont	189	228
Maryland	205	232	Virginia	190	229
Massachusetts	204	239	Washington	172	226
Michigan	192	220	West Virginia	—[a]	214
Minnesota	187	226	Wisconsin	195	223
Mississippi	—[a]	210	Wyoming	190	225
Missouri	189	221			
			United States	188	225

Note. Proficiency levels corresponding to scale scores are Below Basic < 208, Basic 208–237, Proficient 238–267, and Advanced > 267. Data from U.S. Department of Education (2011b).

[a]Standards for reporting were not met.

TABLE 2.5. NAEP Reading Scale Scores by State for ELL and Non-ELL Students, Eighth Grade, 2011

State	ELL students	Non-ELL students	State	ELL students	Non-ELL students
Alabama	—[a]	259	Montana	—[a]	273
Alaska	215	267	Nebraska	—[a]	268
Arizona	—[a]	261	Nevada	215	263
Arkansas	239	260	New Hampshire	—[a]	273
California	220	262	New Jersey	—[a]	276
Colorado	224	274	New Mexico	218	260
Connecticut	224	277	New York	216	268
Delaware	—[a]	266	North Carolina	233	264
District of Columbia	215	244	North Dakota	—[a]	269
Florida	225	264	Ohio	224	269
Georgia	—[a]	263	Oklahoma	—[a]	261
Hawaii	220	260	Oregon	215	267
Idaho	231	269	Pennsylvania	220	269
Illinois	224	267	Rhode Island	219	267
Indiana	235	266	South Carolina	251	261
Iowa	231	266	South Dakota	—[a]	270
Kansas	242	269	Tennessee	—[a]	260
Kentucky	—[a]	269	Texas	225	264
Louisiana	—[a]	255	Utah	222	269
Maine	—[a]	271	Vermont	—[a]	274
Maryland	—[a]	272	Virginia	241	269
Massachusetts	211	277	Washington	222	270
Michigan	237	266	West Virginia	—[a]	256
Minnesota	233	272	Wisconsin	240	269
Mississippi	—[a]	254	Wyoming	—[a]	270
Missouri	—[a]	267	United States	223	266

Note. Proficiency levels corresponding to scale scores are Below Basic < 243, Basic 243–280, Proficient 281–322, and Advanced > 322. Data from U.S. Department of Education (2011b).

[a]Standards for reporting were not met.

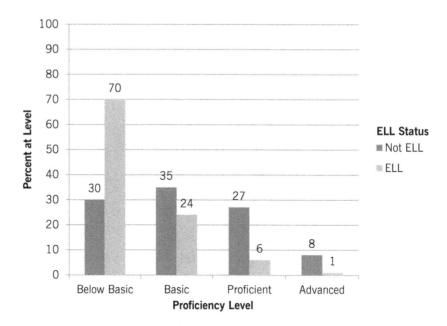

FIGURE 2.1. The percentage of fourth-grade ELLs and non-ELLs at the achievement levels of Below Basic, Basic, Proficient, and Advanced on the 2011 NAEP Reading assessment. Data from U.S. Department of Education, Institute of Education Sciences, National Center for Education Statistics, National Assessment of Educational Progress, 2011 Reading Assessment.

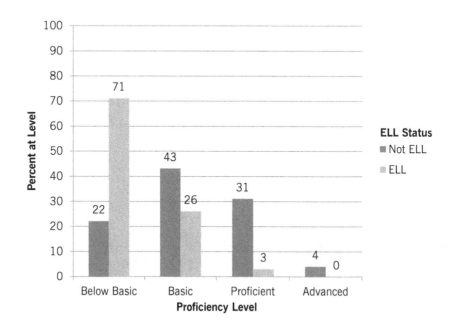

FIGURE 2.2. The percentage of eighth-grade ELLs and non-ELLs at the achievement levels of Below Basic, Basic, Proficient, and Advanced on the 2011 NAEP Reading assessment. Data from U.S. Department of Education, Institute of Education Sciences, National Center for Education Statistics, National Assessment of Educational Progress, 2011 Reading Assessment.

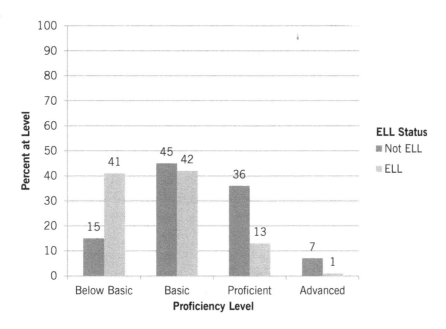

FIGURE 2.3. The percentage of fourth-grade ELLs and non-ELLs at the achievement levels of Below Basic, Basic, Proficient, and Advanced on the 2011 NAEP Mathematics assessment. Data from U.S. Department of Education, Institute of Education Sciences, National Center for Education Statistics, National Assessment of Educational Progress, 2011 Reading Assessment.

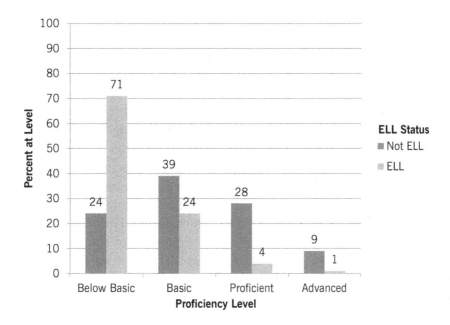

FIGURE 2.4. The percentage of eighth-grade ELLs and non-ELLs at the achievement levels of Below Basic, Basic, Proficient, and Advanced on the 2011 NAEP Mathematics assessment. Data from U.S. Department of Education, Institute of Education Sciences, National Center for Education Statistics, National Assessment of Educational Progress, 2011 Reading Assessment.

57% of non-ELLs scored at the same level or below. In eighth grade, 95% of ELLs scored at the Basic or Below Basic levels, compared to 63% of non-ELLs. Conversely, 5% of fourth-grade ELLs scored at the Proficient or Advanced levels, and 37% of non-ELLs scored at the Proficient or Advanced levels. Thus, it is entirely reasonable to presume that facilitating the acquisition of ELP may very likely enhance the mathematics outcomes of many ELLs.

It is often presumed that ELLs experience heightened risk of poor academic achievement because of the demands of not only learning academic content but also, concurrently, the English language. Clearly, such a dual demand impacts academic performance (e.g., Baker, Kame'enui, & Simmons, 2002); however, ELLs also tend to experience additional environmental demands that further increase their degree of risk for academic underachievement. For example, in 2000, 68% of ELLs enrolled in kindergarten through fifth grade were considered to be from low-income environments, which was almost twice as high as the percentage of non-ELLs living in low-income environments (U.S. Department of Education, 2012c). Research has clearly demonstrated the enhanced risk of experiencing poor academic outcomes for students raised in low-income environments (e.g., McLoyd, 1998; Sirin, 2005). To examine the impact of poverty on ELLs' academic achievement, Kieffer (2008) controlled demographic risk factors, including poverty, to compare English reading growth trajectories in two groups of ELL students: (1) ELLs entering kindergarten who were considered to be proficient in oral English and (2) ELLs entering kindergarten with limited oral English proficiency. The comparison of both groups to native English speakers indicated that ELLs who entered kindergarten with oral English proficiency had similar reading achievement growth to that of native English speakers, whereas those ELLs who entered kindergarten with limited oral English proficiency had lower English reading trajectories than native English speakers, with the differences between these two groups described as large by fifth grade. However, when researchers controlled for poverty, the differences in reading achievement decreased (but did not disappear) for ELLs. These data were interpreted as being clear indicators of the need to provide literacy intervention for students with limited English skills who are entering public schools, and provided justification for early intervention as a way to facilitate the English academic achievement of ELLs.

The challenges for many ELL students are also supported by the well-documented finding that linguistic-minority students tend to be overrepresented in special education programs and underrepresented in advanced courses and in gifted and talented programs (e.g., Artiles, Rueda, Salazar, & Higareda, 2005; Artiles & Trent, 1994; Donovan & Cross, 2002; Ford, 1998; Zhang & Katsiyannis, 2002). In particular, Hispanic students (although not necessarily ELL Hispanic students) have a long history of being overrepresented in the specific learning disability (SLD) category of special education (e.g., Chinn & Hughes, 1987; Donovan & Cross, 2002; Rueda & Windmueller, 2006; Salend, Garrick Duhaney, & Montgomery, 2002). ELL students' linguistic diversity and frequent language barriers are often cited as salient reasons for their overrepresentation and underrepresentation in various special education categories (Klingner, Artiles, & Barletta, 2006; Rueda & Windmueller, 2006). Overrepresentation partially occurs as a result of conducting special education evaluations either when an ELL student displays low levels of English proficiency after a set period of time, or when the ELL student demonstrates academic underachievement and school failure (McCardle, Mele-McCarthy, Cutting, Leos, & D'Emilio, 2005). Artiles and colleagues (2005) examined the identification of ELL students for special education eligibility within California urban school districts. The authors reported that ELL students, particularly those with first and second levels (i.e., low levels) of ELP, were at a greater risk for special education identification and eligibility (compared to ELL students at higher levels of proficiency) as they progress through the grade levels. Results also suggested that special education services were relied on the most for ELL students in English immersion classrooms, whereas ELL students in bilingual educational settings or modified English immersion programs were referred for special education evaluations less frequently. Regarding underrepresentation, evidence suggests that teachers may be hesitant to refer ELL students for a special education evaluation, because they assume that these students' academic difficulties are the result of second-language acquisition difficulties or because they are already receiving ESL services (Klingner et al., 2006; Limbos & Geva, 2002). Thus, it is clear that a student's second-language status has significant implications for his or her eventual educational attainment.

Social–Emotional Outcomes

The difficulties we just outlined regarding the development of basic and advanced academic skills clearly play a significant role in the negative academic and related outcomes experienced by many ELL students and immigrant families. We know that academic skills significantly impact future physical, emotional, and vocational wellness (Brown-Chidsey, 2005; Centers for Disease Control and Prevention [CDC], 2005). For example, limited academic skills have been associated with increased rates of pregnancy (Matson & Haglund, 2000), incarceration (Strom, 2000), mental illness (Harlow, 2003), and poorer health and long-term wellness (CDC, 2005).

The evidence also suggests that many ELL students are at significant risk for emotional difficulties. According to the U.S. Department of Health and Human Services (2001), "Hispanic American youth are at significantly higher risk for poor mental health than white youth are by virtue of higher rates of depressive and anxiety symptoms, as well as higher rates of suicidal ideation and suicide attempts" (p. 11). Linguistically diverse individuals' mental health, according to Gibbs and Huang (1998), can be impacted by their cultural and ethnic background by (1) shaping their belief system about mental health and illness, (2) impacting the way that they cope with mental illness or show symptoms, (3) affecting how parents deal with a child's mental illness and what professionals/paraprofessionals they will bring them to see, and (4) affecting treatment of a mental illness, particularly if the treatment chosen does not match children's ethnic beliefs and traditions. In addition, many minority families may have less access to mental health care services or may choose not to seek help for linguistic or cultural reasons (U.S. Department of Health and Human Services, 2001), such as the view of mental illness as a "dishonor" to the family in some cultures (Esquivel & Keitel, 1990).

ELL students face additional issues affecting mental health. These include factors such as lifestyle changes and separation from family members left behind in their native country

(Gopaul-McNicol & Thomas-Presswood, 1998). Children of migrant farm worker families may face specific challenges requiring professionals to consider their background (e.g., war or other trauma in their native country), including factors (e.g., prejudice or racism in the community) that specifically may hinder their sufficient acquisition of English. School staff members may not always be informed of critical experiences in a child's background history (e.g., traumatic experiences in the native country or during the emigration process) or the additional stressors (e.g., death of a parent or witness to violence) that affect a child's mental health and most certainly require additional investigation by school personnel (e.g., school counselor, school social worker, school psychologist).

SO, NOW WHAT?

We have discussed how it is not uncommon for ELLs—as a group—to struggle in an academic context in the United States; this likely is not news to most readers of this book given the frequent media coverage and political discussion regarding global underachievement within our schools. What may be surprising, however, is the link between the chronic and widespread nature of these difficulties and the corresponding deleterious associations with basic emotional wellness later in life. This clarifies that, without a doubt, the *modus operandi* in schools cannot continue. Nevertheless, the question remains: "Why do ELLs, as a group, struggle to perform at similar achievement levels to non-ELL students?" Of course, this is likely due to multiple interacting factors; however, because of the need to learn Academic English, the question now—and the task that lies ahead for all educators—is how to facilitate this obligatory English language and academic growth. We begin to examine this question in Chapter 3.

CHAPTER 3

Understanding RTI and How It Will Help Your ELLs Succeed

RTI is a conceptual framework that comprises multiple critical activities and components that are integrated into a service delivery model designed to help educators appropriately assess and immediately respond to the needs of *all* students. Typically, RTI activities occur fluidly across multiple intervention tiers, so that across tier levels, there is a progressive increase in the severity of academic needs displayed by students. That is, at Tier 1, most students' academic needs are met without incident. Despite efforts at Tier 1, *some* students continue to display moderate academic need and therefore require the increased intensity of instruction and intervention offered at Tier 2. Moreover, a *few* students continue to struggle at both Tiers 1 and 2, and require the most intense level of intervention and progress monitoring at Tier 3.

Although RTI is a relatively new term in our educational vernacular within the last decade, RTI in its multiple shapes and forms is actually an outgrowth of much earlier educational efforts and theory, including applied behavior analysis, behavioral consultation, instructional consultation, schoolwide intervention teams, and curriculum-based assessment, among others. What all of these earlier efforts and theoretical foundations had in common was that each utilized some form of a problem-solving process characterized by a series of steps, including (1) problem identification, (2) problem definition, (3) the selection and design of intervention plans, and (4) intervention implementation and progress monitoring (e.g., Brown-Chidsey & Steege, 2010). What is also relatively new is the national educational initiative to implement RTI, which has been driven by a number of issues, including dissatisfaction with prior discrepancy approaches for determining special education eligibility and the recognition that too many students were not succeeding academically (or behaviorally); thus, RTI has become an alternative approach for both determining special education eligibility in the area of specific learning disabilities and reshaping our schools to become places that emphasize prevention and early intervention services, as compared to traditional wait-to-fail approaches (i.e., discrepancy models) to students' difficulties. Thus, RTI models have become an extension of broad problem-solving concepts and applications.

Although variations of RTI exist, the primary difference between the most common models relates to its intended outcome, which is either to inform special education identification and eligibility or drive schoolwide reform and improved outcomes for all students. The *ideal* RTI model, however, not only accomplishes *both* of these outcomes—facilitating special education eligibility processes *and* prompting schoolwide and within-classroom reform—but also is designed to address individual students' needs. In this book, we apply RTI to ELLs with the intention of expediting all three of these desirable outcomes. In this chapter, we describe the benefits of implementing RTI models for individual students and at the systems level by outlining critical RTI components that must be implemented for the benefits of RTI to be gained. We also describe how RTI components should be adapted or customized when providing services to ELL students, and how implementing these components benefits ELLs.

RTI MODELS

In RTI theory, all teachers (1) utilize only the highest quality core curricula (e.g., in reading, the curriculum emphasizes phonemic awareness, phonics, fluency, comprehension, and vocabulary); (2) implement excellent instructional strategies and research-based interventions that address the needs of *all* students; and (3) collect frequent formative assessment data (e.g., curriculum-based measurement [CBM]) to monitor students' academic progress and modify instruction/intervention accordingly. Thus, RTI involves an ongoing sequence of assessment and instruction/intervention activities that, first and foremost, are *the responsibility of general education classroom teachers*. These assessment, instructional, and intervention activities are performed across various tiers (usually three), starting with Tier 1, which affects the entire population (e.g., a whole classroom, grade level, building, district). What differentiates the assessment and instruction/intervention activities as one "moves up" the Tiers from Tier 1 to Tier 3 is (1) the *frequency* with which formative assessment is conducted and (2) the *intensity* (e.g., duration *and* frequency) with which instruction/intervention is provided to some students Although these assessment and instruction/intervention activities at Tier 1 include *all* students, *most*—but not all—students respond adequately at Tier 1. Theoretically, 85–90% of all students' academic needs should be addressed adequately at Tier 1, although this will vary among individual schools and districts. Some students (about 10–15%), in addition to Tier 1, require the more *frequent* assessment and *intense* instruction/intervention activities delivered at Tier 2. It is our position in this book that most ELLs require at least a Tier 2 level of support from the beginning to gain the necessary Academic English to be successful in school. A few students at Tier 2 (about 5–10%) will *still* struggle and consequently require even *more* frequent assessment and more intense intervention—at Tier 3—than that provided at Tier 2. It is quite likely that *many* of your ELLs, especially newcomers, will require Tier 3 support. Assessment, instruction, and intervention activities across the multiple tiers, including those for ELLs, *takes place within the general education setting.* During these general education activities, the classroom teacher collects frequent qualitative and quantitative data on students' performance. Careful documentation of what transpires during these processes within each of the tiers allows school-based teams to learn whether a student either (1) responded to the core instruction and supplemental intervention or, alternatively, (2) did not respond to the core instruction and supplemental intervention. In the latter situation, and in a small number of cases, the student may be considered for a special education evaluation, in which the school psychologist and the evaluation team conduct a comprehensive individualized evaluation to understand better what might be causing a student's poor response to intervention. Results of the evaluation, in conjunction with all of the data collected during the RTI process, help the case conference committee, including the parent, determine a student's eligibility and programming for special education services.

THE RTI DIAMOND

Most educators probably have seen the illustrations of how RTI models typically have been conceptualized; most frequently, these models are represented as either as an upright triangle (see Figure 3.1) or an inverted triangle (Figure 3.2). Both versions of the model essentially represent the same critical features described earlier and attempt to convey that RTI comprises tiered components that are implemented at increasing intensity (i.e., intervention) and frequency (i.e., assessment). Figures 3.1 and 3.2 also illustrate a "funneling" of students, in that as the tiers become more intensive (i.e., going from Tier 1 to Tier 2 to Tier 3), the number of students in need of the more intensive services decreases. Both versions of the RTI triangle also suggest that failure to respond adequately to intervention in the more intensive tiers inevitably results in the need to consider whether the student meets eligibility criteria for special education services. We contend that the models represented in Figures 3.1 and 3.2 represent RTI too simplistically and, quite frankly, erroneously, as a way to funnel the small number of students who do not respond adequately into special education.

In contrast to these popular triangular representations of RTI, we prefer to exemplify RTI using the shape of a diamond, as illustrated in Figure 3.3. We prefer such a diamond-shaped model to the triangular models because the diamond-shaped approach shows that determining special education eligibility is only a small portion of the RTI story. The remaining part of the story, and perhaps the more important part, concerns driving school and classwide reform, and improved outcomes for *all* students, which also includes students who demonstrate above-average academic achievement and are in need of differentiated instruction to meet their academic needs. It is our position that RTI should be considered a strengths-based approach rather than one that focuses always only on underachieving students. Within a truly comprehensive service delivery model, such as the one embodied by our diamond-shaped RTI figure, the paramount goal is not to determine special education eligibility, but rather to prompt school- and classwide efforts that effectively meet the needs of *all* students. Granted, this model conceptualization still allows for the determination of special education eligibility; however, special education is not the primary purpose

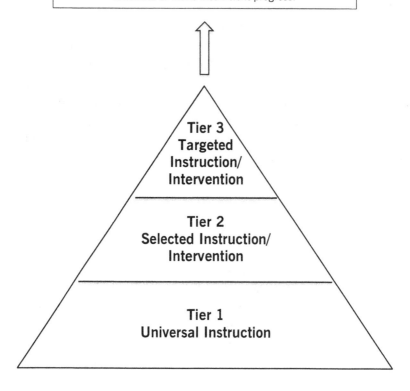

FIGURE 3.1. Illustration of the RTI model for determining special education eligibility.

or outcome of implementing such a model. When viewed in this way, RTI is implemented to *remediate* student difficulties at the first sign of trouble, in an effort to *prevent* significant problems that might otherwise lead to referral of higher numbers of students and perhaps identification for special education services, and it is also a way to meet the different academic needs and further enhance the achievement of those students who, rather than struggling, are succeeding within the classroom.

To illustrate, consider a kindergarten student who has difficulty identifying the letters of the English alphabet and/or naming their corresponding sounds (i.e., mapping, phonemes to their graphemes; whether he or she is an ELL student is irrelevant). Immediate action must be taken to ensure that the student gains proficiency in letter naming and letter–sound identification. There is an urgency in making sure that the student masters letter names and their corresponding letter sounds, because we know that letter and sound identification are causal predictors of later reading success. In this illustration, the teacher needs to use simple, yet effective activities (e.g., interspersing letters the student knows with letters that he or she does not yet know in a stack of flashcards) on a fairly frequent basis (e.g., three times a week for 10 minutes at a time), during which the teacher also monitors the student's progress on letter naming and letter–sound fluency. The student's progress (i.e., both rate of

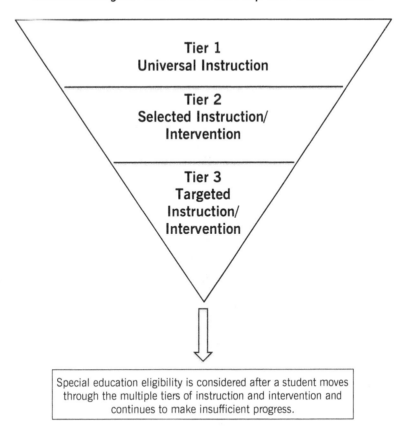

FIGURE 3.2. Equivalent illustration (compared to Figure 3.1) of the RTI model for determining special education eligibility.

improvement and absolute score) indicates to the teacher whether the student is responding (i.e., the raw scores on a graph are going up at an acceptably fast rate) or not responding (i.e., the raw scores on a graph are not going up at an acceptably fast rate) to the intervention. Now consider a different kindergarten student in the same classroom; this student, however, already knows a significant number of high frequency sight words and even is able to adequately sound out and decipher words in beginning basal readers. This student, who is displaying reading skills beyond those displayed by the majority of her classmates, also should be provided with differentiated instruction that might include more advanced reading materials and scaffolded support to continue advancing her literacy skills. Thus, RTI as a diamond-shaped model is intended to facilitate data collection for all students at all levels of achievement, with corresponding instructional modifications and intervention approaches provided to accelerate all students' reading progress.

A note of caution is needed, however. Somewhere along the way, it seems to have become acceptable in some educational circles to view RTI as comprising only three intervention "attempts": one intervention attempt (core/universal instruction) at Tier 1, one at Tier 2, and one at Tier 3. In fact, we believe that Figures 3.1 and 3.2 may inadvertently contribute to this misperception! In reality, however, the "three-attempt model" is a gross and inappro-

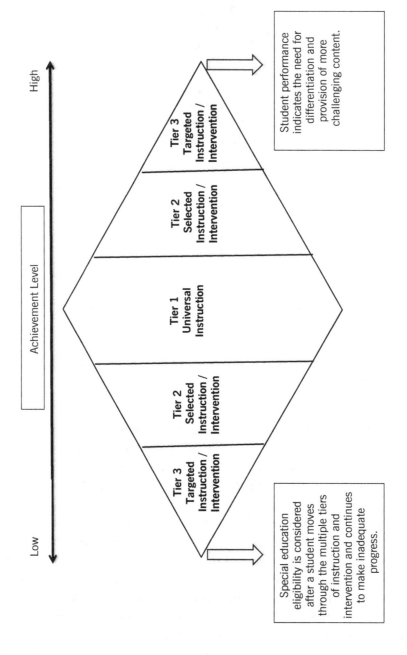

Low ←——————— Achievement Level ——————→ High

Tier 3
Targeted
Instruction /
Intervention

Tier 2
Selected
Instruction /
Intervention

Tier 1
Universal
Instruction

Tier 2
Selected
Instruction /
Intervention

Tier 3
Targeted
Instruction /
Intervention

Student performance indicates the need for differentiation and provision of more challenging content.

Special education eligibility is considered after a student moves through the multiple tiers of instruction and intervention and continues to make inadequate progress.

FIGURE 3.3. The RTI model for schoolwide reform.

priate oversimplification of RTI. Such a view suggests that a student gets "three strikes, then he or she is out (of regular education!)," when in fact the three RTI tiers actually reflect the relative intensity of the intervention approach and frequency of progress monitoring, and should absolutely not be interpreted as being limited to one "attempt" to help a student at each tier. In reality, *multiple* instructional modifications and intervention options should be attempted at *each* tier depending on the student's needs; thus, if a student's skills and performance are significantly low compared to those of peers and where he or she started, the amount of supplemental intervention—and concomitant progress monitoring—provided to that student should be proportional to the difficulty that the student is having. Thus, intervention intensity and progress monitoring frequency are greater at Tier 2 than at Tier 1, but they are even more intense at Tier 3 than at Tiers 1 and 2.

OUTCOMES ASSOCIATED WITH RTI IMPLEMENTATION

Although there are variations in the terminology used to describe educators' activities in RTI, the critical components are essentially the same and consist of (1) sound core instruction for all students, (2) universal screening and progress monitoring procedures that help educators make data-informed decisions, (3) a process for determining movement between intervention tiers and corresponding supplemental interventions, and (4) an emphasis on implementing instructions/interventions as they were intended to be implemented (i.e., intervention fidelity). These components, which are discussed in more detail later in this chapter, are (1) scientifically sound (we trust the research behind them!), (2) common educational practices, and (3) associated with improved student outcomes. However, the true value of RTI is the *implementation* and *integration* of these components with one another. Thus, within RTI models, the expectation is that the whole is greater than the sum of its parts.

General RTI Outcomes

Research clearly has demonstrated the positive outcomes associated with many individual RTI components and activities (e.g., using CBM to screen and monitor progress). Although there is less research examining outcomes associated with complete RTI model implementation (i.e., program evaluation research), increasing evidence demonstrates positive outcomes of whole-model implementation. One of the first comprehensive examinations of RTI model effectiveness was a meta-analysis in which the results of 21 studies indicated a significant reduction in special education referrals and a significant increase in reading achievement scores (Burns, Appleton, & Stehouwer, 2005). Of the 21 articles included in this meta-analysis, 11 of them examined outcomes from (1) the Heartland (Iowa) Area model, (2) the Ohio Intervention-Based Assessment (IBA), (3) Pennsylvania's Instructional Support Team (IST) project, and (4) the Minneapolis (Minnesota) public schools' problem-solving model (MPSM), each of which were considered early implementers of RTI.

The Heartland (Iowa) Area model (e.g., Heartland Area Education Agency 11, 2002; Ikeda, Tilly, Stumme, Volmer, & Allison, 1996; Jankowski & Heartland Area Education

Agency 11, 2003), was designed in 1988 to be a model in which school staff members (e.g., regular education classroom teachers, special education teachers, school psychologists, administrators) and parents utilized a problem-solving process to (1) identify and define student difficulties, (2) assist in implementing interventions, and (3) monitor progress of student performance. Despite the frequent tendency by RTI proponents to reference the Heartland Area model as a successful example of RTI implementation, Fuchs, Morgan, Young, and Rise (2003) cautioned that the relative lack of results demonstrating overall positive student outcomes, combined with the tendency to focus instead on referral and placement numbers, make it difficult to evaluate appropriately the model's overall effectiveness.

The Ohio IBA (e.g., Telzrow, McNamara, & Hollinger, 2000) model initially was implemented in 1992 and utilized a behavioral problem-solving approach combined with collaborative consultation. Telzrow et al. evaluated outcomes associated with implementation of this model, with results suggesting that there was an overall improvement in student performance. Similarly, the Pennsylvania IST model (e.g., Fuchs et al., 2003; Kovaleski, Tucker, & Stevens, 1996), first implemented in 1990, has been credited with lowering referral rates for special education services by more than one-half in schools that implemented the IST model as compared to schools that did not; schools implementing the IST model also saw grade retention rates decrease by up to two-thirds.

The Minneapolis PSM (e.g., Marston, Muyskens, Lau, & Canter, 2003) has been in place since 1993 and was initially implemented as an attempt to utilize a nonbiased assessment system. The PSM included a sequence of problem-solving steps: (1) describing the problem with specificity, (2) implementing strategies for intervention, (3) monitoring student progress and effectiveness of instruction, and (4) repeating the problem-solving steps as appropriate. Although researchers such as Marston et al. have provided data suggesting that the overall model has been effective, Fuchs et al. (2003) emphasized that in their review of studies examining the Minneapolis PSM, there was a lack of evidence that students who participated in the process actually made academic progress. Thus, although there appear to be data indicating that the implementation of the PSM in Minneapolis produced positive outcomes, questions remain regarding its true overall effectiveness.

VanDerHeyden, Witt, and Gilbertson (2007) examined the outcomes associated with the implementation of an RTI model in five schools within a single district. Results indicated that implementation of the System to Enhance Educational Performance (STEEP) process resulted in a reduction in the number of students referred for special education evaluations and a corresponding reduction in the number of students determined to be eligible for special education services. Given the small number of linguistically diverse students that were included in the sample, the authors were unable to make any definitive conclusions regarding the implementation of RTI with ELLs, but instead indicated that a more in-depth analysis of the performance of ELLs was needed.

Despite the growing number of indicators reflecting the potential advantages of RTI implementation, conflicting evidence of the value of RTI also exists. For example, in a recent meta-analysis that examined 13 studies concerning RTI implementation, Tran, Sanchez, Arellano, and Swanson (2011) suggested that although RTI procedures resulted in improvements in reading skills, the achievement gap between low responders and adequate responders was not narrowed. However, Tran et al. emphasized that the significance of

TABLE 3.1. Recommended Resources Relating to Outcomes Associated with RTI Model Implementation

Burns, M., Appleton, J. J., & Stehouwer, J. D. (2005). Meta-analytic review of responsiveness-to-intervention research: Examining field-based and research-implemented models. *Journal of Psychoeducational Assessment, 23*, 381–394.

Griffin, A. J., Parsons, L., Burns, M. K., & VanDerHeyden, A. (2007). *Response to intervention research to practice.* Washington, DC: National Association of State Directors of Special Education.

Tran, L., Sanchez, T., Arellano, B., & Swanson, H. L. (2011). A meta-analysis of the RTI literature for children at risk for reading disabilities. *Journal of Learning Disabilities, 44*, 283–295.

their meta-analysis was that "a clear pattern emerged suggesting that low responders can be identified prior to intervention" (p. 293). From our perspective, the more important result of this meta-analysis was that responders displayed a mean effect size gain of 1.91, and low responders, a mean effect size gain of 0.72, both of which are classified as large. Thus, although the achievement gap *between* the two groups did not disappear, both groups of students demonstrated significant growth associated with their participation in reading interventions. One could even surmise that these results suggest that although RTI might not be a "better" way to determine special education eligibility, it is effective in improving the outcomes of the majority of students who participate in RTI. Table 3.1 provides a list of resources that address outcomes associated with RTI model implementation and should be consulted if more information is desired.

RTI for ELLs

Providing scientifically based core instruction and supplemental interventions, conducting progress monitoring, and utilizing data-based decision making within multi-tiered models increasingly has been supported by research with native English-speaking students. Moreover, federal legislation (e.g., NCLB, Individuals with Disabilities Education Act [IDEA]) has encouraged—and in some cases mandated—the use of these procedures. Although increasing empirical support exists for the use of an RTI approach to address the academic difficulties of non-ELL students, knowledge regarding the effectiveness of complete RTI model implementation to address the unique learning needs of ELLs is only beginning to emerge and increasingly is being examined by researchers.

One of the first published attempts examining the effectiveness of interventions with ELL students within an implied context of RTI investigated reading interventions designed for Spanish-speaking ELL students identified as being at risk for reading disabilities (Vaughn et al., 2006). Vaughn and her colleagues studied the effectiveness of ELLs' specialized reading curricula developed in both Spanish and English compared to the curricula already implemented in the schools. The curricula they used with their ELL participants emphasized the following components of reading instruction known to be supported in the literature for monolingual English speakers: phonemic awareness, letter knowledge, word recognition, reading fluency, and comprehension strategies (i.e., the Five Pillars of

Reading Instruction, discussed in Chapter 5). Included in the Vaughn et al. intervention were instructional practices intended to increase the effectiveness of the core instruction for ELLs, such as the use of visual aids, explicit instruction, vocabulary clarification, facial expressions, repetitive language and routines, and modeling.

After researchers screened potential ELL participants to determine their preintervention reading abilities, students identified as being at risk were randomly assigned to either a Spanish or an English reading intervention group, or to a control group. Assignment to either the Spanish or English intervention group depended on the language of the student's core reading program (i.e., students being taught to read in English at school were assigned to the English intervention group). The investigators provided all participants in the treatment groups in English and Spanish with the reading intervention they created, in addition to the students' regular core reading program. In the intervention that lasted 7 months, students received daily intervention for 50 minutes.

Results indicated that both the Spanish and English intervention groups outperformed the comparison students (i.e., core instruction only) on many of the posttreatment measures in Spanish, such as letter-naming fluency, letter–sound identification, phonological awareness, word attack, passage comprehension, and oral reading fluency. Additionally, both treatment and control groups demonstrated growth on multiple English reading outcomes, thus suggesting that Spanish reading skills may support concomitant English reading skills. Overall, Vaughn and her colleagues (2006) concluded that important instructional components of both the Spanish and English interventions that resulted in academic gains included word study, comprehension strategies, reading fluency, vocabulary development, and phonics instruction. This finding supports the notion that elements of reading instruction demonstrated to be effective for native English speakers are also important elements of reading instruction for ELL students. Additionally, the results of this study are particularly valuable because they indicate that specific instructional methods and strategies (repetition, gestures, vocabulary clarification, etc.) may be necessary to optimize the acquisition of literacy skills of ELL students identified as being at risk for reading difficulties.

Given the growing research support for RTI model implementation with ELL students, our focus in the remainder of this book emphasizes the critical and necessary research-supported *components* of RTI for providing effective educational services to ELLs. Furthermore, in accord with the diamond-shaped RTI model we presented earlier, we conceptualize RTI as a way to ensure that a *comprehensive* and *integrated* set of services is rolled out for all students, but in particular ELLs and students who may need additional academic support.

NECESSARY COMPONENTS FOR IMPLEMENTING RTI MODELS

A number of critical components are essential for implementing high-quality RTI models. Although RTI models can be described using varying terms, all models consist of some combination of the same elements. Generally speaking, to be effective and to meet the needs of all students, RTI models should include the following basic yet critical components:

1. High-quality and scientifically based *core content curriculum and instruction (e.g., in reading, the focus is on phonemic awareness, phonics, fluency, reading comprehension and vocabulary)*.
2. *Data-based procedures* for making decisions regarding curriculum, intervention provision, intervention effectiveness, and overall student performance.
3. *Universal screening procedures.*
4. *Progress monitoring procedures.*
5. A well-defined process for determining *movement between instructional and intervention tiers.*
6. Availability of high-quality and scientifically based *supplemental interventions.*
7. Procedures for evaluating *integrity (i.e., fidelity) of implementation* of classroom instruction and supplemental interventions.
8. Well-defined procedures for *determining special education eligibility.*

Table 3.2 provides a list of resources for each of the various components of RTI model implementation and should be consulted if more in-depth information is desired regarding these topics.

Components 1–8 remain critical for the use of RTI models with ELL students; the primary difference in their application for ELLs versus native English-speaking students is that each of the eight components must incorporate more *explicit consideration of ELP and second-language acquisition* variables. One might adapt these eight components and their application to working with ELL students by revising them in the following ways:

1. High-quality and scientifically based *core content instruction* that allows ELL students to access the general education curriculum. Closely connected to this component, the implemented *language instructional model* must also meet the needs of all ELLs. Instruction must be differentiated to meet the needs of individual ELLs and include respectful tasks that are engaging, challenging, and interesting.
2. *Data-based procedures that take into consideration specific ELP levels* for making decisions regarding curriculum, intervention provision, intervention effectiveness, and overall student performance.
3. *Universal screening procedures* that *account for specific ELP levels.*
4. *Progress monitoring procedures* that *account for specific ELP levels.*
5. A well-defined process *that considers specific ELP levels* when determining *movement between instructional and intervention tiers.*
6. Availability of high-quality and scientifically based *supplemental interventions* that include *appropriate intervention options for ELL students at varying ELP levels.*
7. Procedures for evaluating the *integrity of implementation* of classroom instruction, supplemental interventions, and *language instruction.*
8. Well-defined procedures for *determining special education eligibility that take into consideration ELP levels, background information associated with ELL status, including exclusionary factors, and instructional implications.*

TABLE 3.2. Recommended Resources Relating to Components of RTI Models in General

General RTI implementation

Brown-Chidsey, R. M., & Steege, M. W. (2010). *Response to intervention: Principles and strategies for effective practice* (2nd ed.). New York: Guilford Press.

Broxterman, K., & Whalen, A. J. (2013). *RTI team building: Effective collaboration and data-based decision making.* New York: Guilford Press.

Burns, M. K., & Gibbons, K. A. (2008). *Implementing response-to-intervention in elementary and secondary schools: Procedures to assure scientific-based practices.* New York: Routledge.

Burns, M. K., Kanive, R., & Karich, A. C. (2014). Best practices in implementing school-based teams within a multitiered system of support. In A. Thomas & P. Harrison (Eds.), *Best practices in school psychology: Data-based and collaborative decision making* (6th ed., pp. 569–581). Bethesda, MD: National Association of School Psychologists.

Jimerson, S. R., Burns, M. K., & VanDerHeyden, A. (Eds.). (2007). *Handbook of response to intervention: The science and practice of assessment and intervention.* New York: Springer.

Miller, G., Lines, C., & Fleming, M. (2014). Best practices in family–school collaboration for multitiered service delivery. In A. Thomas & P. Harrison (Eds.), *Best practices in school psychology: Systems-level services* (6th ed., pp. 491–504). Bethesda, MD: National Association of School Psychologists.

Reschly, D. J., & Bergstrom, M. K. (2009). Response to intervention. In T. B. Gutkin & C. R. Reynolds (Eds.), *The handbook of school psychology* (4th ed., pp. 434–460). Hoboken, NJ: Wiley.

Stoiber, K. C. (2014). A comprehensive framework for multi-tiered systems of support in school psychology. In A. Thomas & P. Harrison (Eds.), *Best practices in school psychology: Data-based and collaborative decision making* (6th ed., pp. 41–70). Bethesda, MD: National Association of School Psychologists.

VanDerHeyden, A. M., & Burns, M. K. (2010). *Essentials of response to intervention.* Hoboken, NJ: Wiley.

Content instruction

Literacy

Kamil, M. L., Borman, G. D., Dole, J., Kral, C. C., Salinger, T., & Torgesen, J. (2008). *Improving adolescent literacy: Effective classroom and intervention practices: A practice guide* (NCEE No. 2008-4027). Washington, DC: National Center for Education Evaluation and Regional Assistance, Institute of Education Sciences, U.S. Department of Education.

Martinez, R. S. (2014). Best practices in instructional strategies for reading in general education. In A. Thomas & P. Harrison (Eds.), *Best practices in school psychology: Student-level services* (6th ed., pp. 9–17). Bethesda, MD: National Association of School Psychologists.

National Institute of Child Health and Human Development. (2000). *Report of the National Reading Panel: Teaching children to read: An evidence-based assessment of the scientific research literature on reading and its implications for reading instruction* (NIH Publication No. 00-4769). Washington, DC: U.S. Department of Health and Human Services.

Shanahan, T., Callison, K., Carriere, C., Duke, N. K., Pearson, P. D., Schatschneider, C., et al. (2010). *Improving reading comprehension in kindergarten through 3rd grade: A practice guide* (NCEE No. 2010-4038). Washington, DC: National Center for Education Evaluation and Regional Assistance, Institute of Education Sciences, U.S. Department of Education.

Snow, C. E., Burns, M. S., & Griffin, P. (Eds.). (1998). *Preventing reading difficulties in young children.* Washington, DC: National Academy Press.

(continued)

TABLE 3.2. *(continued)*

Mathematics

Clarke, B., Doabler, C. T., & Nelson, N. J. (2014). Best practices in mathematics assessment and intervention with elementary students. In A. Thomas & P. Harrison (Eds.), *Best practices in school psychology: Data-based and collaborative decision making* (6th ed., pp. 219–232). Bethesda, MD: National Association of School Psychologists.

Gersten, R., Beckmann, S., Clarke, B., Foegen, A., Marsh, L., Star, J. R., et al. (2009). *Assisting students struggling with mathematics: Response to intervention (RtI) for elementary and middle schools* (NCEE No. 2009-4060). Washington, DC: National Center for Education Evaluation and Regional Assistance, Institute of Education Sciences, U.S. Department of Education.

National Mathematics Advisory Panel. (2008). *Foundations for success: The final report of the National Mathematics Advisory Panel.* Washington, DC: U.S. Department of Education.

Siegler, R., Carpenter, T., Fennell, F., Geary, D., Lewis, J., Okamoto, Y., et al. (2010). *Developing effective fractions instruction for kindergarten through 8th grade: A practice guide* (NCEE No. 2010-4039). Washington, DC: National Center for Education Evaluation and Regional Assistance, Institute of Education Sciences, U.S. Department of Education.

Swanson, H. L. (2009). Science-supported math instruction for children with math difficulties. In S. Rosenfield & V. Berninger (Eds.), *Implementing evidence-based academic interventions in school settings* (pp. 85–106). New York: Oxford University Press.

Woodward, J., Beckmann, S., Driscoll, M., Franke, M., Herzig, P., Jitendra, A., et al. (2012). *Improving mathematical problem solving in grades 4 through 8: A practice guide* (NCEE No. 2012-4055). Washington, DC: National Center for Education Evaluation and Regional Assistance, Institute of Education Sciences, U.S. Department of Education.

Zannou, Y., Kettlerlin-Geller, L. R., & Shivraj, P. (2014). Best practices in mathematics instruction and assessment in secondary settings. In A. Thomas & P. Harrison (Eds.), *Best practices in school psychology: Data-based and collaborative decision making* (6th ed., pp. 233–246). Bethesda, MD: National Association of School Psychologists.

Writing

Graham, S., Bollinger, A., Booth Olson, C., D'Aoust, C., MacArthur, C., McCutchen, D., et al. (2012). *Teaching elementary school students to be effective writers: A practice guide* (NCEE No. 2012- 4058). Washington, DC: National Center for Education Evaluation and Regional Assistance, Institute of Education Sciences, U.S. Department of Education.

Malecki, C. K. (2014). Best practices in written language assessment and intervention. In A. Thomas & P. Harrison (Eds.), *Best practices in school psychology: Data-based and collaborative decision making* (6th ed., pp. 187–202). Bethesda, MD: National Association of School Psychologists.

Data-based decision making (universal screening and progress monitoring)

Albers, C. A., & Kettler, R. J. (2014). Best practices in universal screening. In A. Thomas & P. Harrison (Eds.), *Best practices in school psychology: Data-based and collaborative decision making* (6th ed., pp. 121–131). Bethesda, MD: National Association of School Psychologists.

Burns, M. K., Haegele, K., & Petersen-Brown, S. (2014). Screening for discrete early reading skills: Using screening data to guide resources and instruction. In R. J. Kettler, T. A. Glover, C. A. Albers, & K. A. Feeney-Kettler (Eds.), *Universal screening in educational settings: Evidence-based decision making for schools* (pp. 171–197). Washington, DC: American Psychological Association.

(continued)

TABLE 3.2. *(continued)*

Clarke, B., Haymond, K., & Gersten, R. (2014). Mathematics screening measures for the primary grades. In R. J. Kettler, T. A. Glover, C. A. Albers, & K. A. Feeney-Kettler (Eds.), *Universal screening in educational settings: Evidence-based decision making for schools* (pp. 199–221). Washington, DC: American Psychological Association.

Hamilton, L., Halverson, R., Jackson, S., Mandinach, E., Supovitz, J., & Wayman, J. (2009). *Using student achievement data to support instructional decision making* (NCEE No. 2009-4067). Washington, DC: National Center for Education Evaluation and Regional Assistance, Institute of Education Sciences, U.S. Department of Education.

Hixson, M. D., Christ, T. J., & Bruni, T. (2014). Best practices in the analysis of progress monitoring data and decision making. In A. Thomas & P. Harrison (Eds.), *Best practices in school psychology: Foundations* (6th ed., pp. 343–354). Bethesda, MD: National Association of School Psychologists.

Hosp, M. K., Hosp, J. L., & Howell, K. W. (2007). *The ABCs of CBM: A practical guide to curriculum-based measurement.* New York: Guilford Press.

Kettler, R. J., Glover, T. A., Albers, C. A., & Feeney-Kettler, K. A. (Eds.). (2014). *Universal screening in educational settings: Evidence-based decision making for schools.* Washington, DC: American Psychological Association.

McConnell, S., Bradfield, T., & Wackerle-Hollman, A. (2014). Early childhood literacy screening. In R. J. Kettler, T. A. Glover, C. A. Albers, & K. A. Feeney-Kettler (Eds.), *Universal screening in educational settings: Evidence-based decision making for schools* (pp. 141–170). Washington, DC: American Psychological Association.

National Center on Response to Intervention. *www.rti4success.org.*

Riley-Tillman, T. C., Burns, M. K., & Gibbons, K. (2013). *RTI applications: Vol. 2. Assessment, analysis, and decision making.* New York: Guilford Press.

Shapiro, E. S., & Guard, K. B. (2014). Best practices in setting progress monitoring goals for academic skill improvement. In A. Thomas & P. Harrison (Eds.), *Best practices in school psychology: Student-level services* (6th ed., pp. 51–66). Bethesda, MD: National Association of School Psychologists.

Stewart, L. H. (2014). Best practices in developing academic local norms. In A. Thomas & P. Harrison (Eds.), *Best practices in school psychology: Foundations* (6th ed., pp. 301–314). Bethesda, MD: National Association of School Psychologists.

Supplemental interventions

General

Begeny, J. C., Schulte, A. C., & Johnson, K. (2012). *Enhancing instructional problem solving: An efficient system for assisting struggling learners.* New York: Guilford Press.

Burns, M. K., Riley-Tillman, T. C., & VanDerHeyden, A. M. (2012). *RTI applications: Vol. 1. Academic and behavioral interventions.* New York: Guilford Press.

Forman, S. G., Lubin, A. R., & Tripptree, A. L. (2014). Best practices in implementing evidence-based school interventions. In A. Thomas & P. Harrison (Eds.), *Best practices in school psychology: Systems-level services* (6th ed., pp. 43–55). Bethesda, MD: National Association of School Psychologists.

Riley-Tillman, T. C., & Burns, M. K. (2009). *Evaluating educational interventions: Single-case design for measuring response to intervention.* New York: Guilford Press.

Stormont, M., Reinke, W. M., Herman, K. C., & Lembke, E. S. (2012). *Academic and behavior supports for at-risk students: Tier 2 interventions.* New York: Guilford Press.

(continued)

TABLE 3.2. *(continued)*

Literacy

Daly, E. J., III, Neugebauer, S., Chafouleas, S., & Skinner, C. H. (2015). *Interventions for reading problems: Designing and evaluating effective strategies* (2nd ed.). New York: Guilford Press.

Daly, E. J., III, O'Connor, M. A., & Young, N. D. (2014). Best practices in oral reading fluency interventions. In A. Thomas & P. Harrison (Eds.), *Best practices in school psychology: Student-level services* (6th ed., pp. 115–128). Bethesda, MD: National Association of School Psychologists.

Gersten, R., Compton, D., Connor, C. M., Dimino, J., Santoro, L., Linan-Thompson, S., et al. (2008). *Assisting students struggling with reading: Response to Intervention and multi-tier intervention for reading in the primary grades. A practice guide.* (NCEE No. 009-4045). Washington, DC: National Center for Education Evaluation and Regional Assistance, Institute of Education Sciences, U.S. Department of Education.

Joseph, L. M. (2014). Best practices on interventions for students with reading problems. In A. Thomas & P. Harrison (Eds.), *Best practices in school psychology: Student-level services* (6th ed., pp. 97–113). Bethesda, MD: National Association of School Psychologists.

Mathematics

Clarke, B., Doabler, C. T., & Nelson, N. J. (2014). Best practices in mathematics assessment and intervention with elementary students. In A. Thomas & P. Harrison (Eds.), *Best practices in school psychology: Data-based and collaborative decision making* (6th ed., pp. 219–232). Bethesda, MD: National Association of School Psychologists.

Gersten, R., Beckmann, S., Clarke, B., Foegen, A., Marsh, L., Star, J. R., et al. (2009). *Assisting students struggling with mathematics: Response to Intervention (RtI) for elementary and middle schools* (NCEE No. 2009-4060). Washington, DC: National Center for Education Evaluation and Regional Assistance, Institute of Education Sciences, U.S. Department of Education.

Writing

Malecki, C. K. (2014). Best practices in written language assessment and intervention. In A. Thomas & P. Harrison (Eds.), *Best practices in school psychology: Data-based and collaborative decision making* (6th ed., pp. 187–202). Bethesda, MD: National Association of School Psychologists.

Integrity/fidelity of implementation

Durlack, J. A., & DuPre, E. P. (2008). Implementation matters: A review on the influence of implementation on program outcomes and the factors affecting implementation. *American Journal of Community Psychology, 41,* 327–350.

Roach, A. T., Lawton, K., & Elliott, S. N. (2014). Best practices in facilitating and evaluating the integrity of school-based interventions. In A. Thomas & P. Harrison (Eds.), *Best practices in school psychology: Data-based and collaborative decision making* (6th ed., pp. 133–146). Bethesda, MD: National Association of School Psychologists.

Sanetti, L. M. H., & Kratochwill, T. R. (2013). Treatment integrity assessment within a problem-solving model. In R. Brown-Chidsey & K. J. Andren (Eds.), *Assessment for intervention: A problem-solving approach* (2nd ed., pp. 297–318). New York: Guilford Press.

Sanetti, L. M., & Kratochwill, T. R. (Eds.). (2014). *Treatment integrity: A foundation for evidence-based practice in applied psychology.* Washington, DC: American Psychological Association.

Table 3.3 provides a summary of resources relating to the various components of RTI model implementation with ELLs. We discuss next in greater detail each of the eight critical components of RTI models for ELL students.

High-Quality Core Instruction

As we noted earlier, RTI models are most frequently conceptualized as occurring across three tiers (e.g., Fuchs, & Fuchs, 2006; Peterson, Prasse, Shinn, & Swerdlik, 2007; Vaughn & Fuchs, 2003). Tier 1 services include the academic and behavioral programming that all children in a school receive; thus, Tier 1 is closely associated with the basic curriculum (which should be of high quality). Educators should expect this core programming to meet the needs of the majority of their students (e.g., 75–80%). More individualized, supplemental support is needed to close the learning and/or behavioral gap for the 20–25% of students not succeeding at this first tier. In Chapter 5 we examine Tier I and sound core instruction for ELLs in more detail.

Data-Based Decision Making

Data-based, or data-informed, decision making consists of using data to guide instructional improvement and to make decisions regarding student performance and overall classroom, grade-level, school, and district performance. We believe that the data empower educators' practices in every way. According to Ikeda, Neesen, and Witt (2008), if your assessment efforts are not directly linked to school improvement efforts, then your efforts are basically worthless. Assessing progress is only half the battle; making informed decisions that lead to individual student and school improvements based on the assessment results is the real goal.

Two types of assessment commonly are practiced in RTI models: universal screening (i.e., benchmarking) and progress monitoring. These are the RTI assessment practices frequently associated with data-based decision making. Generally, the same assessment tools or procedures are used for both universal screening and progress monitoring (e.g., letter-naming fluency, reading curriculum-based measurement [R-CBM]). The difference between universal screening and progress monitoring lies in the *purpose and frequency* of assessments. In universal screening, all students receive assessments, usually two or three times per academic year. In progress monitoring, the assessments are given more frequently, such as monthly or even weekly. To illustrate the concepts of universal screening and progress monitoring, we like to use an example that is familiar to all readers. Each time you visit the doctor, whether for a regular checkup or because indeed you are sick, a nurse takes your temperature. *All* patients get their temperature checked (i.e., the population is screened), just to make sure that the thermometer is registering right at about 98.6 degrees Fahrenheit. In contrast, progress monitoring assessments are given more frequently, as determined by patient need (i.e., the greater the need, the more frequent the progress monitoring) and, obviously, only to *some* patients. Following the preceding temperature example, say that you have a fever when you go in for your regular checkup. This temperature—or screener—tells the doctor that *something* is going on; the thermometer cannot tell the doctor *what* is

TABLE 3.3. Recommended Resources Relating to Components of RTI Models Specific to ELLs

General

Carvalho, C., Dennison, A., & Estrella, I. (2014). Best practices in the assessment of English language learners. In A. Thomas & P. Harrison (Eds.), *Best practices in school psychology: Foundations* (6th ed., pp. 75–87). Bethesda, MD: National Association of School Psychologists.

Proctor, S. L., & Meyers, J. (2014). Best practices in primary prevention in diverse schools and communities. In A. Thomas & P. Harrison (Eds.), *Best practices in school psychology: Foundations* (6th ed., pp. 33–47). Bethesda, MD: National Association of School Psychologists.

Xu, Y., & Drame, E. (2007). Culturally appropriate context: Unlocking the potential of response to intervention for English language learners. *Early Childhood Education Journal, 35,* 305–311.

Literacy and English language instruction

August, D., & Shanahan, T. (Eds.). (2006). *Developing literacy in second-language learners: Report of the National Literacy Panel on Language-Minority Children and Youth.* Mahwah, NJ: Erlbaum.

Baker, S., Lesaux, N., Jayanthi, M., Dimino, J., Proctor, C. P., Morris, J., et al. (2014). *Teaching academic content and literacy to English learners in elementary and middle school* (NCEE No. 2014-4012). Washington, DC: National Center for Education Evaluation and Regional Assistance (NCEE), Institute of Education Sciences, U.S. Department of Education.

Cheung, A. C. K., & Slavin, R. E. (2012). Effective reading programs for Spanish-dominant English language learners (ELLs) in the elementary grades: A synthesis of research. *Review of Educational Research, 82,* 351–395.

Fien, H., Smith, J. L. M., Baker, S. K., Chaparro, E., Baker, D. L., & Preciado, J. A. (2011). Including English learners in a multitiered approach to early reading instruction and intervention. *Assessment for Effective Intervention, 36,* 143–157.

Gersten, R., Baker, S. K., Shanahan, T., Linan-Thompson, S., Collins, P., & Scarcella, R. (2007). *Effective literacy and English language Instruction for English learners in the elementary grades: A practice guide* (NCEE No. 2007-4011). Washington, DC: National Center for Education Evaluation and Regional Assistance, Institute of Education Sciences, U.S. Department of Education.

Li, G., & Edwards, P. A. (Eds.). (2010). *Best practices in ELL instruction.* New York: Guilford Press.

Vanderwood, M. L., & Socie, D. (2014). Best practices in assessing and improving English language learners' literacy performance. In A. Thomas & P. Harrison (Eds.), *Best practices in school psychology: Foundations* (6th ed., pp. 89–98). Bethesda, MD: National Association of School Psychologists.

Data-based decision making (universal screening and progress monitoring)

Albers, C. A., & Mission, P. L. (2014). Universal screening of English language learners: Language proficiency and literacy. In R. J. Kettler, T. A. Glover, C. A. Albers, & K. A. Feeney-Kettler (Eds.), *Universal screening in educational settings: Evidence-based decision making for schools* (pp. 275–304). Washington, DC: American Psychological Association.

Richards-Tutor, C., Solari, E. J., Leafstedt, J. M., Gerber, M. M., Filippini, A., & Aceves, T. C. (2012). Response to intervention for English learners: Examining models for determining response and nonresponse. *Assessment for Effective Intervention, 38,* 172–184.

(continued)

TABLE 3.3. *(continued)*

Supplemental interventions

Albers, C. A., Mission, P. L., & Bice-Urbach, B. J. (2013). Considering diverse learner characteristics in problem-solving assessment. In R. Brown-Chidsey & K. J. Andren (Eds.), *Assessment for intervention: A problem-solving approach* (2nd ed., pp. 101–122). New York: Guilford Press.

August, D., & Shanahan, T. (Eds.). (2006). *Developing literacy in second-language learners: Report of the National Literacy Panel on Language-Minority Children and Youth*. Mahwah, NJ: Erlbaum.

Gersten, R., Baker, S. K., Shanahan, T., Linan-Thompson, S., Collins, P., & Scarcella, R. (2007). *Effective literacy and English language instruction for English learners in the elementary grades: A practice guide* (NCEE No. 2007-4011). Washington, DC: National Center for Education Evaluation and Regional Assistance, Institute of Education Sciences, U.S. Department of Education.

Jones, J. (2014). Best practices in providing culturally responsive interventions. In A. Thomas & P. Harrison (Eds.), *Best practices in school psychology: Foundations* (6th ed., pp. 49–60). Bethesda, MD: National Association of School Psychologists.

going on (that would require further assessment), but it certainly signals that *something* is awry. Say your doctor sends you home with a prescription for antibiotics (i.e., a research-based intervention/treatment). In the coming hours and days, you are likely to monitor your own progress or response to the antibiotics by frequently taking your temperature to make sure the number on the thermometer goes down. You monitor your fever's progress until the problem is eliminated (i.e., you no longer have a fever), and you will know the fever is gone when both the temperature is back to approximately 98.6 degrees Fahrenheit *and* you start to feel better. Within the context of RTI, universal screening and progress monitoring are similar to the previous body temperature example with the difference being that RTI is applied to academic standing and academic progress.

Within RTI models, universal early academic screening is an absolutely necessary prerequisite to providing critical prevention and intervention services for all students, including ELLs (e.g., Albers, Glover, & Kratochwill, 2007; Albers & Mission, 2014; Kettler, Glover, Albers, & Feeney-Kettler, 2014; Parisi, Ihlo, & Glover, 2014). To be effective, universal screening systems need to be appropriate (e.g., compatible with local needs, aligned with constructs of interest, supported theoretically and empirically), technically adequate (in terms of norms, reliability, and validity), and usable (e.g., feasible, acceptable to teachers; Glover & Albers, 2007). Specific to ELLs, unfortunately, the majority of universal screening procedures fails to consider specific ELP levels adequately when estimating the degree of risk for current and future academic difficulties. To address this concern, in Chapter 5, we outline specific procedures for incorporating ELP levels, what language instructional model is in place, and other critical issues to bear in mind when conducting universal screening procedures with ELLs.

Progress monitoring includes procedures that help educators and families know what each student is learning. Progress monitoring results also help educators and parents analyze potential explanations for any failure to meet expectations and identify a new course of action. An example would be a student who persistently is reading below the 25th percentile on a reading fluency task (i.e., R-CBM) despite participating in frequent, intense, targeted, research-based interventions to bolster reading fluency (e.g., repeated reading or choral reading). To implement RTI models fully, it behooves schools to select common and relatively simple procedures for monitoring student progress and performance using CBMs and other data. We recommend many of the more common and widely accessible assessments and data management systems available today (e.g., AIMSweb and Dynamic Indicators of Basic Early Literacy Skills [DIBELS]). Universal screening should be embedded within the progress monitoring system, such that the same instruments or procedures utilized for universal screening are used also for progress monitoring (in our earlier medical example, a thermometer was used to check temperatures for both the universal screening and the progress monitoring procedures). More frequent progress monitoring at Tiers 2 and 3 allows a collaborative team to decide whether an intervention is effective (in the medical example, the dropping temperature on the thermometer indicates that the antibiotics are working).

Implementation of Research-Based Interventions

Within RTI models, educators (e.g., classroom teachers, classroom aides, special education teachers, school psychologists, and support staff) provide a range of instructional strategies and interventions to ensure that the academic and behavioral needs of all students are met. However, before RTI models as a whole can be implemented effectively with ELLs, it is necessary to have validated interventions for use with ELLs at each tier. In other words, an ELL (or any student) should only be identified as needing additional intervention supports after failing to respond to an intervention *empirically shown to be effective with other ELLs*. In other words, say that a teacher decides to implement a strategy or intervention for which he or she has no knowledge about whether it has been studied by researchers and determined to be effective with ELLs, but he or she has the materials to implement it, so he or she does so anyway. And say that his or her student does not respond favorably (and the teacher knows this to be true because the student's progress monitoring data do not indicate improvement) to that particular strategy or intervention. It would be highly inappropriate for the teacher to decide that the student did not respond well to this particular intervention because the student has an underlying deficit. *We cannot determine lack of responsiveness unless the intervention we use has been studied by researchers and deemed to be effective in students similar to the student receiving the intervention in your classroom.* In the earlier fever example, we would never want a doctor to prescribe a treatment (i.e., antibiotics) that were not proven in past research actually to work—especially in humans!

We recognize that currently the number of identified evidence-based interventions for ELLs is relatively small, particularly in the area of reading, which makes it difficult to select and implement from a wide range of appropriate supplemental interventions for ELL students. What's more, research that is available is rarely definitive and often is conflicting. Nevertheless, there *are* feasible options for intervention available, as we discuss in Chapters 5 and 6. Both native English-speaking students who do not respond adequately to the core instruction, which should constitute a much smaller proportion of the students (e.g.,

10–15%) in the classroom, and most ELLs are often best served by Tier 2 interventions provided in smaller groups. The smaller group size increases individual students' opportunities to respond and receive corrective feedback.

For those students, including some ELLs, who fail to respond to interventions at Tier 2, even more intensive, targeted interventions (and more frequent progress monitoring) must be the next course of action. It is important to note that interventions at the Tiers 2 and 3 are not meant to replace core universal curriculum and instruction; rather, students should receive the supplemental services *in addition to* the core curriculum. Simply stated, one should never pull a student out of the core reading curriculum so that he or she can participate in a small-group reading intervention! The student must participate in both the core reading curriculum *and* the small-group reading intervention. Schoolwide decisions must be made about what to sacrifice in the schedule to make this possible. The key is determining whether a student is able to improve his or her skills and performance when provided instruction and intervention that is adequate in duration, intensity, and frequency. Flexible movement between intervention tiers therefore makes educational service delivery more systematic and responsive to the needs of individual students.

Instructional and Intervention Integrity

A critical yet often underappreciated and poorly understood component of RTI models is the degree to which the universal curriculum and corresponding supplemental interventions are implemented as intended, which is referred to as *instructional and intervention integrity,* or *fidelity.* For many students, learning will not occur if the curriculum is not implemented as intended (e.g., if it is not delivered in the recommended format or at the recommended frequency), nor will improvement be seen if supplemental interventions are not implemented as they were designed to be implemented. In our earlier medical example, say you are supposed to take your antibiotics twice a day for 10 days, but you decide to stop taking them after 4 days because you start feeling much better. Shortly thereafter, not surprisingly, you get sick again. You cannot then blame the intervention (i.e., the antibiotics) for not working, because you chose not to take them as they were intended to be taken (based on clinical trials in medical research). Likewise, in schools, when the core curriculum and supplement interventions are not put into practice as intended, it is not possible to determine whether a student is "responding" to instruction and intervention. Given the additional challenge facing ELLs who are learning English concurrently with academic content, implementation fidelity is an even more critical component impacting RTI model implementation.

RTI IMPLEMENTATION APPROACHES

There are two broad ways to implement RTI interventions at Tiers 2 and 3: (1) standard protocol approaches or (2) problem-solving approaches. Both of these are discussed in greater detail below.

Standard Protocol Approaches

Standard protocol RTI approaches implement predetermined, evidence-based interventions for students who do not respond adequately to core instruction and thereby experience difficulties in the same academic content area or skill (e.g., phonemic awareness, reading fluency, reading comprehension, mathematics, and writing). For example, a school might decide to use repeated readings for all students struggling with reading fluency or incremental rehearsal for all students struggling with single-digit multiplication facts. Because of the predetermined nature of the intervention options, each student who receives additional supports thus receives the identical interventions as any other student identified as needing additional supports in the same area. A perceived advantage of a standard protocol approach is that educators are trained to implement a limited and predetermined number of interventions, increasing the likelihood that educators will become highly skilled at implementing these specific interventions. Additionally, standard protocol approaches utilize school resources more efficiently, because a *group* of students can simultaneously participate in research-based interventions (Fuchs et al., 2003).

Problem-Solving Approaches

Conversely, problem-solving approaches rely on a team of educators to analyze student problems systematically and develop appropriate individualized intervention plans to address the identified difficulties. As described by Deno (2013), "the term *problem solving* is used whenever people act to eliminate a difference between what they currently sense or perceive and alternative conditions that they value" and "refers to the activities undertaken to reduce or eliminate the perceived discrepancies" (p. 11). The problem-solving approach to intervention planning is intended to be more sensitive to individual differences (Fuchs et al., 2003) than the standard protocol approach, and it is critical for students who are experiencing difficulties that cannot or have not been adequately addressed by standard protocol interventions. Given the benefits of utilizing both standard protocol interventions and interventions derived from the problem-solving process, the majority of RTI models described in the literature use a combination of these two approaches (Jimerson, Burns, & VanDerHeyden, 2007), which typically means using the standard protocol approach at Tier 2 and the problem-solving approach at Tier 3.

The problem-solving model described by Deno (2013) encapsulates the primary components of most problem-solving models. Specifically, this problem-solving model includes a series of five steps:

1. Identifying the problem.
2. Defining the problem.
3. Exploring alternative solutions.
4. Applying the selected intervention.
5. Looking at the effects.

This problem-solving model, often referred to as the IDEAL (i.e., Identify, Define, Explore, Apply, and Look) model, was considered as a multi-tiered system of support, which essentially was an early version of modern RTI models. Given the relative lack of evidence-based interventions and prepackaged intervention approaches that have been demonstrated to be effective for use with ELLs (as we see in Chapters 5 and 6), RTI approaches based on problem solving likely are more applicable to the implementation of RTI with ELLs, especially considering the heterogeneity within this population.

Consideration of Ecological Factors

A critical feature of problem-solving models is their emphasis on evaluating ecological variables that may be associated with students' academic difficulties (e.g., McCurdy, Coutts, Sheridan, & Campbell, 2013). For example, Rosenfield (1987) referred to students whose needs were not being met by the implemented curriculum and instructional approaches as "curriculum casualties" (p. 27); we would actually take this sentiment one step further and suggest that many ELLs are not only "curriculum casualties" but actually are also "*ecological* academic casualties" in that multiple ecological variables encountered by this population of students increase the likelihood of chronic academic underachievement. The true value of implementing an RTI model with ELLs—particularly a model that utilizes a problem-solving approach—is that the RTI process should, from the beginning, consider the impact of these ecological variables and explore ways to minimize their impact within and outside the school setting.

Utilizing an RTI model to provide services to the student body population is intended to ensure that environmental or ecological variables—or those variables not *internal* to a student—are not the sources of a student's academic difficulties. Stated differently, RTI models are quasi-standardized approaches designed to rule out environmental and ecological factors as the primary determinant of the student's difficulties. We cannot emphasize enough the importance of considering these factors when determining what *might* be causing a student, and in particular an ELL student, to struggle in school (and as we see in Chapter 7, these factors become even more important when considering special education eligibility). There is an implicit assumption that the use of RTI procedures will compel educators to examine the relative influence of *ecological* factors as the source of the student's difficulties, and that if there is evidence that these factors are relevant, the school will intervene to lessen the impact of these factors on a child's academic success. The ecological factors of greatest relevance include (see Table 3.4 for specific examples of these variables):

1. Lack of appropriate instruction.
2. Curriculum factors.
3. Classroom and school factors.
4. Cultural factors.
5. Economic factors.
6. Environmental factors.

TABLE 3.4. Specific Examples Associated with Ecological Variables

Lack of appropriate instruction

- Failure to implement evidence-based reading programs
- Lack of instruction in mathematics
- Lack of exposure to relative cognitive tasks
- Failure to use progress monitoring and formative assessment to inform instruction at classroom and individual levels
- Student not taught at appropriate instructional level
- Inappropriate mismatch between ELP level and instruction
- Lack of opportunities for active responding
- Lack of quality instructional planning
- Interfering problem behaviors are not addressed, thus impacting students' attention to learning

Curriculum factors

- Failure to implement evidence-based curricula
- Lack of consistency in curriculum between grade levels
- Insufficient opportunity to learn
- Lack of appropriate supplemental intervention opportunities
- Failure to utilize appropriate accommodations
- Students' language skills (first vs. second language) do not allow for comprehension of content

Classroom and school factors

- Lack of appropriately trained classroom teachers and support staff
- Lack of language instruction resources
- Large class sizes
- Lack of technology in classrooms
- Lack of schoolwide behavior program
- Lack of communication with parents/guardians

Cultural factors

- Use of assessments not validated for use with student characteristics (e.g., language)
- Conflicting/inconsistent educational and behavioral expectations between parents/guardians and school
- Limited parental involvement in school activities due to cultural and communication barriers
- Limited exposure and opportunities to learn in previous educational settings

Economic factors

- Single-parent household potentially resulting in fewer parental school involvement opportunities
- Parental work responsibilities
- Exposure to community violence and crime
- Homelessness/frequent mobility
- Lack of health care and related services
- Lack of appropriate nutrition
- Limited community resources

Environmental factors

- Difficulties in parents/guardians being actively engaged in student's education
- Student responsibilities at home that detract from school performance
- Limited access to educational resources
- Limited community resources or limited access to community resources

Consideration of these ecological factors is perhaps even more applicable when considering ELL students, as their limited ELP and academic performance are significantly impacted by each of these six factors. Clearly, it is essential that ecological factors be considered during the problem-solving process, so that the optimal academic instruction and intervention services can be identified for all students, especially ELLs.

Ecological Factors Worksheets

To assist RTI teams in evaluating the potential influence of ecological factors on a student's school performance, we created a series of worksheets to guide you in reference to the ecological factors. As you can see in Appendices 3.1–3.7 (at the end of the chapter) the worksheets are designed to facilitate data collection for instruction and intervention planning regarding multiple relevant ecological factors, including those in the areas covering the following seven domains:

1. Learner Domain
2. Lack of Appropriate Instruction
3. Core Curriculum
4. Classroom/School Disadvantage
5. Cultural Factors
6. Economic Factors
7. Environmental Factors

In conjunction with the RTI program participation worksheets, which are presented in Chapter 6, the ecological factors worksheets can provide excellent guidance for school RTI teams. For each of the seven domains, there are multiple areas of consideration. First, the problem-solving/RTI team is asked to consider potential factors contributing to school difficulties for individual ELL students within a particular domain. In the Learner Domain example (Appendix 3.1), the team considers whether factors such as existing disability, emotional difficulties, or drug/alcohol use are present. Next, the team identifies specific examples of the contributing factor, if present. So, in the Learner Domain, if a physical condition is impacting learning, a member of the team checks off the specific condition or conditions, such as visual impairment, chronic health condition, and medication side effects. Third, the team indicates the sources of evidence corroborating the information. The following columns in the worksheet contain four questions in which the team evaluates: (1) whether the factor is present, (2) how long the factor has been present (if known), (3) the degree to which the factor is contributing to student's difficulties, and (4) the degree to which the team members believe the student's difficulties would continue to exist if this factor were no longer present. The last column refocuses the team toward a possible solution by encouraging the team members to brainstorm how they will address the issue.

CHALLENGES IN IMPLEMENTING PREVENTION
AND EARLY INTERVENTION SERVICES WITH ELLs

As it does with all students, RTI potentially has multiple benefits for providing early intervention and support to ELLs who may be struggling academically and behaviorally. The use of data, benchmark testing or universal screening, and progress monitoring to determine which students may be at risk in reading, for example, and to determine intervention outcomes for struggling students provides a key advantage of RTI. The increased emphasis on core instruction and acknowledgment of the need to meet the varying challenges associated with providing services to students who are not proficient in English also serve these students well. The implementation of RTI models also should assist in reallocating resources, so that ELL students can receive additional support *before* determining whether they qualify for special education services.

Current research examining RTI implementation has been conducted primarily with monolingual English-speaking populations. Thus, it is sometimes challenging to generalize the existing findings to more diverse populations, such as ELLs (Vaughn, Mathes, Linan-Thompson, & Francis, 2005; Xu & Drame, 2008). Specifically, the efficacy of certain reading interventions, especially in English, often has not been tested with ELL students, making it difficult to establish a thorough evidence base. All too frequently, interventions that are considered evidence-based are implemented with diverse students, without consideration of the population that is being served. Although some interventions and programs have been found to improve outcomes for both ELLs and native English-speaking students, it is important to note that diversity must be considered when choosing the most appropriate curriculum or intervention. As an example, in one study, a group of ELL students struggling in English reading was provided with Reading Recovery (Linan-Thompson, Vaughn, Prater, & Cirino, 2006; Orosco & Klinger, 2010), a short-term (and very costly) intervention for first graders performing below the 10th percentile in reading. Although this intervention has demonstrated improvements for native English-speaking students, it was found to be ineffective in producing sufficient progress for ELL students at risk for reading difficulties. Considering that differentiated instruction is critical within an RTI framework, the core curriculum often is structured toward what will benefit the majority of students. Because many schools have native English speakers as the majority population, this means that the core reading curriculum all students receive would more likely be geared toward non-ELL students. This also means that teachers and school staff need to be cognizant of the effectiveness of interventions chosen, based on each student's individual, diverse background, and unique academic and linguistic needs.

A final challenge in the use of RTI for ELL populations has to do with teacher training. Often, teachers feel unprepared to work with diverse populations of students. Regrettably, many teachers have not received adequate training to teach ELL students effectively within the general education classroom (Orosco & Klinger, 2010; Xu & Drame, 2008). Teachers often lack knowledge regarding the process of second-language acquisition, which may limit the quality of instruction and supplemental intervention that they can and do provide to ELLs. In addition to a lack of data-supported interventions and needs that differ from those of the majority population, ELL students also may struggle because their teachers are unaware of the strategies needed to provide additional support *within* the general education classroom (which we describe in detail in Chapter 5). Further training of current teachers and support within teacher education programs is critical to help improve the educational outcomes for ELL students. We hope in this book to provide at least a cursory primer for classroom teachers who are unsure of how best to provide appropriate instruction and intervention for their ELL students.

Unfortunately, school personnel all too frequently do not identify students with learning difficulties or provide individualized services until these students are in second or third grade (Wagner, Francis, & Morris, 2005). Limited English language abilities that impede the academic performance of students appear to delay further the identification of the learning difficulties that hinder progress. Data reveal that schools are identifying learning difficulties in the ELL population at increased rates in grades 4–6, 2 to 3 years *after* they are typically detecting similar difficulties in monolingual English-speaking students (McCardle, Mele-McCarthy, Cutting, et al., 2005). These data highlight the difficulty educators have in distinguishing between issues of language acquisition and skills deficits commonly associated with true specific learning disabilities. Thus, remediation of difficulties is delayed because interventions are not provided until a student's academic performance has fallen significantly behind grade-level expectations. This delay can have a direct impact on students' behavior by putting them beyond the reach of the academic success that can serve as a protective factor against behavioral and emotional difficulties (Walker & Shinn, 2002). Unfortunately, by the time appropriate services are made available to ELLs, it is likely that the school will have to provide costly and intensive remedial services (e.g., special education), and still it may be difficult or nearly impossible for the student to catch up with peers.

We recognize that there is a great need for future research on RTI implementation with ELL populations; at the same time, we cannot wait for all of the questions to be answered, as students are struggling *today*. As we hope you will see in the remainder of this book, our goal is to provide guidance—based on what we already know—on how to implement RTI with ELL students.

Ecological Factor 1 Worksheet: Learner Domain

Possible contributing factor	Example	Evidence source(s)	Is this factor present?
☐ Physical condition impacting learning	Student records, teacher/parent/guardian/ student report indicate: ☐ Visual impairment ☐ Hearing impairment ☐ Motor impairment ☐ Chronic health condition ☐ Transient health condition ☐ Medication side effects ☐ Other		NO YES
☐ Existing disability (e.g., autism)	Student records, teacher/parent/ guardian/student report indicate presence of existing disability ☐ Other		NO YES
☐ Impaired cognitive functioning	Student records, teacher/parent/ guardian report indicate presence of impaired cognitive functioning ☐ Other		NO YES
☐ Emotional difficulties	Student records, teacher/parent/guardian/ student report indicate symptoms of: ☐ Anxiety ☐ Depression ☐ Stress ☐ Emotional withdrawal ☐ Other		NO YES

(continued)

Ecological Factor 1 Worksheet: Learner Domain *(page 2 of 3)*

Possible contributing factor	Example	Evidence source(s)	Is this factor present?
☐ Behavioral difficulties	☐ Student records, teacher/parent/guardian/student report indicate: ☐ Office disciplinary referrals ☐ Disciplinary actions within classroom/school setting ☐ Other		NO YES
☐ School adjustment difficulties	☐ Teacher/parent/guardian/student report indicating school adjustment difficulties ☐ Other		NO YES
☐ Existence of transient or chronic crisis	☐ Death of parent/ guardian/ family member/relative/friend ☐ Parent/guardian/family member/relative/friend illness (chronic or transient) ☐ Parental/guardian marital difficulties ☐ Other		NO YES
☐ Drug/alcohol use	☐ Teacher/parent/guardian/student report and/or records indicating possible drug/alcohol use ☐ Other		NO YES

(continued)

52

Ecological Factor 1 Worksheet: Learner Domain (page 3 of 3)

If you circled YES in column 4 identifying that a factor is of significant concern, continue below:

Learner domain factors present	Specific examples in which this factor is of concern	For how long has this factor been present?[a]	Is this factor contributing to the student's difficulties?[b]	Would this student's difficulties continue to exist if this factor were addressed/remedied?[c]	How will this be addressed/remedied?
		1 2 3 4	1 2 3	1 2 3 4 5	
		1 2 3 4	1 2 3	1 2 3 4 5	
		1 2 3 4	1 2 3	1 2 3 4 5	
		1 2 3 4	1 2 3	1 2 3 4 5	
		1 2 3 4	1 2 3	1 2 3 4 5	
		1 2 3 4	1 2 3	1 2 3 4 5	
		1 2 3 4	1 2 3	1 2 3 4 5	
		1 2 3 4	1 2 3	1 2 3 4 5	

[a]1—From the beginning of the student's educational experiences; 2—For more than one academic year, but not the entire time of the student's educational experiences; 3—For only the current academic year; 4—Recently (not present at beginning of academic year, but began at some point after the beginning of the year).

[b]1—Yes; 2—Partially; 3—No.

[c]1—Yes, definitely; 2—Yes, the student's difficulties would decrease as a result, but would still remain significant; 3—The student's difficulties would decrease, but it is unknown to what degree the difficulties would still be present; 4—No, the removal of this factor would make a significant difference in the child's difficulties; 5—No, the removal of this factor would result in the student's difficulties no longer being present.

Ecological Factor 2 Worksheet: Lack of Appropriate Instruction

Appropriate instruction factors to consider	Example	Evidence source(s)	Is this factor present?
☐ Good attendance	☐ Full-day absences ☐ Partial-day absences ☐ Tardies ☐ In-school suspension days ☐ Other absences		NO YES
☐ Frequent mobility	☐ Number of moves ☐ Number of schools in which the student was enrolled ☐ Inconsistent academic standards at grade levels in different schools in which the student was enrolled ☐ Other		NO YES
☐ Use of non-scientifically based curricula	☐ Review by independent organization (e.g., What Works Clearinghouse) documenting effectiveness ☐ District/school-level data indicating curriculum effectiveness ☐ Other		NO YES
☐ Academic mismatch between grade-level curricula and student's skills level	☐ ELP scores and instructional implications ☐ Progress monitoring data not used to determine student progress and instructional/intervention needs ☐ Reading ☐ Math ☐ Writing ☐ Other		NO YES

(continued)

Ecological Factor 2 Worksheet: Lack of Appropriate Instruction *(page 2 of 4)*

Appropriate instruction factors to consider	Example	Evidence source(s)	Is this factor present?
☐ Inappropriate match between ELP level and instruction	☐ Failure to use ELP scores in considering instructional implications ☐ Use of old ELP scores in determining services ☐ Progress monitoring data not used to determine student progress and instructional/intervention needs ☐ Other		NO YES
☐ Quality instructional planning	☐ Reading ☐ Math ☐ Writing		NO YES
☐ Goals and objectives are aligned with student's skills level	☐ Appropriate instructional grouping ☐ Use of differentiation		NO YES
☐ Lack of prerequisite skills necessary to complete assigned tasks	☐ Performance in prior grade levels/courses ☐ Necessary skills identified through skills analysis ☐ Consideration of instructional ratios ☐ Other		NO YES
☐ Lack of progress-monitoring procedures	☐ Reading ☐ Math ☐ Writing ☐ Other		NO YES

(continued)

Ecological Factor 2 Worksheet: Lack of Appropriate Instruction *(page 3 of 4)*

Appropriate instruction factors to consider	Example	Evidence source(s)	Is this factor present?
☐ Lack of quality instructional planning	☐ Reading ☐ Math ☐ Writing ☐ Other		NO YES
☐ Student's behavior is deterrent to learning	☐ Office disciplinary referrals ☐ Suspensions from school ☐ Observations regarding time on or off task ☐ Other		NO YES
☐ Goals and objectives not aligned with student's skills level	☐ Appropriate instructional grouping ☐ Use of differentiation ☐ Other		NO YES
☐ Tasks relevant to the student's background and experience not utilized	☐ Instructional materials ☐ Classroom materials ☐ Assignments ☐ Other		NO YES
☐ Lack of opportunities for active responding	☐ Reading ☐ Math ☐ Writing ☐ Other		NO YES

(continued)

Ecological Factor 2 Worksheet: Lack of Appropriate Instruction (page 4 of 4)

If you circled YES in column 4 identifying that a factor is of significant concern, continue below:

Lack of appropriate instruction factors of significant concern	Specific examples in which this factor is of concern	For how long has this factor been/not been present?[a]	Is this factor contributing to the student's difficulties?[b]	Would this student's difficulties continue to exist if this factor was addressed/remedied?[c]	How will this be addressed/remedied?
		1 2 3 4	1 2 3	1 2 3 4 5	
		1 2 3 4	1 2 3	1 2 3 4 5	
		1 2 3 4	1 2 3	1 2 3 4 5	
		1 2 3 4	1 2 3	1 2 3 4 5	
		1 2 3 4	1 2 3	1 2 3 4 5	
		1 2 3 4	1 2 3	1 2 3 4 5	
		1 2 3 4	1 2 3	1 2 3 4 5	

[a]1—From the beginning of the student's educational experiences; 2—For more than one academic year, but not the entire time of the student's educational experiences; 3—For only the current academic year; 4—Recently (not present at beginning of academic year, but began at some point after the beginning of the year).

[b]1—Yes; 2—Partially; 3—No.

[c]1—Yes, definitely; 2—Yes, the student's difficulties would decrease as a result, but would still remain significant; 3—The student's difficulties would decrease, but it is unknown to what degree the difficulties would still be present; 4—No, the removal of this factor would make a significant difference in the child's difficulties; 5—No, the removal of this factor would result in the student's difficulties no longer being present.

Ecological Factor 3 Worksheet: Core Curriculum

Core curriculum factors to consider	Examples	Evidence source(s)	Is this factor a significant concern?
☐ Use of non-scientifically based curriculum	☐ Review by independent organization (e.g., What Works Clearinghouse) documenting effectiveness ☐ District/school-level data indicating curriculum effectiveness ☐ Other		NO YES
☐ Lack of data-based process to document ongoing effectiveness of curriculum	☐ Percentage of students at proficient/nonproficient categories ☐ Performance of student subgroups ☐ Other		NO YES
☐ Lack of consistency in curriculum between grade levels	☐ Reading ☐ Math ☐ Writing ☐ Other		NO YES
☐ Insufficient opportunity to respond	☐ Reading ☐ Math ☐ Writing ☐ Other		NO YES

(continued)

Ecological Factor 3 Worksheet: Core Curriculum *(page 2 of 3)*

Core curriculum factors to consider	Examples	Evidence source(s)	Is this factor a significant concern?
☐ Lack of frequent formative assessment and progress monitoring	☐ Reading ☐ Math ☐ Writing ☐ Other		NO YES
☐ Lack of multi-tiered intervention opportunities	☐ Reading ☐ Math ☐ Writing ☐ Other		NO YES
☐ Failure to use accommodations when appropriate	☐ Reading ☐ Math ☐ Writing ☐ Other		NO YES
☐ Student's language skills (first vs. second language) do not allow for adequate comprehension of content	☐ Reading ☐ Math ☐ Writing ☐ Other		NO YES
☐ Lack of evidence regarding language instructional model effectiveness	☐ Reading ☐ Math ☐ Writing ☐ Other		NO YES

(continued)

59

Ecological Factor 3 Worksheet: Core Curriculum (*page 3 of 3*)

If you circled YES in column 4 identifying that a factor is of significant concern, continue below:

Core curriculum factors of significant concern	Specific examples in which this factor is of concern	For how long has this factor been/not been present?[a]	Is this factor contributing to the student's difficulties?[b]	Would this student's difficulties continue to exist if this factor was addressed/remedied?[c]	How will this be addressed/remedied?
		1 2 3 4	1 2 3	1 2 3 4 5	
		1 2 3 4	1 2 3	1 2 3 4 5	
		1 2 3 4	1 2 3	1 2 3 4 5	
		1 2 3 4	1 2 3	1 2 3 4 5	
		1 2 3 4	1 2 3	1 2 3 4 5	
		1 2 3 4	1 2 3	1 2 3 4 5	
		1 2 3 4	1 2 3	1 2 3 4 5	
		1 2 3 4	1 2 3	1 2 3 4 5	
		1 2 3 4	1 2 3	1 2 3 4 5	

[a]1—From the beginning of the student's educational experiences; 2—For more than one academic year, but not the entire time of the student's educational experiences; 3—For only the current academic year; 4—Recently (not present at beginning of academic year, but began at some point after the beginning of the year).

[b]1—Yes; 2—Partially; 3—No.

[c]1—Yes, definitely; 2—Yes, the student's difficulties would decrease as a result, but would still remain significant; 3—The student's difficulties would decrease, but it is unknown to what degree the difficulties would still be present; 4—No, the removal of this factor would make a significant difference in the child's difficulties; 5—No, the removal of this factor would result in the student's difficulties no longer being present.

Ecological Factor 4 Worksheet: Classroom/School Disadvantage

Classroom/school disadvantage factors to consider	Example	Evidence source(s)	Is this factor a significant concern?
☐ Use of non-scientifically based curriculum	☐ Review by independent organization (e.g., What Works Clearinghouse) documenting effectiveness ☐ District/school-level data indicating curriculum effectiveness		NO YES
☐ Lack of appropriately trained teachers	☐ Evidence of teacher certifications, including bilingual staff		NO YES
☐ Lack of bilingual programs/quality	☐ Language instructional model ☐ District/school-level data regarding effectiveness of language instructional model		NO YES

(continued)

Ecological Factor 4 Worksheet: Classroom/School Disadvantage *(page 2 of 3)*

Classroom/school disadvantage factors to consider	Example	Is this factor a significant concern?
☐ Large class sizes	☐ District/school records	NO YES
☐ Lack of technology use in classroom	☐ District/school records ☐ Teacher report	NO YES
☐ Lack of schoolwide behavior program	☐ Schoolwide and classroom behavioral data	NO YES
☐ Lack of clear classroom rules and routines	☐ Schoolwide and classroom behavioral data	NO YES

(continued)

Ecological Factor 4 Worksheet: Classroom/School Disadvantage *(page 3 of 3)*

If you circled YES in column 4 identifying that a factor is of significant concern, continue below:

School/classroom factors of significant concern	Specific examples in which this factor is of concern	For how long has this factor not been present?[a]	Is this factor contributing to the student's difficulties?[b]	Would this student's difficulties continue to exist if this factor was addressed/remedied?[c]	How will this be addressed/remedied?
		1 2 3 4	1 2 3	1 2 3 4 5	
		1 2 3 4	1 2 3	1 2 3 4 5	
		1 2 3 4	1 2 3	1 2 3 4 5	
		1 2 3 4	1 2 3	1 2 3 4 5	
		1 2 3 4	1 2 3	1 2 3 4 5	
		1 2 3 4	1 2 3	1 2 3 4 5	
		1 2 3 4	1 2 3	1 2 3 4 5	

[a]1—From the beginning of the student's educational experiences; 2—For more than one academic year, but not the entire time of the student's educational experiences; 3—For only the current academic year; 4—Recently (not present at beginning of academic year, but began at some point after the beginning of the year).

[b]1—Yes; 2—Partially; 3—No.

[c]1—Yes, definitely; 2—Yes, the student's difficulties would decrease as a result, but would still remain significant; 3—The student's difficulties would decrease, but it is unknown to what degree the difficulties would still be present; 4—No, the removal of this factor would make a significant difference in the child's difficulties; 5—No, the removal of this factor would result in the student's difficulties no longer being present.

Ecological Factor 5 Worksheet: Cultural Factors

Cultural factors to consider	Example	Evidence source(s)	Is this factor a significant concern?
☐ Conflicting educational and behavioral expectations between students, and/or parents/guardians and school	☐ School reports apparent lack of parental interest in student's educational performance ☐ Parents/guardians report lack of understanding on part of school ☐ Other		NO YES
☐ Lack of communication or miscommunication between parents and school	☐ School reports limited follow-up from student's parents/guardians ☐ Parents/guardians report lack of communication from school ☐ Other		NO YES

(continued)

Ecological Factor 5 Worksheet: Cultural Factors *(page 2 of 3)*

Cultural factors to consider	Example	Evidence source(s)	Is this factor a significant concern?
☐ Limited parental involvement in school due to cultural and communication barriers	☐ Parents/guardians indicate importance of other expectations in place of or in addition to education ☐ Parents/guardians indicate limited desire to be involved in school activities ☐ Parents/guardians indicate barriers to being involved with school activities ☐ School indicates limited success in actively involving parents/guardians ☐ Other		NO YES
☐ Limited exposure and opportunities to learn in previous educational settings	☐ Student's records indicate a lack of quality educational experiences in other schools and/or countries ☐ Student's prior educational experiences were in a foreign country where education system is not strong ☐ Other		NO YES
☐ Use of assessments not validated for use with student characteristics (e.g., language)	☐ Use of inadequate or outdated scores to determine instruction, intervention, and/or services ☐ Assessment of achievement in language other than student's first language ☐ Record of prior evaluations with inadequate consideration of language/cultural factors ☐ Other		NO YES

(continued)

Ecological Factor 5 Worksheet: Cultural Factors *(page 3 of 3)*

If you circled YES in column 4 identifying that a factor is of significant concern, continue below:

Cultural factors of significant concern	Specific examples in which this factor is of concern	For how long has this factor been/not been present?[a]	Is this factor contributing to the student's difficulties?[b]	Would this student's difficulties continue to exist if this factor was addressed/remedied?[c]	How will this be addressed/remedied?
		1 2 3 4	1 2 3	1 2 3 4 5	
		1 2 3 4	1 2 3	1 2 3 4 5	
		1 2 3 4	1 2 3	1 2 3 4 5	
		1 2 3 4	1 2 3	1 2 3 4 5	
		1 2 3 4	1 2 3	1 2 3 4 5	

[a]1—From the beginning of the student's educational experiences; 2—For more than one academic year, but not the entire time of the student's educational experiences; 3—For only the current academic year; 4—Recently (not present at beginning of academic year, but began at some point after the beginning of the year).

[b]1—Yes; 2—Partially; 3—No.

[c]1—Yes, definitely; 2—Yes, the student's difficulties would decrease as a result, but would still remain significant; 3—The student's difficulties would decrease, but it is unknown to what degree the difficulties would still be present; 4—No, the removal of this factor would make a significant difference in the child's difficulties; 5—No, the removal of this factor would result in the student's difficulties no longer being present.

Ecological Factor 6 Worksheet: Economic Factors

Possible contributing factor	Example	Evidence source(s)	Is this factor a significant concern?
☐ Single-parent/guardian household	☐ Parent/guardian/student report suggests difficulties with parent/guardian assisting with homework activities due to limited time availability ☐ Other		YES NO
☐ Parent(s) work multiple jobs/work during times when student is at home	☐ Parent/guardian/student report suggests difficulties with parent/guardian assisting with homework activities due to limited time availability ☐ Other		YES NO
☐ Exposure to community violence/crime	☐ Parent/guardian/student report that access to community resources is limited due to concerns regarding violence/crime ☐ Other		YES NO
☐ Homelessness and/or frequent mobility	☐ Parent/guardian/student report and/or records suggest lack of stability in prior educational experiences ☐ Other		YES NO

(continued)

Ecological Factor 6 Worksheet: Economic Factors *(page 2 of 3)*

Possible contributing factor	Example	Evidence source(s)	Is this factor a significant concern?
☐ Lack of health care and other health-related services	☐ Lack of insurance ☐ Limited access to community health resources (e.g., physical, mental health) ☐ Other		YES NO
☐ Possible lack of appropriate nutrition	☐ Lack of nutrition leading to increased illness ☐ Lack of nutrition leading to student difficulties in maintaining attention		YES NO
☐ Limited community resources or limited access to community resources	☐ Parent/guardian/student report that access to community resources is limited ☐ Other		YES NO
☐ Student employment	☐ Parent/guardian/student report that student works on evenings and/or weekends		YES NO

(continued)

Ecological Factor 6 Worksheet: Economic Factors (page 3 of 3)

Economic factors of significant concern	Specific examples in which this factor is of concern	For how long has this factor been/not been present?[a]	Is this factor contributing to the student's difficulties?[b]	Would this student's difficulties continue to exist if this factor was addressed/remedied?[c]	How will this be addressed/remedied?
		1 2 3 4	1 2 3	1 2 3 4 5	
		1 2 3 4	1 2 3	1 2 3 4 5	
		1 2 3 4	1 2 3	1 2 3 4 5	
		1 2 3 4	1 2 3	1 2 3 4 5	
		1 2 3 4	1 2 3	1 2 3 4 5	
		1 2 3 4	1 2 3	1 2 3 4 5	
		1 2 3 4	1 2 3	1 2 3 4 5	
		1 2 3 4	1 2 3	1 2 3 4 5	

[a]1—From the beginning of the student's educational experiences; 2—For more than one academic year, but not the entire time of the student's educational experiences; 3—For only the current academic year; 4—Recently (not present at beginning of academic year, but began at some point after the beginning of the year).

[b]1—Yes; 2—Partially; 3—No.

[c]1—Yes, definitely; 2—Yes, the student's difficulties would decrease as a result, but would still remain significant; 3—The student's difficulties would decrease, but it is unknown to what degree the difficulties would still be present; 4—No, the removal of this factor would make a significant difference in the child's difficulties; 5—No, the removal of this factor would result in the student's difficulties no longer being present.

Ecological Factor 7 Worksheet: Environmental Factors

Environmental factors to consider	Example	Evidence source(s)	Is this factor a significant concern?
☐ Difficulties in parents/ guardians being actively engaged in student's education	☐ Attendance at parent–teacher conferences ☐ Attendance at school activities (e.g., math night, science night) ☐ Responsiveness to school notes, messages, etc. ☐ Communication from school to home and from home to school ☐ Evidence of parental monitoring of home work assignments		NO YES
☐ Student has significant responsibilities at home that detract from school performance	☐ Single-parent household ☐ Existence of household member with chronic illness, disability, etc. ☐ Presence of younger siblings whose care requires student's assistance ☐ Other		NO YES

(continued)

Ecological Factor 7 Worksheet: Environmental Factors *(page 2 of 3)*

Environmental factors to consider	Example	Evidence source(s)	Is this factor a significant concern?
☐ Limited access to books, games, computers, and other resources at home	☐ Limited access to educational materials at home		NO YES
☐ Limited community resources or limited access to community resources	☐ Limited access to educational materials in community ☐ Limited access to libraries, after-school programs, YMCA, etc. ☐ Other		NO YES
☐ Student employment	☐ Parent/guardian/student report that student works on evenings and/or weekends		NO YES

(continued)

Ecological Factor 7 Worksheet: Environmental Factors *(page 3 of 3)*

If you circled YES in column 4 identifying that a factor is of significant concern, continue below:

Environmental domain factors present	Specific examples in which this factor is of concern	For how long has this factor not been present?[a]	Is this factor contributing to the student's difficulties?[b]	Would this student's difficulties continue to exist if this factor was addressed/remedied?[c]	How will this be addressed/remedied?
		1 2 3 4	1 2 3	1 2 3 4 5	
		1 2 3 4	1 2 3	1 2 3 4 5	
		1 2 3 4	1 2 3	1 2 3 4 5	
		1 2 3 4	1 2 3	1 2 3 4 5	
		1 2 3 4	1 2 3	1 2 3 4 5	

[a]1—From the beginning of the student's educational experiences; 2—For more than one academic year, but not the entire time of the student's educational experiences; 3—For only the current academic year; 4—Recently (not present at beginning of academic year, but began at some point after the beginning of the year).

[b]1—Yes; 2—Partially; 3—No.

[c]1—Yes, definitely; 2—Yes, the student's difficulties would decrease as a result, but would still remain significant; 3—The student's difficulties would decrease, but it is unknown to what degree the difficulties would still be present; 4—No, the removal of this factor would make a significant difference in the child's difficulties; 5—No, the removal of this factor would result in the student's difficulties no longer being present.

CHAPTER 4

The Critical Variable

Academic Language Proficiency and Its Impact on Students Learning English as a Second Language

Although we consider English language proficiency (ELP) to be an ELL foundational concept that could have been included in Chapter 2, we believe that the critical and essential nature of this variable, as well as other closely related variables, dictates that we discuss this concept in a separate chapter. Although the science surrounding ELP is relatively limited, research conducted in the past couple of decades has advanced our understanding of this important variable. Thus, our hope is to provide a summary of ELP for those of you with knowledge in this area; at the same time, we recognize that much of this content may be new to educators who have not been involved in educating ELLs in the past. We therefore hope also to provide a straightforward introduction of ELP to those of you in this situation for the first time. Consequently, in this chapter we do not focus on implementation of response to intervention (RTI) per se; rather, our intent is to emphasize the importance of ELP, so that all of its aspects can be considered and integrated within RTI procedures, as we will see in more detail in subsequent chapters.

A critical component of successfully implementing RTI with ELLs relates to their development of Academic English, which can be defined as the language used in classrooms that facilitates the development of knowledge and corresponding academic skills. Two critical components associated with Academic English development for ELLs include (1) ELP *assessment*, and (2) corresponding English language *instruction*. Whereas in past years it was presumed that ESL teachers and bilingual specialists alone were responsible for ensuring that ELL students obtain proficiency in the English language and in academic skills in English, it is becoming increasingly clear that *all* educators share in this critical responsibility. It is *especially* important for the general education teacher to partake in this responsibility—and perhaps even take the lead. Nevertheless, we again want to emphasize the role that *all* adults in a school district play in supporting ELLs' educational progress, including the significant growth needed in oral language proficiency and academic language proficiency. Underlying our position that all adults in a school are responsible for the academic progress of ELLs is the notion that the teaching and learning of the English language—or any language for that matter—cannot be restricted to only certain times of the school day; this means that all educators—including district and school administrators, classroom teachers, classroom aides and assistants, art teachers, music teachers, physical education instructors, coaches, school psychologists, counselors, speech–language pathologists, and other school staff—*must become both knowledgeable about and invested in helping their ELLs attain ELP.*

To this end, we introduce and dedicate a whole chapter to the concept of ELP. As a primer, we review some of the history that informs knowledge of this topic. Given the growing recognition of the need for standards-based instruction (i.e., Common Core State Standards [CCSS]), which applies both to content instruction and language instruction, we examine how ELP standards are applied in present-day schools. A discussion of ELP would not be complete without an overview of the assessments designed to measure progress toward these standards; thus, we explore the role that ELP assessments play in educational settings and how these assessments and standards should interact to improve instruction and ELLs' outcomes—at least in theory. Given the significance of using ELP assessments to determine participation in ELL-related services (e.g., ESL, bilingual instruction),[1] we then examine eligibility and exit criteria for these services.

BASIC INTERPERSONAL COMMUNICATIVE SKILLS, COGNITIVE ACADEMIC LANGUAGE PROFICIENCY, AND ACADEMIC LANGUAGE

To be successful in the prototypical U.S. English-dominant public school, ELLs must not only learn communicative (i.e., social) English, but they must also master academic language, which, according to experts, can take 7 to 10 years or more (Dixon, et al., 2012; Thomas & Collier, 1997). Simply stated, academic success in the United States necessitates a command of the English language (particularly academic language) as well as competence in reading in the English language. Indeed, all students, including ELLs who are educated in the United States, are required to learn to read at grade level in English (NCLB, 2002).

There is a long historical and legal precedent for meeting the needs of language diverse students. As we enter into a discussion of second-language acquisition, we introduce three key concepts: (1) *basic interpersonal communicative skills* (BICS), (b) *cognitive academic language proficiency* (CALP), and (3) *academic language* (AL). These concepts originate in the discipline of linguistics and are applied within the field of education. Again, we recog-

---

[1] Not to be confounded with special education eligibility and services, which is an entirely separate issue.

nize that some—perhaps even many—educators may be familiar with these critical ideas; however, we are just as confident that not everyone is in the situation of deeply understanding these concepts and how they relate to the everyday schooling of ELLs. Because many educators report that they feel poorly prepared to work with ELLs (O'Neal, Ringler, & Rodriguez, 2008), our goal in this chapter is to offer readers a foundation of understanding about ELP and ELLs upon which subsequent learning can be anchored. The concepts associated with BICS, CALP, and AL are integral to understanding what it is like for ELLs who are learning English as a second language, and for planning and implementing appropriate instruction and intervention activities.

ELL students are as heterogeneous *within* language groups as they are *across* language groups. *This fact must permeate all aspects of how educators approach all ELL students.* Indeed, no two students—ELLs or native English speakers—are alike. To illustrate, an ELL student who is a recent immigrant may make incredible strides in English in his or her first year in the United States, whereas a second-generation, U.S.-born ELL student may struggle considerably with Academic English despite being educated exclusively in U.S. schools. There are myriad factors—some of which are quite complex—that shape the speed and accuracy with which ELL students acquire ESL and academic language. Thus, it is imperative for teachers to differentiate their instruction and assessment goals according to the strengths and needs of *individual* ELLs. For this to be possible, educators who work with ELL students must be aware of the *general* process of ESL acquisition, to which we turn next.

The second-language model perhaps most widely cited in the literature is based on the work of Jim Cummins (1984, 2000). In his research, Cummins explained the elaborate process of learning ESL in terms of two recognizable stages. He described the first 2 to 3 years of second-language acquisition as a period when learners demonstrate an imperfect but emerging level of language proficiency, which Cummins named *basic interpersonal communicative skills.* Sometimes referred to as "survival language," BICS encompasses the language proficiency necessary to "get by" in the second language. Hence, BICS includes everyday language such as social commands (e.g., "That is my pencil"; "I don't want to go to the library") and questions (e.g., "May I use the restroom?"; "Can you say that again, please?"). To make the concept of BICS more readily comprehensible, we provide the following example.

Consider the situation in which you do not speak a word of French. However, you decide to take an overseas teaching assignment in Bordeaux, France, a small province where nobody (it seems) speaks English. Early on, surely you will learn enough French (out of necessity, if anything) to survive in your new surroundings. For example, it is only a matter of time before you learn to communicate (in your best French) with the townspeople, asking questions such as, "Where is the local school?" and "Can you point me in the direction of the bakery?" This emerging language ability reflects your developing BICS in French. Over the coming weeks and months, you likely will take increasing language risks in practicing your French with the new people you are meeting. In the first year or so, you may make great strides in your acquisition of French, and it may seem to some of the locals that you have been in Bordeaux longer than you actually have been. Similarly, some ELLs who have been in U.S. schools for a only few years may *seem* very proficient in English—so much so that teachers expect them to perform comparably to their native English-speaking peers. Consider in the Bordeaux example (fast forward 3 years) that you were asked to teach a class—not your regular English class (which is what you went to Bordeaux to teach in the first place) but a class for local native French-speaking children—in French. You have been in Bordeaux for a few years, after all, and you *sound* like you have mastered the intricacies of the language; furthermore, you *are* a teacher by training, so why shouldn't you be able to teach French children in French? Well, according to Cummins, second-language learners must develop a *profound and complex level* of language proficiency in order to be successful in an *academic setting* in that same language; Cummins calls this advanced degree of language proficiency CALP. In the Bordeaux example, although you can easily find your way around town—especially the bakeries and flea markets—it does not mean that you have acquired the specific professional (i.e., academic) language necessary to be a successful French teacher of native French-speaking children. You may be a teacher by training and you may be able to speak conversational French, but knowledge of pedagogy and professional teaching constructs in French is not something to which you have been exposed, a fact that will make it extremely difficult for you to teach in French as effectively as a native French-speaking teacher (at least at this early stage of your residency in Bordeaux). Indeed, although estimates vary, CALP usually takes 5–10 years to acquire, above and beyond the initial 2–3 years that are requisite to acquiring BICS. For ELL students in U.S. schools, this means it takes *at least* 7 years or more to acquire the academic language needed to function completely independently in academic material. Consequently, to be successful in the academic material presented in school, supportive teaching practices and scaffolded learning opportunities *must* be provided to all ELLs in the general education classroom and by the general education teacher for up to 10 years.

We know that BICS develops only in highly relevant and contextualized settings (e.g., finding the local bakery when you are hungry for breakfast), whereas CALP develops in much more decontextualized settings and requires study and great effort (e.g., learning pedagogical foundations of teaching native French speakers in French). Teachers who work with ELLs must understand that the second-language acquisition process is highly complex—and can proceed at vastly different rates from one student to the next. However, one thing is certain: It is highly inappropriate to assume that an ELL student who has made great strides in the first year or two in the United States (i.e., has great BICS) is prepared linguistically or academically to participate independently in higher level academic tasks (e.g., comprehending a textbook chapter on the Civil War, understanding a lecture on photosynthesis, or taking a standardized test in English); that student still must be provided with explicit and sustained scaffolding and support to be successful in school.

The concept of AL (for a more in-depth review of AL as a construct, see Anstrom et al., 2010) is associated with CALP, whereas BICS is associated with social language (SL). The terms AL and SL have been used in schools more frequently since they appeared in NCLB in 2001.

ELP STANDARDS

NCLB required states to establish ELP standards (also referred to as English language development [ELD] standards) that were aligned with each state's academic content standards (i.e., English language arts, mathematics, science) within the domains of speaking, listening, reading, and writing. To assist states in implementing these NCLB requirements, a number of multistate consortia were developed, allowing individual states to avoid having to develop ELP standards and assessments independently. As of 2015, the largest of the consortia (i.e., the World-Class Instructional Design and Assessment [WIDA] Consortium) included 36 states plus the District of Columbia. Of these, 34 states and the District of Columbia have adopted the WIDA ELP standards and administer the WIDA ELP assessment (i.e., Assessing Comprehension and Communication in English State to State for English Language Learners [ACCESS for ELLs]), and 2 states (i.e., Florida and Idaho) that have adopted the WIDA ELP standards but do not administer the ACCESS for ELLs. Non-WIDA states either joined smaller consortia or developed their own state-specific ELP standards and corresponding assessments.

Since the release of the original version in 2004, the WIDA ELP standards have undergone numerous revisions, most notably in 2007 and most recently in 2012. The 2012 version of the ELP standards, entitled the *2012 Amplification of the ELD Standards* (available at *www.wida.us/standards/eld.aspx*), is an enhancement of the 2007 ELP standards. The 2012 ELP standards now contain connections to state content standards, including the CCSS (*www.corestandards.org*) and the Next Generation Science Standards (*www.nextgenscience.org*). These amplified standards were designed to represent the SL, AL, and instructional language necessary for ELLs to actively engage with peers, educators, and the school's curriculum. There are five standards that specify the language necessary to enable ELLs (1) to communicate for social and instruction purposes within the school setting; (2) to communicate information, ideas, and concepts necessary for academic success in the content area of language arts; (3) to communicate information, ideas, and concepts necessary for academic success in the content area of mathematics; (4) to communicate information, ideas, and concepts necessary for academic success in the content area of science; and (5) to communicate information, ideas, and concepts necessary for academic success in the content area of social studies (WIDA, 2012a). These standards address the areas of speaking, listening, reading, and writing, and separate standards exist for each grade level between kindergarten and grade 12. Specific ELP levels are defined as existing on a continuum from Level 1 to Level 6, with Level 6 representing proficiency in English. The definitions of specific ELP levels are described in more detail in Figures 4.1 (listening and reading) and 4.2 (speaking and writing).

Within each ELP standard and within each domain (i.e., listening, speaking, reading, and writing) there is a description of what an ELL student should know and be able to do at each ELP level; Figures 4.3 and 4.4 illustrate the WIDA Consortium's Standard 2 for grade-level clusters 3–5 within each domain of listening, speaking, reading, and writing. For example, within the area of language arts, an ELL student in grade 3 who is considered

	Discourse Level	Sentence Level	Word Level
	Linguistic Complexity	**Language Forms and Conventions**	**Vocabulary Usage**
Level 6: Reaching—Language that meets all criteria through Level 5: Bridging			
Level 5: Bridging	• Rich descriptive discourse with complex sentences • Cohesive and organized related ideas	• Compound, complex grammatical constructions (e.g., multiple phrases and clauses) • A broad range of sentence patterns characteristic of particular content areas	• Technical and abstract content-area language, including content-specific collocations • Words and expressions with shades of meaning across content areas
Level 4: Expanding	• Connected discourse with a variety of sentences • Expanded related ideas	• A variety of complex grammatical constructions • Sentence patterns characteristic of particular content areas	• Specific and some technical content-area language • Words or expressions with multiple meanings across content areas
Level 3: Developing	• Discourse with a series of extended sentences • Related ideas	• Compound and some complex (e.g., noun phrase, verb phrase, prepositional phrase) grammatical constructions • Sentence patterns across content areas	• Specific content language, including expressions • Words and expressions with common collocations and idioms across content areas
Level 2: Emerging	• Multiple related simple sentences • An idea with details	• Compound grammatical constructions • Repetitive phrasal and sentence patterns across content areas	• General content words and expressions, including cognates • Social and instructional words and expressions across content areas
Level 1: Entering	• Single statements or questions • An idea within words, phrases, or chunks of language	• Simple grammatical constructions (e.g., commands, *Wh-*questions, declaratives) • Common social and instructional forms and patterns	• General content-related words • Everyday social and instructional words and expressions

FIGURE 4.1. WIDA performance definitions for listening and reading, grades K–12. Reprinted with permission from WIDA (2012a).

	Discourse Level	Sentence Level	Word Level
	Linguistic Complexity	Language Forms and Conventions	Vocabulary Usage
Level 6: Reaching—Language that meets all criteria through Level 5: Bridging			
Level 5: Bridging	• Multiple, complex sentences • Organized, cohesive, and coherent expression of ideas	• A variety of grammatical structures matched to purpose • A broad range of sentence patterns characteristic of particular content areas	• Technical and abstract content-area language, including content-specific collocations • Words and expressions with shades of meaning across content areas
Level 4: Expanding	• Short, expanded, and some complex sentences • Organized expression of ideas with emerging cohesion	• A variety of grammatical structures • Sentence patterns characteristic of particular content areas	• Specific and some content-area language • Words and expressions with expressive meaning through use of collocations and idioms across content areas
Level 3: Developing	• Short and some expanded sentences with emerging complexity • Expanded expression of one idea or emerging expression of multiple related ideas	• Repetitive grammatical structures with occasional variation • Sentence patterns across content areas	• Specific content language, including cognates and expressions • Words or expressions with multiple meanings used across content areas
Level 2: Emerging	• Phrases or short sentences • Emerging expression of ideas	• Formulaic grammatical structures • Repetitive phrasal and sentence patterns across content areas	• General content words and expressions • Social and instructional words and expressions across content areas
Level 1: Entering	• Words, phrases, or chunks of language • Single words used to represent ideas	• Phrase-level grammatical structures • Phrasal patterns associated with common social and instructional situations	• General content-related words • Everyday social and instructional words and expressions

FIGURE 4.2. WIDA performance definitions for speaking and writing, grades K–12. Reprinted with permission from WIDA (2012a).

		Level 1: Entering	Level 2: Beginning	Level 3: Developing	Level 4: Expanding	Level 5: Bridging	
Listening	**Example Genre** **Mysteries**	Match pictures to individual clues based on oral statements	Identify pictures associated with solutions to short mysteries read aloud	Make predictions based on pictures of clues/pieces of evidence from mysteries and oral descriptions	Sequence pictures of clues/pieces of evidence from mysteries read aloud	Apply to students' lives analogies of events or characters in mysteries read aloud	**Level 6: Reaching**
	Example Topic **Explicit and inferential information**	Match oral statements from narrative or expository material to their illustrated representations	Determine literal meanings of oral passages from narrative or expository materials and match to illustrations	Project next in a sequence from oral discourse on narrative or expository material supported by illustrations	Identify cause–effect in oral discourse from narrative or expository material supported by illustrations	Make connections and draw conclusions from oral discourse using grade-level materials	
Speaking	**Example Genre** **Fantasies**	Answer *Wh*-questions to distinguish between pictures of real and imaginary people, objects, or situations	Describe pictures of imaginary people, objects, or situations	Provide details of pictures of imaginary people, objects, or situations	Complex scenarios from pictures of imaginary people, objects, or situations	Make up fantasies about imaginary people, objects, or situations	
	Example Topic **Story elements and types of genres**	Name story elements of various genres (e.g., nonfiction works, fairy tales, myths, fables or legends) depicted visually	Describe story elements of various genres supported by illustrations	Summarize story line, issues, or conflicts in various genres supported by illustrations	Discuss relationships among ideas or offer opinions on issues in various genres supported by illustrations	Propose options or solutions to issues in various genres and support responses with details	

FIGURE 4.3. WIDA English Language Proficiency Standard 2, Language Arts, in the areas of listening and speaking, grades 3–5. Reprinted with permission from WIDA (2007a).

		Level 1: Entering	Level 2: Beginning	Level 3: Developing	Level 4: Expanding	Level 5: Bridging	
Reading	**Example Genre** **Biographies and autobiographies**	Find identifying information on biographies from illustrations, words, or phrases	Sequence events in biographical sketches using illustrations and graphic organizers (e.g., timelines)	Sort relevant from irrelevant biographical information using illustrations and graphic organizers	Compare–contrast biographical information of two persons using illustrations and graphic organizers	Synthesize biographical information of two persons from grade-level material to form opinions on people	**Level 6: Reaching**
	Example Topic **Main ideas and details**	Find identifying information illustrative of main ideas from illustrations, words, or phrases	Sort main ideas and details from sentences using visual support and graphic organizers	Match main ideas with their details from paragraphs using visual support and graphic organizers	Interpret text to identify main ideas and details from multiple paragraphs using visual or graphic support	Form or infer main ideas from details using grade-level materials	
Writing	**Example Genre** **Narratives**	Respond to illustrated events using words or phrases based on models	List illustrated events using phrases or short sentences based on models	Depict a series of illustrated events using related sentences in narrative form based on model	Sequence a series of illustrated events using paragraph transitions in narrative form based on models	Produce grade-level narrative stories of reports	
	Example Topic **Conventions and mechanics**	Identify basic conventions or mechanics in text (e.g., use of capital letters)	Differentiate uses of conventions or mechanics in illustrated sentences (e.g., those that end in periods or question marks)	Relate when to use conventions or mechanics in illustrated passages (e.g., commas to indicate a series)	Revise illustrated paragraphs according to use of specified conventions or mechanics (e.g., combine sentences to make appositives)	Provide examples and reasons for use of specified conventions or mechanics (e.g., "Why do we need commas?")	

FIGURE 4.4. WIDA English Language Proficiency Standard 2, Language Arts, in the areas of reading and writing, grades 3–5. Reprinted with permission from WIDA (2007a).

to be at an ELP Level 2 (i.e., beginning) in the listening domain should be able to "identify pictures associated with solutions to short mysteries read aloud." For states that are not part of the WIDA Consortium, each respective state's ELP standards are similar in content and are intended to assist in making sure that ELLs attain ELP levels that will lead to academic success. Thus, ELP standards must play a significant role in providing services within an RTI model that incorporates ELLs.

To assist educators in utilizing ELP standards and implementing the standards within classrooms, the WIDA Consortium also developed what are referred to as "Can Do" descriptors (WIDA, 2012b). These "Can Do" descriptors describe how ELLs process and use language as a function of specific ELP levels and are applicable across all ELP standards, thus providing educators the opportunity to link language development within each of the academic areas. Examples of these descriptors are provided in Figure 4.5 (listening and speaking) and Figure 4.6 (reading and writing).

ELP ASSESSMENT

Assessment Instruments

Prior to NCLB, ELP assessments involved administration of commercially marketed ELP assessment instruments that are now commonly referred to as "off-the-shelf" measures (e.g., *Idea Proficiency Test* [IPT], *Language Assessment Scales* [LAS], *Maculaitis Assessment of Competencies Test of English Language Proficiency* [MAC]). As described earlier, NCLB required that states not only develop ELP standards, but that each state administer an annual ELP assessment that examines AL proficiency. Thus, the consortia that were developed to address these requirements created a number of ELP assessments, with the largest number of states joining the WIDA Consortium and thereby administering the WIDA Consortium ELP assessment, known as ACCESS for ELLs. As indicated in Table 4.1, as of 2015, 34 states plus the District of Columbia administer the ACCESS for ELLs on an annual basis, with 5 states administering a version of the *English Language Development Assessment* (ELDA), 1 state administering the *LAS Links K–12 Placement Test*, and 1 state administering the *English Language Development Assessment* (ELPA). The remaining 9 states administer state-specific ELP assessments.

Within the near future, the landscape of ELP assessment again will be changing. Due to the implementation of the CCSS and the Next Generation Science Standards (NGSS), the U.S. Department of Education encouraged states to develop new ELP assessments that incorporated components of the CCSS and NGSS into the assessments. As a result, two large consortia of states were formed; these consortia included (1) the Assessment Services Supporting ELs [English Learners] through Technology Systems (ASSETS; *http://assets. wceruw.org*), and (2) ELPA21 (*www.elpa21.org*). Table 4.1 identifies which states belong to each of the consortia and which states have decided to remain independent of consortium membership. The ASSETS Consortium will be utilizing a revised and updated version of the ACCESS for ELLs that will be computer administered and renamed the ACCESS for ELLs 2.0, beginning in the 2015–2016 academic year. The ELPA21 Consortium, which

	Level 1: Entering	Level 2: Beginning	Level 3: Developing	Level 4: Expanding	Level 5: Bridging	
Listening	• Point to stated pictures, words, or phrases • Follow one-step oral directions (e.g., physically or through drawings) • Identify objects, figures, people from oral statements or questions (e.g., Which one is a rock?") • Match classroom oral language to daily routines	• Categorize content-based pictures or objects from oral descriptions • Arrange pictures or objects per oral information • Follow two-step oral directions • Draw in response to oral descriptions • Evaluate oral information (e.g., about lunch options)	• Follow multi-step oral directions • Identify illustrated main ideas form paragraph-level oral discourse • Match literal meanings of oral descriptions or oral reading to illustrations • Sequence pictures form oral stories, processes, or procedures	• Interpret oral information and apply to new situations • Identify illustrated main ideas and supporting ideas form oral discourse • Infer from and act on oral information • Role-play the work of authors, mathematicians, scientists, historians from oral readings, videos, or multimedia	• Carry out oral instructions containing grade-level, content-based language • Construct models or use manipulatives to problem-solve based on oral discourse • Distinguish between literal and figurative language in oral discourse • Form opinions of people, places, or ideas from oral scenarios	**Level 6: Reaching**
Speaking	• Express basic needs or conditions • Name pre-taught objects, people, diagrams, or pictures • Recite words or phrases from pictures of everyday objects and oral modeling • Answer yes–no and choice questions	• Ask simple, everyday questions (e.g., "Who is absent?") • Restate content-based facts • Describe pictures, events, objects, or people using phrases or short sentences • Share basic social information with peers	• Answer simple content-based questions • Re/tell short stories or events • Make predications or hypotheses from discourse • Offer solutions to social conflict • Present content-based information • Engage in problem solving	• Answer opinion questions with supporting details • Discuss stories, issues, and concepts • Give content-based oral reports • Offer creative solutions issues/problems • Compare/contrast content-based functions and relationships	• Justify/defend opinions or explanations with evidence • Give content-based presentations using technical vocabulary • Sequence steps in grade-level problem solving • Explain in detail results of inquiry (e.g., scientific experiments)	

FIGURE 4.5. WIDA English Language "Can-Do" descriptors for grades 3–5, listening and speaking. Reprinted with permission from WIDA (2007b).

	Level 1: Entering	Level 2: Beginning	Level 3: Developing	Level 4: Expanding	Level 5: Bridging	
Reading	• Match icons or diagrams with words/concepts • Identify cognates from first language, as applicable • Make sound–symbol–word relations • Math illustrated words/phrases in differing contexts (e.g., on the board, in a book)	• Identify facts and explicit messages from illustrated text • Find changes to root words in context • Identify elements of story grammar (e.g., characters, setting) • Follow visually supported written directions (e.g., "Draw a star in the sky.")	• Interpret information or data from charts and graphs • Identify main ideas and some details • Sequence events in stories or content-based processes • Use context clues and illustrations to determine meaning of words/phrases	• Classify features of various genres of text (e.g., "and they lived happily ever after"; fairy tales) • Match graphic organizers to different texts (e.g., compare–contrast with Venn diagram) • Find ideas that support main ideas • Differentiate between fact and opinion in narrative and expository text	• Summarize information from multiple related sources • Answer analytical questions about grade-level text • Identify, explain, and give examples of figures of speech • Draw conclusions from explicit and implicit text at or near grade level	**Level 6: Reaching**
Writing	• Label objects, pictures, or diagrams from word/phrase banks • Communicate ideas by drawing • Copy words, phrases, and short sentences • Answer oral questions with single words	• Make lists from labels or with peers • Complete–produce sentences from word/phrase banks or walls • Fill in graphic organizers, charts, and tables • Make comparisons using real-life or visually supported materials	• Produce simple expository or narrative text • String related sentences together • Compare–contrast content-based information • Describe events, people, processes, procedures	• Take notes using graphic organizers • Summarize content-based information • Author multiple forms of writing (e.g., expository, narrative, persuasive) from models • Explain strategies or use of information in solving problems	• Produce extended responses of original text approaching grade level • Apply content-based information to new contexts • Connect or integrate personal experiences with literature/content • Create grade-level stories or reports	

FIGURE 4.6. WIDA English Language "Can-Do" descriptors for grades 3–5, reading and writing. Reprinted with permission from WIDA (2007b).

TABLE 4.1. Current ELP Measures Used by Each State, and Consortium Membership for New ELP Measures Aligned with the CCSS

State	Current ELP assessments[a]						Consortium membership[c]		
	ACCESS	ELDA	ELPA	CELLA	LAS links	SSM[b]	ASSETS	ELPA21	NM[d]
Alabama	X						X		
Alaska	X						X		
Arizona						AZELLA			X
Arkansas		X						X	
California						CELDT			X
Colorado	X						X		
Connecticut					X				X
Delaware	X						X		
District of Columbia	X						X		
Florida				X				X	
Georgia	X								X
Hawaii	X								X
Idaho						IELA	X		
Illinois	X						X		
Indiana	X								X
Iowa		X				I-ELDA		X	
Kansas						KELPA		X	
Kentucky	X						X		
Louisiana		X						X	
Maine	X						X		
Maryland	X						X		
Massachusetts	X						X		
Michigan	X						X		
Minnesota	X						X		
Mississippi	X						X		
Missouri	X						X		
Montana	X						X		
Nebraska		X						X	
Nevada	X						X		

(continued)

TABLE 4.1. *(continued)*

State	Current ELP assessments[a]						Consortium membership[c]		
	ACCESS	ELDA	ELPA	CELLA	LAS links	SSM[b]	ASSETS	ELPA21	NM[d]
New Hampshire	X						X		
New Jersey	X						X		
New Mexico	X						X		
New York						NYSESLAT			X
North Carolina	X						X		
North Dakota	X						X		
Ohio						OTELA		X	
Oklahoma	X						X		
Oregon			X					X	
Pennsylvania	X						X		
Rhode Island	X						X		
South Carolina	X						X		
South Dakota	X						X		
Tennessee	X						X		X
Texas						Multiple measures allowed			X
Utah	X						X		
Vermont	X						X		
Virginia	X						X		
Washington						WELPA		X	
West Virginia		X[e]						X	
Wisconsin	X						X		
Wyoming	X						X		

[a]ACCESS for ELLs, Assessing Comprehension and Communication in English State-to-State for English Language Learners; ELDA, English Language Development Assessment; ELPA, English Language Proficiency Assessment; CELLA, Comprehensive English Language Learning Assessment; LAS Links, Language Assessment Scales.

[b]SSM, state-specific measure; AZELLA, Arizona English Language Learner Assessment; CELDT, California English Language Development Test; IELA, Idaho English Language Assessment; I-ELDA, Iowa–English Language Development Assessment; KELPA, Kansas English Language Proficiency Assessment; NYSESLAT, New York State English as a Second Language Achievement Test; OTELA, Ohio Test of English Language Acquisition; WELPA, Washington English Language Proficiency Assessment.

[c]ASSETS, Assessment Services Supporting ELs through Technology Systems; ELPA21, English Language Proficiency Assessment for the 21st Century.

[d]NM, not a member of either ASSETS or ELPA21 consortia.

[e]Officially called the West Virginia Test of English Language Learning.

will be utilizing a revised and updated version of the ELPA, is scheduled to be ready for administration during the 2016–2017 academic year.

Uses of ELP Measures

ELP measures are designed for a variety of purposes that include (1) determination of participation in ELL-related services, (2) NCLB accountability requirements, (3) utility for classroom planning and instruction, and (4) assistance in intervention design and implementation (Albers, Kenyon, & Boals, 2009). Each of these purposes is now discussed briefly; we discuss the implications for instruction and intervention in more detail in later chapters.

Determination of Participation

Note that when we talk about determining whether an ELL student is able to receive ELL-related services, we are not talking about eligibility for special education services. These are two separate issues, even though participating in ELL-related services may have multiple implications for special education eligibility, which we discuss in later chapters. Whether a student is able to receive ELL-related services (again, in contrast to eligibility for services for special education programming) is determined upon his or her entry into the school system (Albers & Mission, 2014). The first component of this determination for ELL-related services is the completion of a home-language survey (HLS); if the HLS—or any other information—suggests that the student's primary home language is not English, school personnel administer either the regular ELP assessment (see Table 4.1), or, in the case of WIDA Consortium states, an abbreviated version of their regular ELP assessment (i.e., the ACCESS for ELLs), which is the WIDA ACCESS Placement Test (W-APT). Although states utilize at least one ELP measure as a component of the initial determination for ELL-related services, each state utilizes different score requirements for determining what level of ELP performance qualifies a student for ELL-related services. Thus, when combined with the fact that states use any number of ELP assessments, clearly there are different criteria for determining whether a student is even classified as an ELL, and whether he or she is determined to be eligible for ELL-related services.

ELP measures are also utilized as one component of determining when a student is no longer eligible to receive ELL-related services. As indicated in Table 4.2, each state utilizes scores obtained from the ELP measure as one component of its exit criteria. However, once again, each state is provided flexibility in determining what level of performance on the ELP measure is required for a student to be considered proficient in English. For example, Alabama only requires an ACCESS for ELLs proficiency composite score of greater than 4.8, whereas Alaska requires an ACCESS for ELLs proficiency composite score greater than 5.0 *plus* scores of at least 4.0 on each domain (reading, writing, speaking, and listening). Thus, a student with an ACCESS for ELLs proficiency composite score of 4.9 and who is receiving ELL-related services in Alaska who then moves to Alabama may no longer be eligible to receive these particular services. To determine whether students should no longer receive ELL-related services, states typically require, in addition to specific ELP scores, (1) a certain level of performance on the state's summative academic achievement test, (2) a parent consultation, and (3) a teacher and/or academic review. Finally, states are allowed the flexibility to require that other criteria be met; for example, Ohio requires a composite proficiency level of at least 5.0 on the state ELP measure (i.e., OTELA) in order to be exited from services; however, a student who scores between a 4.0 and 4.9 and then completes a trial period of mainstream instruction and obtains a score of 4.0 or above on the OTELA can be exited from services. ELL students in Ohio cannot be removed from ELL-related services prior to third grade.

The most basic use of ELP measures is to determine ELLs' *current* level of ELP, as required by the NCLB. The student's performance on the measure is reported as a scale score within each of the domains (i.e., listening, speaking, reading, and writing), and a proficiency level is then assigned to correspond with the scale score. Within the ACCESS for ELLs, composite scores are calculated in the areas of oral language (listening and speaking domain scores), literacy (reading and writing domain scores), comprehension (listening and reading domain scores), and an overall composite (WIDA, 2012c). The critical issue to appreciate when interpreting these scores is the contribution of the language domains to each of the composite scores, as these contributions vary by ELP measure. Again, using the ACCESS for ELLs as an example, Table 4.3 contains the percentages of contribution by language domains. ELP composite scores are compensatory, which means that a student may obtain a high enough composite score to exit ELL services, yet not be proficient in one or more language domains (i.e., high scores in one domain [e.g., speaking] can compensate for a lower score within a different domain [e.g., writing]). Thus, it is possible for an ELL to have a composite score that is considered proficient, yet have domain scores that are relatively lower. This is why some states have ELP assessment exit requirements (e.g., Table 4.2) that consider domain scores in combination with the overall composite score.

NCLB Accountability Requirements

Students' scores on ELP measures serve as the foundation for determining whether districts and states are making progress toward the requirements of Annual Measurable Achievement Objectives (AMAOs) one and two (see Chapter 2). As a reminder, these AMAOs are as follows:

- AMAO 1: Annual increases in the number or percentage of ELLs making progress in learning English (i.e., Are ELLs *progressing* toward English proficiency?).
- AMAO 2: Annual increases in the number or percentage of ELLs attaining ELP (i.e., Are ELLs *attaining* English proficiency?).

Given the complexity of these AMAO calculations, we avoid any further discussion of these accountability requirements. Instead, we recommend that readers interested in more information consult more authoritative resources, such as the accountability offices of the relevant state education agency.

TABLE 4.2. ELL Exit Criteria by State

State	Minimum ELP measure requirements	Achievement test required?	Parent consultation?	Other requirements and considerations
AL	ACCESS for ELLs overall composite score ≥4.8	No	No	
AK	ACCESS for ELLs overall composite score ≥5.0 and 4.0 score or higher in each domain (i.e., Reading, Writing, Speaking and Listening)	No	No	
AZ	AZELLA overall composite score = proficient and intermediate or proficient on Total Combined Proficiency, Reading Level Proficiency, and Writing Level Proficiency	No	No	Teacher evaluation of student performance required
AR	ELDA overall composite score = 5.0 and 5.0 scores in each domain (i.e., Reading, Writing, Speaking, and Listening)	Yes	Yes	Teacher evaluation of student performance and passing grades required
CA	CELDT = overall performance level is Early Advanced or higher and Intermediate or higher in each domain (i.e., Reading, Writing, Speaking, and Listening)	Yes	Yes	Teacher evaluation of student performance required
CO	ACCESS for ELLs overall composite score ≥5.0 and Literacy score ≥5.0	Yes	Yes	Teacher evaluation of student performance required
CT	LAS Links Overall Level ≥4 and Reading score ≥4 and Writing score ≥4	No	No	
DE	ACCESS for ELLs overall composite score 5.0	No	No	ACCESS for ELLs individual domain scores (i.e., Reading, Writing, Speaking, and Listening) should be reviewed and all factors considered before exiting student from services.
DC	ACCESS for ELLs overall composite score ≥5.0	No	No	
FL	CELLA = composite and domain scores (Reading, Writing, Speaking, and Listening) must be at proficient level	Yes (for students in grades 3–12)	No	School ELL Committee can exit student based on holistic evaluation of student's academic record.
GE	ACCESS for ELLs overall composite score ≥5.0	Yes	No	For students who score at proficient level on either the ACCESS for ELLs or the academic achievement test, but not both, has eligibility determined through a Language Assessment Conference.

(continued)

TABLE 4.2. *(continued)*

State	Minimum ELP measure requirements	Achievement test required?	Parent consultation?	Other requirements and considerations
HI	ACCESS for ELLs overall composite score ≥6.0 results in automatic exit from services	No	No	Student also may be exited if ACCESS for ELLs overall composite score ≥4.8 and Literacy score ≥4.2, demonstrates satisfactory grades, and receives recommendations for exit by all appropriate teachers.
ID	IELA composite score ≥4.0 (Early Fluent) and each domain score ≥4.0 (Early Fluent)	Yes	No	And at least one of the following: (1) Idaho Reading Indicator score of at least 3.0; (2) Idaho Standards Achievement Test score Basic level; (3) Demonstrate access to core content with a student portfolio using work samples from at least two core content areas that demonstrate a Level 4 (Expanding) as defined by WIDA's Performance Definition Rubrics and Can Do Descriptors.
IL	ACCESS for ELLs overall composite score ≥4.8, literacy subscore ≥4.2, and writing proficiency subscore ≥4.1	No	No	
IN	ACCESS for ELLs overall composite score ≥5.0	No	No	
IA	I-ELDA composite score ≥6.0 and all domain scores ≥3.1	Yes	No	Students must also meet three of the following four exit criteria: (1) Success in regular classroom, (2) Language Instruction Education Program support not required, (3) Sustainability of success, (4) Score proficient on districtwide and statewide assessments in reading, mathematics, and science.
KS	KELPA overall composite score ≥fluent and all domain scores ≥fluent for 2 consecutive years.	No	No	Building Leadership Team or Student Improvement Team can recommend exit after 1 year of KELPA scores fluent; decision must be unanimous and be based on the best interest of the student.
KY	ACCESS for overall composite score ≥5.0 and literacy composite score ≥4.0	No	No	Student cannot be exited in kindergarten.
LA	Grades K–2: ELDA overall composite score = level 5 for 2 consecutive years or, in the same year, ELDA overall composite score = level 5 and at grade-level/benchmark/low-risk on a standardized reading assessment, such as DIBELS Next. For grades 3–8: ELDA overall composite score = level 5 or, in the same year, ELDA overall composite score = level 4 and at proficient on the English language arts state content assessment.	Yes	No	

(continued)

State	Exit criteria			Additional criteria / notes
ME	For grades 9–12: ELDA overall composite score = level 5 or, in the same year, ELDA overall composite score = level 4 and at proficient on the English state content assessment in the most recent academic year. ACCESS for ELLs overall composite score ≥6.0	No	No	District Lau Plans must stipulate a Level 6 composite score on the ACCESS for ELLs.
MD	ACCESS for ELLs overall composite score ≥5.0 and literacy composite score ≥4.0	No	No	
MA	ACCESS for ELLs overall composite score ≥4.0 and scored at least proficient on the MCAS ELA test and demonstrate the ability to perform ordinary class work in English; or ACCESS for ELLs overall composite score ≥5.0 and Reading and Writing scores ≥4.0 and demonstrate the ability to perform ordinary classwork in English, or ACCESS for ELLs overall composite score ≥6.0.	Yes	No	
MI	ACCESS for ELLs overall composite score ≥5.0 and must perform ≥proficient or advanced proficient in reading and math on the state approved academic achievement tests	Yes	No	
MN	ACCESS for ELLs overall composite score ≥5.0 in most cases	Yes	Yes	Specific exit criteria are determined by local educational agencies.
MS	Grades 3–5: ACCESS for ELLs overall composite score ≥5.0 on Tier B or ≥4.5 on Tier C; Grades 6–8: ACCESS for ELLs overall composite score ≥5.0 on Tier B or ≥4.0 on Tier C; Grades 9–12: ACCESS for ELLs overall composite score ≥4.0 on either Tier B or C.	Yes	No	ACCESS for ELLs specified overall composite scores plus proficient level on state language arts proficiency examination.
MO	ACCESS for ELLs overall composite score ≥6.0 on Tier C; or overall composite score ≥5.0 on Tier C and ≥Basic level on state English Language Arts assessment and some additional criteria from those listed in last column; or overall composite score ≥4.7 on Tier C and ≥Basic level on state English Language Arts assessment and all additional criteria from those listed in last column.	Yes	Yes	Additional criteria: (1) district benchmark or interim assessments (in multiple content areas), (2) writing performance assessments scored with the Missouri standardized rubric, (3) writing samples, (4) academic records such as semester and course grades, and (5) agreement between ESL teacher, classroom teacher(s), other relevant staff, and parents/guardians that language is no longer a barrier to the student's ability to access academic content.
MT	ACCESS for ELLs overall composite score ≥5.0 and literacy composite score ≥4.0	Yes	No	Additional required measures of reading, writing, or language development available from school assessments and input from general education and content teachers

TABLE 4.2. *(continued)*

State	Minimum ELP measure requirements	Achievement test required?	Parent consultation?	Other requirements and considerations
NE	ELDA composite score = proficient	Yes	No	Grades K–2 also requires teacher recommendation. For grades 3–12, in lieu of ELDA proficient score, student can be exited if meeting or exceeding the standard on the state content reading assessment.
NV	ACCESS for ELLs overall composite score ≥5.0 and literacy composite ≥5.0	No	No	
NH	ACCESS for ELLs overall composite score ≥5.0 and domain (Reading, Writing, Speaking, and Listening) ≥4.0	No	No	
NJ	ACCESS for ELLs overall composite score ≥4.5 if multiple criteria support the decision to exit the student	Yes	Yes	Examples of multiple criteria supporting decision to exit the student include classroom grades, teacher recommendations, achievement scores, etc.
NM	ACCESS for ELLs overall composite score ≥5.0 on Tier B or Tier C	No	No	
NY	NYSESLAT = Proficient or Commanding level; or NYSESLAT = Advanced or Expanding level and 3+ on a grade 3–8 English language arts assessment or 65+ on the Regents Exam in English	Yes	No	
NC	ACCESS for ELLs overall composite score ≥4.8, with at least a 4.0 on the reading subtest and a 4.0 on the writing domain	No	No	
ND	ACCESS for ELLs overall composite score ≥5.0 and domain (Reading, Writing, Speaking, and Listening) scores ≥3.5	No	No	
OH	OTELA composite score ≥5.0	No	No	If a student obtains an OTELA composite score between 4.0 and 4.9 and subsequently completes a trial period of mainstream instruction and continues to obtain an OTELA composite score of ≥4 during the trial period, he or she can be exited from services. Students are not to be exited prior to Grade 3.
OK	ACCESS for ELLs overall composite score ≥5.0 and a literacy domain score ≥4.5 on the Tier B or Tier C form	Yes	No	Also requires additional information (e.g., classroom achievement, benchmark assessments, state content assessments)

State	Criteria			Notes
OR	O-ELPA composite score ≥5.0	No	No	Student also can be exited if O-ELPA composite ≥4.0 if evidence indicates that a student is able to successfully participate in grade-appropriate content and continues to perform on par with his or her peers.
PA	ACCESS for ELLs ≥overall composite score of 5.0	No	Yes	Additional criteria include a Pennsylvania System of School Assessment (PSSA) score ≥Basic; or ACCESS for ELLs overall composite score ≥4.5 if PSSA score ≥Proficient; and one of the following two criteria: (1) final grades of C or better in mathematics, language arts, science, and social studies; (2) scores on districtwide assessments that are comparable to the BASIC performance level on the PSSA.
RI	ACCESS for ELLs overall composite score ≥4.5 and Comprehension composite score ≥5.0, and a speaking score above a district-established minimum	No	Yes	Alternative exit criteria include NECAP Reading score ≥3 and ACCESS for ELLs overall composite score above a district established minimum. All students require three of the following criteria: (1) Passing grades in all core content classes, or (2) ESL/bilingual education teacher recommendation, or (3) at least two general education core content teacher recommendations, or (4) at least three writing samples demonstrating skill not more than 1 year below grade level, or (5) score on a district reading assessment not more than 1 year below grade level as defined by the publisher or the district. Kindergartners are not eligible for exit.
SC	ACCESS for ELLs overall composite score ≥5.0	No	No	No students in K–2 can be exited from services.
SD	ACCESS for ELLs overall composite score 4.7 and reading domain score ≥4.5 and writing domain score of ≥4.1	No	No	
TN	Exit requirements to be determined		No	
TX	Multiple ELP measures allowed[a]	Yes	Yes	In addition to scoring proficient on ELP measure, student must demonstrate adequate achievement on English reading and English writing assessments and obtain a recommendation to exit services based on a subjective teacher evaluation.
UT	ACCESS for ELLs overall composite score ≥5.0	No	No	

(continued)

TABLE 4.2. *(continued)*

State	Minimum ELP measure requirements	Achievement test required?	Parent consultation?	Other requirements and considerations
VT	ACCESS for ELLs overall composite score ≥5.0 and reading domain ≥4.0 and writing domain ≥4.0	No	No	
VA	ACCESS for ELLs overall composite score ≥5.0 and literacy domain score ≥5.0 on Tier 1	No	No	
WA	WELPA proficiency level ≥4	No	No	
WV	ELDA[b] composite = 5.0 for 2 consecutive years	Yes	No	Student must also score at mastery or above on the West Virginia Educational Standards Test, reading language arts assessment (grades 3–8, 10) or reading language arts end of course exams (grades 9 and 11).
WI	ACCESS for ELLs overall composite score ≥5.0	Yes	No	ACCESS for ELLs overall composite score = 6.0 results in student automatically exiting services; ACCESS for ELLs overall composite score between 5.0–5.9 can be exited if (1) the student is at least in fourth grade, (2) the student has sufficiently developed the academic language to demonstrate his or her understanding in English, and (3) the district has evaluated at least two pieces of evidence of academic ELP (e.g., district benchmark examinations, writing samples, state assessment, course grades).
WY	ACCESS for ELLs overall composite score ≥5.0 and domain scores (Speaking, Reading, Writing, Listening) ≥4.0	No	No	

94

Note. ACCESS for ELLs, Assessing Comprehension and Communication in English State-to-State for English Language Learners; AZELLA, Arizona English Language Learner Assessment; CELDT, California English Language Development Test; CELLA, Comprehensive English Language Learning Assessment; ELDA, English Language Development Assessment; ELPA, English Language Proficiency Assessment; IELA, Idaho English Language Assessment; I-ELDA, Iowa–English Language Development Assessment; KELPA, Kansas English Language Proficiency Assessment; LAS Links, Language Assessment Scales; NYSESLAT, New York State English as a Second Language Achievement Test; OR, Oregon English Language Proficiency Assessment; OTELA, Ohio Test of English Language Acquisition; WELPA, Washington English Language Proficiency Assessment.

[a]For list of allowable ELP measures, see *http://tea.texas.gov/index4.aspx?id=25769814359.*

[b]Officially called the West Virginia Test of English Language Learning.

TABLE 4.3. ACCESS for ELLs Composite Scores and the Percentage Contribution of Each Language Domain

Composite score	Domain contribution (percentage) to composite score			
	Listening	Speaking	Reading	Writing
Oral	50	50	—	—
Literacy	—	—	50	50
Comprehension	30	—	70	—
Overall	15	15	35	35

Note. Data from WIDA (2012c).

Classroom Planning, Instruction, and Assisting in Intervention Design and Implementation

ELP measures inform classroom teachers and other educators regarding the specific level of ELP at which each of their ELLs is performing overall, as well as students' ELP levels within the specific domains of listening, speaking, reading, and writing. Thus, a classroom teacher armed with this information is able to differentiate lesson plans for ELL students within the classroom setting. For actual examples of how ELP standards and ELP levels can be integrated within classroom planning, we encourage you to review actual lesson plans that are available within WIDA's "Lesson Plan Share Space" (*www.wida.us/getin-volved/lessonplan-sharespace.aspx*). The important point to remember is that without the necessary AL, discussion in the typical classroom—as well as textbooks, worksheets, and other tasks containing language components—is equivalent to that taking place in a foreign language, even for native English speakers. Consequently, it is essential that data obtained from ELP measures be appropriately utilized to assist in instructional differentiation that is consistent with the AL needs of each individual ELL.

ENGLISH LANGUAGE INSTRUCTIONAL MODELS

Due to the diversity within and across ELLs, as we have mentioned previously, it is unlikely that one English language instructional model is a good fit for all students and all schools. Thus, it is important that decision makers (i.e., you!) consider questions about the unique needs of your particular students and unique community. In this process, consideration should be given to the diversity of linguistic backgrounds present, the language resources that are available (e.g., interpreters and translators), teachers' experience in working with ELLs, and the community's attitudes regarding bilingualism (Moughamian, Rivera, & Francis, 2009). Despite our desire to be able to answer unequivocally the question of which language instructional model produces the most positive outcomes for ELLs, and despite claims by multiple researchers as to the "best" model, the fact remains that there are many unanswered questions (e.g., August & Hakuta, 1997; Lindholm-Leary & Borsato, 2006). Thus, we do not advocate for one language instructional model over another; rather, we remain true to the beliefs we stated at the outset, that ELLs ultimately need to obtain *proficiency in the English language* to have the highest likelihood of experiencing academic success in U.S. schools. No matter what language instructional model is in place within a specific school, RTI models can be implemented, because RTI is not a program but rather is a process that can be applied across multiple settings under varying circumstances and conditions.

The three most common ELL English language instructional models are (1) *English-only* programs in which students develop skills solely in English, (2) *bilingual* programs in which students develop skills in two languages at the same time, and (3) *transitional* programs in which students transition from a bilingual to an English-only model after reaching a certain grade level or English competency level. Depending on the source, research supports each one of these models as being the most effective. The National Literacy Panel's extensive meta-analysis of studies on the effectiveness of various instructional models indicates that bilingual education models seem to have a positive, small-to-moderate effect on English reading outcomes (August & Shanahan, 2006). Similarly, Goldenberg (2008) concluded from the results of five separate meta-analyses that "teaching students to read in their first language promotes higher levels of reading achievement in English" (p. 14). The implication here is that, if possible, it is ideal for all students to have the opportunity to develop skills in their first language in addition to learning English, in order to reach higher levels of AL proficiency in both languages.

English-Only Models

The goal of this approach is to increase ELL's academic knowledge by using English as the primary or sole means of instruction. Within this framework, teachers provide instruction in English, and ELLs receive pullout supports or may even be placed in a special English language development classroom. The focus of these classrooms is on building students' English language skills to proficiency so they can access academic content in their general education classrooms. Additionally, ELLs may stay in general education classrooms in which teachers use a form of sheltered instruction (SI; i.e., separate from the mainstream) to enable students to grasp both the English *language* and English *academic content* (Moughamian et al., 2009). In an SI environment which we discuss next, teachers modify the language demands of the content areas that they are teaching. For example, teachers might use simplified texts or have vocabulary explicitly defined using realia (i.e., teaching materials drawn from everyday life such as a skein of yarn and knitting needles). Additionally, in SI, there are clear language objectives alongside content objectives, both of which are stated explicitly and featured prominently (e.g., written on the board) prior to and during instruction. To illustrate, students' academic content objective may include knowledge about the Civil War, and the corresponding language objectives would be writing and orally reciting three sentences in English about the Civil War (Echevarria, Vogt, & Short, 2008).

Sheltered Instruction

The SI method, which helps ELLs acquire content material in their classes, is a whole-class approach that seeks to make classroom content comprehensible to ELLs (Beacher, 2011). It is based in language acquisition theory and focuses on the interactions of the student with both content and language objectives (Echevarria et al., 2008). The SI approach takes content material and breaks down the language components in an effort to assist in transferring the information to students. This manipulation of material is done through building background knowledge, encouraging collaborative peer groups, using hands-on activities, and using the students' first language (L1) as a support mechanism (e.g., using cognates, allowing students to respond in L1). SI also places a strong emphasis on weaving explicit language instruction into all lessons. For example, teachers might write specific language goals for each lesson, and students are given time to demonstrate the knowledge they have gained in a particular lesson through reading, writing, or speaking in English. Specific instructional methods used in the SI approach have been found to be effective for both ELLs and mainstream students (Echevarria et al., 2008).

Dual-Language Models

In a dual-language approach, the student's L1 is used to help develop his or her knowledge in the targeted second language (L2), English. The dual-language approach is based on the idea that there are transferable skills from knowledge of an L1 that can be used to acquire an L2, such as higher order vocabulary skills and an understanding of syntax (August & Shanahan, 2006; Leafstedt & Gerber, 2005). Within this model there are two main methods of instruction. The first is a bilingual transition program in which students receive L1 instruction for a limited amount of time to help them gain transferable skills that assist them in learning English. In early-exit bilingual programs, students are taught in their L1 for as little as 2 years, then are quickly are transitioned into English-only classrooms. Students within late-exit bilingual programs are taught in their L1 for upward of 6 years, then transition into mainstream English-only classrooms. The main goal of these programs in both examples is to allow the student to gain enough rich exposure in their L1 to be able to transfer those skills to learning the L2 (Echevarria et al., 2008). In the second method of dual-language instruction, bilingual immersion, the goal is for students to develop proficiency in L1 and L2 simultaneously. Students are taught in both languages, and the classroom student body comprises approximately equal numbers of students who speak native English and those who speak a different language (e.g., Spanish, Chinese).

Research on the use of dual-language models or English-only models has shown mixed results (Barnett, Yarosz, Thomas, Jung, & Blanco, 2007; Lindholm-Leary & Hernandez, 2011; Lopez & Tashakkori, 2006). However, Collier and Thomas (2004) conducted a comprehensive longitudinal study comparing different types of instructional approaches for ELLs. Their study spanned 18 years and examined data from 23 school districts across 15 different states. Overall findings indicated that ELLs made the most academic growth in bilingual immersion programs. The study also found little support to indicate that English-only instruction actually benefited the students. When the authors compared the state achievement data for students whose parents refused ESL services and those who received English-only services, Collier and Thomas found that there was no significant difference between students' scores. Other studies have demonstrated that students who were formerly in bilingual immersion programs performed as well or better than their English-only counterparts on state tests (Genesee, Lindholm-Leary, Saunders, & Christian, 2006; Lindholm-Leary & Hernandez, 2011; Lopez & Tashakkori, 2006). In 2006, the National Literacy Panel on Language-Minority Children and Youth conducted a meta-analysis on the current research on instructional models for ELLs. The authors released an executive summary indicating that students perform better on English reading proficiency measures when they are in bilingual programs rather than English-only programs (August & Shanahan, 2006).

THE IMPORTANCE OF ACADEMIC ENGLISH

The trend of foreign and U.S.-born ELL students struggling in U.S. schools and the evidence that AL development is key to the academic success of ELL students are both clear. However, scientifically based evidence to determine what educators should do about these issues remains relatively inconclusive at this time. Thus, it is important to focus on the limited number of evidence-based approaches that *are* currently known in order to ensure that up-to-date best practices are being used and to guide future research in a direction that will appropriately fill the gaps in our knowledge.

Indicative of the importance of acquiring Academic English, the Institute of Education Sciences has published a number of practice guides (e.g., Baker et al., 2014; Gersten et al., 2007) that emphasize the essential role of Academic English in not only literacy but also other content areas. Recommendations associated with literacy and language instruction (Gersten et al., 2007) included (1) screening for reading problems and the monitoring of progress, (2) providing intensive small-group reading interventions, (3) providing extensive and varied vocabulary instruction, (4) developing Academic English, and (5) using regular peer-assisted learning opportunities. Similarly, Baker et al. (2014) recommended a number of strategies for enhancing literacy instruction and other academic content areas; this practice guide not only expanded on much of the content addressed in the earlier practice guide (i.e., Gersten et al., 2007) but also extended the recommendations to the middle school level. These updated recommendations included (1) teaching academic vocabulary words intensively across several days, utilizing a variety of instructional methods; (2) integration of oral and written English language instruction into content-area teaching; (3) provision of regular and structured opportunities to develop written language skills; and (4) provision of small-group instructional intervention for students struggling with literacy and Academic English language development. In addition to merely providing recommendations, Baker et al. (2014) provided specific examples of how to accomplish these activities. As you will see, all of these recommendations are core elements of RTI and are emphasized throughout the remainder of this book.

The first four chapters have established the foundation for the implementation of RTI models with ELLs. Chapter 1 provided a broad overview of multiple issues associated with RTI implementation with ELLs. Chapter 2 examined key demographic variables, emphasized that teachers throughout the United States need to be prepared to work effectively with ELLs, and provided a context in which multiple education-related outcomes need to be considered when working with ELLs. Chapter 3 overviewed RTI models and also identified key considerations when implementing RTI with ELLs, and Chapter 4 has established the importance of ELP and AL. The remainder of this book examines core instructional practices and supplemental interventions for enhancing academic skills and facilitating the trajectory in which these academic skills are obtained.

CHAPTER 5

Best Practices in Assessment and Instruction for ELLs at Tier 1

In Chapter 3, we introduced RTI and discussed how this dynamic model of assessment and intervention can help ELLs and their teachers experience academic success. We also described RTI in the context of a diamond-shaped approach to serving ELL students (and, really *all* students). Recall that our diamond-shaped approach to RTI, in contrast to popular triangle-shaped approaches, epitomizes the principal goals in RTI, which are to wield schoolwide and classwide reform efforts to meet the needs of *all* students, and only secondarily to assist in special education evaluation and eligibility practices. Thus, our diamond-shaped approach is figurative in that as a model, it embraces schoolwide and classwide reform efforts that meet the needs of *all* students, embodying a brilliant (pun intended!) and systemic approach to education. By adhering to an approach that allows educators to focus most of their energy on *preventing* and *remediating* academic problems, students with true, underlying learning disorders, including specific learning disabilities (SLD), become more easily identifiable. Our diamond-shaped approach to RTI is also symbolic, however, in that just as diamonds are *the* finest of all gemstones, we deem the RTI model described here to be the soundest of all population-based service delivery models, especially for addressing the academic needs of ELLs.

This chapter is a primer on best practices in assessment and instruction/intervention at Tier 1. Tier 1 includes *all* students. The term *all students* includes those with identified special needs, ELLs, general education students, and gifted and talented students. In regard to assessment at Tier 1, we discuss universal screening, progress monitoring, and early identification of ELLs who are not making projected gains in English language acquisition, ELP, and/or grade-level academic skills. In Chapter 1 we described our guiding philosophy for this text, noting that while we staunchly advocate for maintenance of ELLs' native language and culture, we also deem mastery of the English language and Academic English to be the linchpins for personal, academic, and vocational success in the United States. In this chapter we begin by emphasizing the importance of universal screening and progress monitoring to examine *English* reading proficiency. Readers interested in assessment in the native language are encouraged to read Carvalho, Dennison, and Estrella (2014), Olvera and Gómez-Cerrillo (2014), and Rhodes, Ochoa, and Ortiz (2005).

Given the importance of instruction/intervention at Tier 1, we feel that it is critical to spend a significant amount of time examining the importance of a sound core curriculum. We discuss how to review curriculum quality, so that the reader can evaluate a school's curriculum and/or actively participate in curriculum adoption discussions and decisions. Because academic standards drive curriculum decisions, we briefly discuss what currently is one of the hottest and most controversial topics in education, the national Common Core State Standards Initiative (CCSS) (*www.corestandards.org*), its role in curriculum selection, and the corresponding implications for ELLs.

Core curriculum quality is only part of the equation when trying to increase the academic achievement of our students. Consequently, we draw from various literatures in instructional pedagogy to describe universal principles and best practices in instruction. These principles are not necessarily or exclusively intended for teaching ELLs; rather, they are tenets for excellent teaching of *all* students. Where possible and appropriate, we describe the application of each principle to ELLs. We also discuss instructional approaches described in the literature as being specifically geared toward promoting learning for ELLs. These latter guidelines are drawn primarily from the L2 literature and are intended for teachers who want to include these strategies in addition to the general ones that are described first. All of the strategies we present in this chapter promote a powerful, child-centered, teacher-empowered learning environment that promises to provide the necessary foundation, so that each and every child, including ELL students, can succeed academically.

Finally, we focus on reading—the gateway skill to all learning—in a discussion of the *five pillars of reading instruction,* whole language versus phonics approaches to teaching reading, and what needs to be considered in reading instruction at the secondary level for both ELLs and struggling native English speakers.

DATA-BASED DECISION MAKING

Throughout the first four chapters of this book, we frequently have referred to the importance of making decisions based on data (i.e., data-based or data-informed decision making). This decision-making criterion was also recognized as essential by the U.S. Department of Education, such that the Institute of Education Sciences (IES) produced a practice guide titled *Using Student Achievement Data to Support Instructional Decision Making* (Hamilton et al., 2009). Within this practice guide, the IES established the following five strategic recommendations for the use of data to inform instruction:

1. Making data part of an ongoing cycle of instructional improvement.
2. Teaching students to examine their own data and set learning goals.

3. Establishing a clear vision for schoolwide data use.
4. Providing supports that foster a data-driven culture within the school.
5. Developing and maintaining a districtwide data system.

As discussed next, we believe that each of these five recommendations can be put into place through the adoption of both universal screening and progress monitoring assessment procedures. We discuss each of these data collection processes below.

UNIVERSAL SCREENING

In our discussion of data-based decision making in Chapter 3, we briefly described the concepts of universal screening, progress monitoring, and research-based interventions/treatments, using an example in real life with which our readers surely are familiar. Specifically, we commented that each time a person visits the doctor, standard protocol typically dictates that a health care provider, generally a nurse, takes the patient's temperature. The idea that *everyone* who goes to the doctor gets his or her temperature checked—whether the person shows signs of illness or not—represents the concept of universal screening (other examples of universal screening within a doctor's office includes having one's blood pressure checked, being weighed, having lymph nodes inspected, etc.). Within schools, a typical term that is used interchangeably with universal screening is *benchmarking;* these terms essentially mean the same thing. However, the term *benchmarking* also includes the concept of progress monitoring; thus, benchmarking typically refers to concepts of both universal screening *and* progress monitoring. To simplify the discussion in this book, we interchangeably use (1) *universal screening* and *benchmarking*, and (2) *progress monitoring* and *benchmarking* when discussing procedures designed to determine how students are doing academically. In the context of RTI, universal screening involves *briefly* assessing *everyone* in a population to get a *snapshot* of the *academic health* of that population. Universal screening is by definition very brief (e.g., it takes less than a minute to get a temperature reading with a thermometer), and it is administered to *everyone* in the defined population. Furthermore, the screener provides a brief snapshot that tells us *something*. It does not tell us everything, but it can be a red flag that indicates when something is not quite right (e.g., body temperature of 103 degrees). Finally, in the context of RTI, we consider universal screening or benchmarking as a means to get an overall picture of the academic health of the population of interest (e.g., all students across the district, in a school building, within a grade level, or within a single classroom). Thus, in implementing RTI with ELLs, two key questions are associated with data-based decision making:

1. What is the academic health of the ELL population in your classroom, grade level, school, and/or district?
2. What is the academic health of the ELL population when you consider specific levels of ELP in your classroom, grade level, school, and/or district?

Before adopting a universal screening approach with ELLs, the expectation is that the universal screening measure will meet the requirements outlined by Glover and Albers (2007), who indicated that measures must be (1) appropriate for their intended use, (2) result in technically adequate (i.e., valid and reliable) decisions, and (3) useable (i.e., teacher- or user-friendly). If the selected measure or measures do not meet these minimum requirements, the results of the universal screening process will incorrectly identify students for supplemental instructional and intervention services, fail to identify students who actually are in need of these services, or a combination of both. Additional resources (e.g., Albers & Kettler, 2014; Kettler et al., 2014) offer more details on how to conduct universal screening within the general population of students and within areas other than the literacy domain; we now turn to one of the focuses of our book, however, which is how to conduct universal screening with ELLs.

Universal Screening with ELLs

To encourage efficiency in data collection and to minimize the costs (in terms of both monetary and personnel costs associated with administering the measures), we advocate for an integrated universal screening and progress monitoring system in which the same assessment tools or measures are used for both universal screening and progress monitoring. The benefits of using the same measures for universal screening and progress monitoring are numerous, including reduced costs in purchasing materials, fewer administration training requirements, fewer data interpretation training requirements, and the ability to track student progress specifically from the time of the initial universal screening through the most recent progress monitoring administration. However, these frequent administration requirements dictate that the universal screening process needs not only to meet the criteria outlined by Glover and Albers (2007; i.e., appropriateness, technical adequacy, and usability) but also to be easily and quickly administered to curtail any significant loss of instructional time (as we see later in the chapter, opportunity to learn is critical, so we don't want to shortchange these valuable instructional opportunities by administering an overabundance of assessments). All of these factors point to the use of curriculum-based measurement (CBM; for an in-depth discussion of CBM administration and interpretation, see Hosp, Hosp, & Howell, 2007; Shinn, 2008) as a viable— and perhaps most appropriate—tool to conduct universal screening and progress monitoring with ELLs. Although other assessment tools have been adopted for universal screening purposes, we stand behind the evidence supporting CBM as the optimal assessment tool for tracking progress in academic skills.

Researchers and practitioners have examined the use of CBM procedures for over three decades, resulting in an evidence base that is substantially broad in scope and size (for a summary, see Reschly, Busch, Betts, Deno, & Long, 2009; Shinn, 2008). This evidence is more than sufficient to meet the requirements of appropriateness, technical adequacy, and usability, particularly when using CBM with non-ELLs. Although the evidence base for using CBM with ELLs is nowhere near as large as support for the use of CBM with non-ELLs, there is increasing evidence that these same measures can be used with ELLs to conduct universal screening and ongoing progress monitoring (e.g., Albers & Mission, 2014; Albers, Mission, & Bice-Urbach, 2013; Baker & Good, 1995; Gutierrez & Vanderwood, 2013; Wiley & Deno, 2005).

As we indicated in Chapter 4, ELP (as measured by ELP assessments) is a critical variable to consider when implementing RTI models with ELLs; perhaps one of the clearest indicators of the need to be familiar with ELP levels occurs when considering how to conduct universal screening of ELLs' English reading skills. As emphasized by Albers and Mission (2014), there are two critical variables to consider when conducting universal screening with ELLs: (1) specific ELP levels and (2) the language instructional model being used in the child's classroom. We examine each of these variables below.

ELP-Level Considerations

The ELP level of ELLs is a significant factor to consider when interpreting data obtained from CBM procedures. As an illustration of this significance, Figure 5.1 demonstrates the English reading fluency performance of Martín, a second-grade ELL, during the fall benchmark assessment of AIMSweb (*www.aimsweb.com*) oral reading fluency (ORF). As

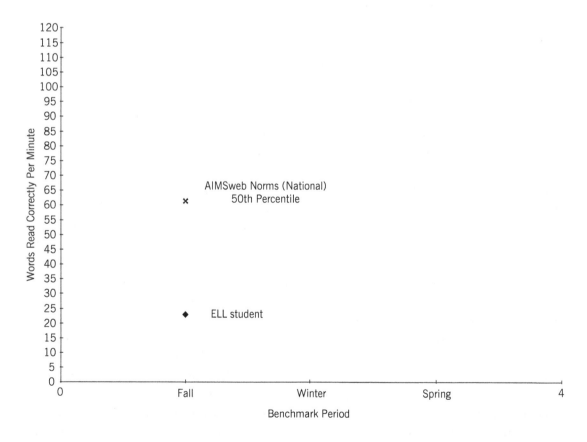

FIGURE 5.1. ORF score for an ELL during the fall benchmark period as compared to the 50th percentile rank according to AIMSweb (national) norms.

indicated in Figure 5.1, Martín was reading approximately 24 words read correctly per minute (WRCM); also indicated in the graph is the ORF 50th percentile rank within the AIMSweb norms (national) group that may (or may not) include ELLs (approximately 62 WRCM). One's immediate reaction when seeing this graph likely would be to suggest that Martín is significantly behind his peers in English reading skills as measured by ORF and would be considered to be at risk of academic failure associated with reading skills.

However, let's examine Martín's ORF in a different way and consider his performance, taking into account what we know about his ELP level. Suppose that the district in which Martín was enrolled had been collecting local norms during the previous 5 years. *Local norms* are norms created by a local school or district that are based on the scores obtained from the population sample within the school or district (for additional information about developing local norms, see Stewart, 2014). For example, some high-achieving schools may choose to compare individual students' scores to local norms, whereas another district may develop local norms based on their ELL student scores. Now compare Martín's score to this set of local norms; here we see that Martín's ORF score is still significantly below the average performance of *other ELL students within the district during the prior 5 years* (see Figure 5.2). Martín's classroom teacher questioned whether he should be considered a "typical"

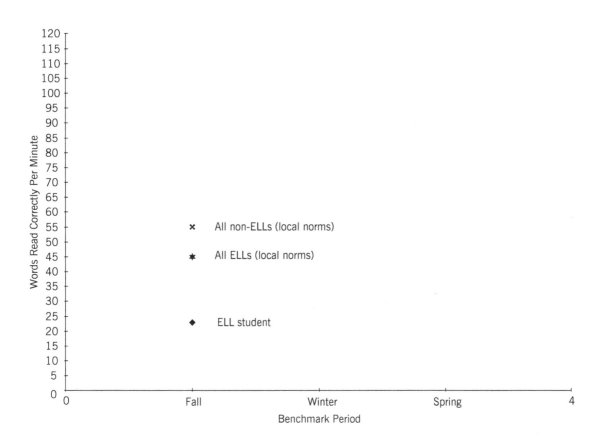

FIGURE 5.2. ORF score for an ELL during the fall benchmark period as compared to local norms for non-ELLs and ELLs.

ELL student given that his latest ELP assessment indicated that his overall ELP composite level was 2.0, which places him within the beginning stages of language acquisition.

Given the growing evidence regarding the significance of specific ELP levels in understanding an ELL's academic performance, combined with the classroom teacher's hesitation in classifying this student as a "typical" ELL student, the district decided to reexamine its norms and its decision to classify ELLs' ELP only in a dichotomous manner (i.e., non-ELL vs. ELL). With these new local norms (i.e., specific to ELP levels), and knowing that Martín had a composite ELP of approximately 2.0, the intervention team came to a different decision regarding his score of 24 WRCM. As can be seen in Figure 5.3, Martín's performance indicated that he actually was reading at or above the levels obtained by other ELLs at ELP level 2 within the district in the past 5 years. Thus, the district personnel decided not to provide supplemental interventions (i.e., because the student was demonstrating adequate progress compared to peers in the district), but rather to continue with the excellent classroom instruction Martín was receiving and to continue monitoring his progress frequently to be sure that his gains in English reading skills continued.

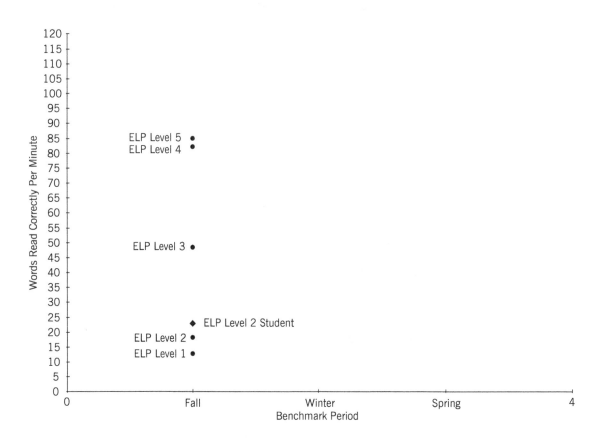

FIGURE 5.3. ORF score for an ELL during the fall benchmark period as compared to the 50th percentile rank (local norms) by specific ELP levels.

Language Instructional Model Considerations

As we indicated in our initial discussion of universal screening, knowing an ELL's specific ELP level is a necessary but not sufficient component for conducting valid and reliable benchmarks and interpreting scores. The second critical variable is consideration of the type of language instructional model to which the student is being exposed. For example, consider an ELL who is enrolled in a school that utilizes a Spanish–English dual-language immersion (DLI) model. In this model, kindergarten students receive 90% of their instruction in Spanish and 10% in English. In first-grade Spanish instruction decreases and English instruction increases at an approximate ratio of 80/20, in second grade it changes to 70/30, in third grade it is 60/40, and in fourth grade it balances to approximately 50/50, so that half of the instruction is provided in Spanish and half is provided in English. Within such a model, it would seem that using CBM ORF procedures in English, then using norms developed with students who received all of their instruction in English (i.e., the national norming sample or the aggregate norms sample) would not be reliable, valid, or equitable for the second-grade students who have received only approximately 20% of their instruction in English during their 3-year academic career. Stated differently, it would not be appropriate to test students on something they have not been taught (i.e., reading in English). The district, then, would have two feasible options for the appropriate screening and progress monitoring of its ELL students; the district could either develop separate norms for students participating with the DLI program *and/or* utilize Spanish CBM measures.

Over the past decade, two versions of CBM materials in Spanish have become commercially available; these include the *Indicadores Dinámicos del Éxito en la Lectura* (IDEL) and the *Medidas Incrementales de Destrezas Esenciales* (MIDE). Both versions were developed to allow educators to determine native Spanish-speaking students' basic literacy skills in Spanish. Being able to determine ELLs' Spanish literacy skills—presuming that their native language is Spanish (and that they have received instruction or schooling in Spanish) —allows educators to determine which Spanish literacy skills the students have acquired. This is important information to have, especially if a student is a recent immigrant to the United States and/or he or she has a history of attending school in a country that is primarily Spanish speaking. If the student demonstrates language proficiency in Spanish *and* he or she has acquired literacy skills in Spanish, our confidence in his or her ability to acquire literacy skills successfully in English significantly increases. With these four data sources (i.e., Spanish language proficiency, ELP, literacy skills in Spanish, and literacy skills in English), a relative degree of risk can be determined. Albers and Mission (2014) outlined the possible risk status implications for ELLs with Spanish language origins based on various combinations of scores within these four data domains, as indicated in Table 5.1. We want to emphasize that interpretation of the various levels of risk can and will vary by a myriad of factors, such as grade level, specific ELP levels, CBM measure utilized, and even native language proficiency levels, so please interpret the recommendations with care. Whether to provide supplemental services to students identified in this manner as at risk will need to be a local decision based on relative contextual variables.

TABLE 5.1. Interpretation of ELP in Spanish and English and Risk Status on CBM-R Measures in Spanish and English

Spanish CBM-R risk status	English CBM-R risk status	Interpretation[a]
		Proficient in Spanish language, proficient in English language
No/minimal risk	No/minimal risk	• No/minimal risk • Ongoing progress monitoring
No/minimal risk	At risk	• Likely not at risk due to acquiring literacy skills in native language • Continue progress monitoring to determine risk status or whether more time is needed to acquire English literacy skills
At risk	No/minimal risk	• Likely not at risk due to acquiring English literacy skills • Ongoing progress monitoring
At risk	At risk	• Likely at risk as did not acquire literacy skills in either native or non-native language, yet is proficient in both languages • Continue progress monitoring to determine risk status
		Proficient in Spanish language, not proficient in English language
No/minimal risk	No/minimal risk	• No/minimal risk • Ongoing progress monitoring • Monitor ELP development
No/minimal risk	At risk	• Likely not at risk due to acquiring literacy skills in native language • Continue progress monitoring to determine risk status or whether more time is needed to acquire English literacy skills • Monitor ELP development
At risk	No/minimal risk	• Likely not at risk due to acquiring English literacy skills • Ongoing progress monitoring • Monitor ELP development
At risk	At risk	• Likely at risk as did not acquire literacy skills in either native or non-native language • Continue progress monitoring to determine risk status or whether more time is needed to acquire English literacy skills • Monitor ELP development

(continued)

TABLE 5.1. *(continued)*

Spanish CBM-R risk status	English CBM-R risk status	Interpretation[a]
	Not proficient in Spanish language, proficient in English language	
No/minimal risk	No/minimal risk	• No/minimal risk • Ongoing progress monitoring
No/minimal risk	At risk	• Likely not at risk due to acquiring literacy skills in native language • Likely needs additional time to acquire English literacy skills • Ongoing progress monitoring
At risk	No/minimal risk	• Likely not at risk due to acquiring ELP and English literacy skills • Ongoing progress monitoring
At risk	At risk	• Likely at risk as did not acquire literacy skills in either native or non-native language, yet is considered to be proficient in English language • Continue progress monitoring to determine risk status or whether more time is needed to acquire English literacy skills
	Not proficient in Spanish language, not proficient in English language	
No/minimal risk	No/minimal risk	• Likely not at risk due to acquiring literacy skills in native and non-native languages • Ongoing progress monitoring • Monitor ELP development
No/minimal risk	At risk	• Likely not at risk due to acquiring literacy skills in native language • Ongoing progress monitoring • Monitor ELP development
At risk	No/minimal risk	• Likely not at risk due to acquiring English literacy • Ongoing progress monitoring • Monitor ELP development
At risk	At risk	• Likely at risk as did not acquire literacy skills in either native or non-native language, and is not proficient in either language • Continue progress monitoring to determine risk status or whether more time is needed to acquire English literacy skills

Note. From Albers and Mission (2014). Adapted with permission from the American Psychological Association. Copyright 2014.

[a]Interpretation can vary by grade level, instructional program, specific ELP levels, mobility, etc.

Progress Monitoring with ELLs

When CBM procedures are adopted for the universal screening of ELLs at Tier 1, we strongly recommend that CBM procedures also be adopted to monitor progress at Tiers 2 and 3. Using the same assessment procedures across all tiers in the RTI model provides familiarity, consistency, and more reliable and valid decisions. As with universal screening, consideration of individual ELL students' ELP levels and corresponding language instructional model exposure remain relevant when interpreting the performance of ELLs on CBM progress monitoring measures. To illustrate this point, we again focus on the impact of ELP levels and the need to interpret CBM scores using norms that are based on specific ELP levels.

Recall that in the earlier example of universal screening we introduced Martín, a second-grade student whose ELP skills were estimated to be a composite level 2, which is within the beginning range of English language acquisition. If the school obtained ORF scores for Martín during the three typical benchmark periods (i.e., fall, winter, spring), and then evaluated his performance in comparison to the regular (national or aggregate) norms

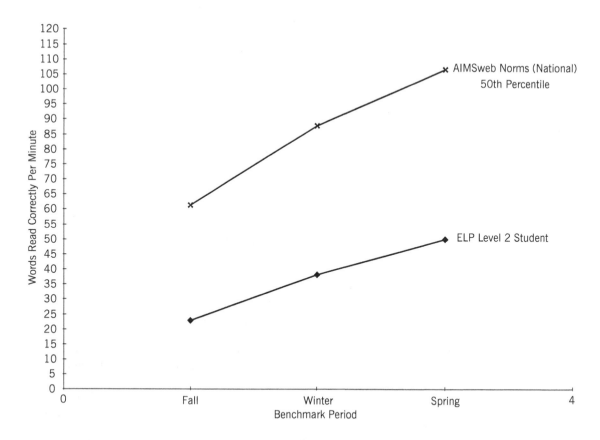

FIGURE 5.4. ORF scores for an ELL during the fall, winter, and spring benchmark periods as compared to the 50th percentile rank according to AIMSweb (national) norms.

provided by AIMSweb, we would see (as illustrated in Figure 5.4) a significant discrepancy between Martín's performance and the 50th percentile rank for students within the aggregate norm sample.

Similar issues arise when comparing Martín's CBM scores against local norms based on non-ELL versus ELL samples, as indicated in Figure 5.5. In contrast, comparing Martín's benchmark scores to local norms based on ELLs by specific ELP levels (see Figure 5.6) suggests that he is making adequate progress in obtaining English literacy skills, which indicates that he should continue receiving the excellent classroom instruction that appears to be facilitating his acquisition of English literacy skills.

To conclude our discussion of universal screening and progress monitoring at Tier 1, we introduce a flowchart (see Figure 5.7) that illustrates how both universal screening and progress monitoring data, as well as ELP assessment data, inform the fluid movement of students between instructional and intervention tiers. With regard to a currently enrolled student, it is necessary to know whether the student is an ELL (in most circumstances, this already has been determined). If the student is a native English speaker, he or she will receive core instruction and participate in universal screening and progress monitoring

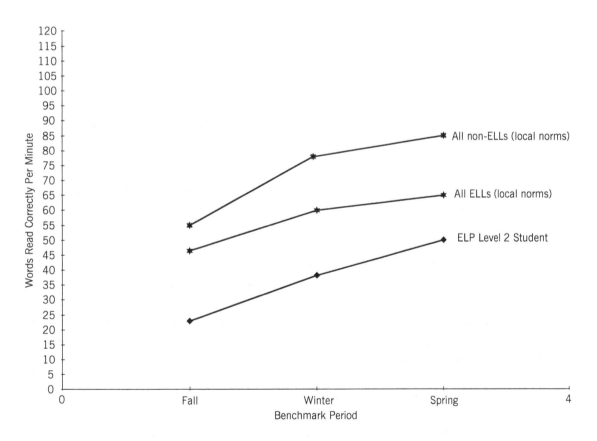

FIGURE 5.5. ORF scores for an ELL during the fall, winter, and spring benchmark periods as compared to local norms for non-ELLs and ELLs.

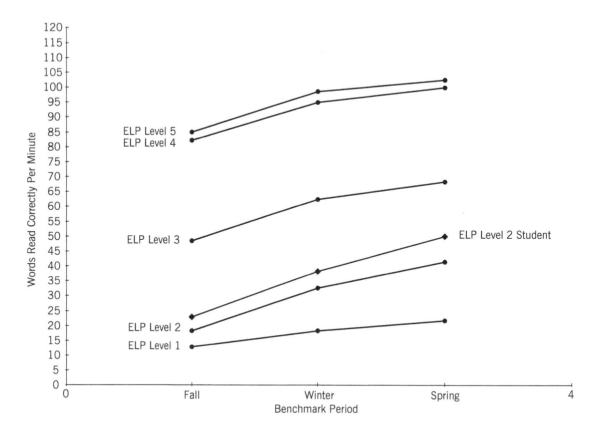

FIGURE 5.6. ORF scores for an ELL during the fall, winter, and spring benchmark periods as compared to the 50th percentile rank (local norms) by specific ELP levels.

activities at each of the benchmark periods. The data obtained from the universal screening will determine whether that student should continue receiving core instruction as is, or whether he or she will receive supplemental interventions. This process continues throughout the year, with the student receiving core instruction in Tier 1 and supplemental support in Tier 2 as needed and indicated by progress monitoring. For the ELL student, the process is similar, with the primary difference being the need to monitor not only academic skills but also English language proficiency. Additionally, specific ELP levels should be considered when interpreting universal screening and progress monitoring data; if the ELL is not making sufficient progress, then it is necessary to consider whether the core instruction being delivered is appropriate for the ELL's ELP level and current academic skills. If the core instruction is not appropriate for the ELL's current levels, then it should be modified to meet that student's needs, with supplemental services added as needed to facilitate the student's academic and language achievement. For a student new to the school, the process is quite similar, except that first it is necessary to determine whether the student is an ELL, and if so, his or her ELP level. The obtained level then provides information to the school staff regarding what types of support may be needed to assist the student in making academic and English language development progress.

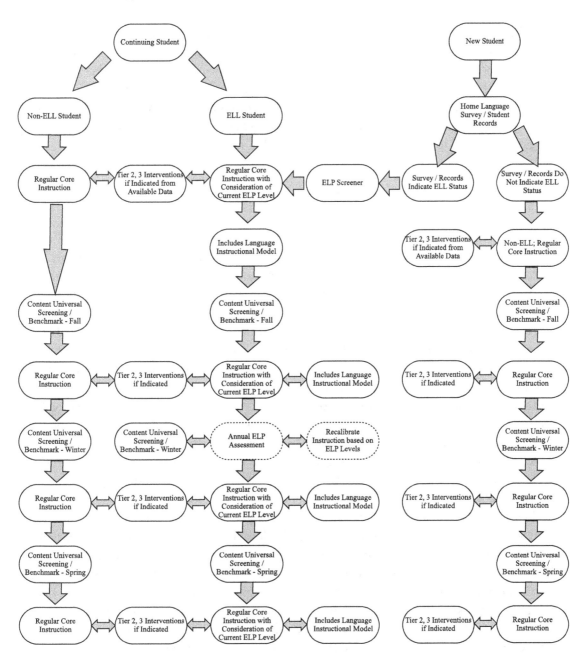

FIGURE 5.7. Instruction and assessment at Tier 1.

We again want to remind the reader that a student who is currently receiving Tier 2 or Tier 3 supports *additionally receives the same core curriculum* that everyone else receives. In other words, the student whose data indicate a relative lack of progress will *also* receive any number of additional *supplemental* interventions and support (which we examine in more detail in Chapter 6). Now that we have examined the significant role that data (whether academic or language data) should play in identifying and monitoring student progress, we turn our attention to the critical linchpin within RTI models: Tier 1 instruction.

INSTRUCTION AT TIER 1

Within an RTI program, instruction at Tier 1 represents *classroom* instruction (Fuchs & Deshler, 2007). In other words, Tier 1 represents both the curriculum (the *what*) and instruction (the *how*) that general education classroom teachers deliver to all students on a daily basis. Even though classroom teachers use the curriculum and, obviously, teach on a daily basis, we wish to emphasize is that not all classroom curricula and instruction are created equally. In the world of curricula, and the instructional strategies available to deliver it to students, there are "good bets" and there are "bad bets" (Foorman, 2007; Fuchs & Deshler, 2007). *Good bets* refer to curricula and instructional practices that have been scientifically validated. That is, rigorous research has been conducted on the program or method, and one or more research studies have reported that the curriculum and/or the strategy is effective—that it worked for the sample of participants included in the study or studies. *Bad bets* are curricula and instructional strategies that have not been rigorously or scientifically tested. In early reading, for example, bad bets might include curricula that focus minimally or only incidentally on the skill of separating and blending speech sounds and instruction that is based on what teachers "feel" is best for kids, not what is *known* to be best for kids (e.g., direct instruction for teaching reading). Even so, no curriculum or instructional strategy is certain to work for all kids in all settings and under all circumstances, thus re-emphasizing the importance of continual progress monitoring. Fuchs and Deshler emphasize that good bets are just that—good bets—and there is no assurance that curricula and instructional strategies that are known to be good bets will work for all struggling students. Nevertheless, as with anything we do in our personal and professional lives, we *always* want to begin with what we know to be the good bets. And when we are dealing with children's education, going with the good bets is the *only* appropriate option.

Academic Standards: The CCSS, NGSS, and ELLs

An examination of Tier 1 instruction must consider the role that academic standards play in classroom instruction. Simply stated, standards articulate what students should learn and be able to do. Thus, Tier 1 instruction, as well as corresponding supplemental services, should be the driving force between what we (i.e., parents, educators, policymakers) want our children and students to be able to do, and what they eventually know and are able to do, whether it is being ready to attend college or technical school to further their education and training or going directly from high school into the workforce and becoming a productive member of society. However, there historically has been a lack of consensus regarding what these academic standards should be.

In an attempt to obtain consensus regarding academic standards within the United States, the CCSS were developed to serve as universal standards in English language arts and mathematics. The CCSS are intended to be a rigorous, consistent set of academic standards to be met by all students across the country to prepare them for vocational training, college, and careers. Prior to the development of the CCSS, states developed their own curricular standards, resulting in 50 different sets of state standards. This approach to standard development became problematic, because such an approach (1) often presented too many standards to realistically cover in the classroom, (2) led to inconsistent use across states, (3) did not hold students to high expectations, and (4) failed to prepare students for the rigors of college and vocational careers (Quay, 2010). A major benefit of the CCSS for the states that have adopted them is that they provide a consistent framework—a clear road map for what to learn and be able to do in order to be successful in college and careers—for *all* students across *all* parts of the country in kindergarten through 12th grade. Although the number of states that ultimately will utilize the CCSS is constantly changing for any number of reasons, including the fact that the standards have become politically charged, the majority of states have voluntarily adopted the CCSS. A significantly smaller number of states (i.e., fewer than 15) have adopted the closely associated NGSS.

The impact of the CCSS implementation on ELLs has yet to be determined, with predictions ranging from the CCSS and NGSS being yet an additional challenge for ELLs to overcome (Coleman & Goldenberg, 2012), to being a positive development that should enhance ELL achievement levels in multiple areas (e.g., Lee, Quinn, & Valdes, 2013; Quay, 2010). Although there has been much speculation about the impact of these standards, the reality is that we do not have any data indicating what the impact actually will be. What we do know is that many educators are experiencing some degree of uncertainty as to the impact of the CCSS and NGSS and few would disagree with the value of high standards and the explicit goal that all students should be held to the same high standards and expectations. However, there is a general consensus that the increased language and literacy demands will be challenging for all students, but especially so for ELLs (Bunch, 2013). Thus, the question is of how to enable educators to enhance classroom instruction and intervention efforts to increase the likelihood that ELLs will be able meet these higher standards.

We propose that the implementation of the CCSS and NGSS will make the implementation of RTI with ELLs even more critical. Relying on language specialists, such as ESL teachers, to be responsible for meeting the academic needs of ELLs will be insufficient; rather, the education of ELLs must be the responsibility of everyone within the school setting, which happens to be a core component of RTI models that we have emphasized throughout the book. This requirement will also necessitate that *all* classroom teachers— and *all* educators—become familiar with the most efficient methods for teaching ELLs. Data-based decision making, frequent formative assessment, high-quality core instruction, and supplemental instructional supports will be necessities in facilitating ELLs' successful acquisition of content represented in the CCSS and NGSS. Thus, we encourage you become more familiar with the CCSS and take these standards into consideration as we discuss Tier 1 instruction in more detail.

Starting Off on the Right Foot: The Learning Environment

Before we delve deeply into describing what good (and bad) bets in curriculum and instruction might look like, we want to discuss how to start off on the right foot in terms of providing a maximally effective learning experience for ELLs—before curriculum and instruction are even considered. We acknowledge that establishing a learning environment that is warm, welcoming, and conducive to the learning of all students, including ELLs, is a surefire first great bet if you want your students to succeed academically. There is no question that school and classroom environments that are perceived by students as warm, welcoming, and "safe" are healthier than those not perceived to be that way. Children who feel a sense of connection or belonging at school are more emotionally and behaviorally engaged (Furrer & Skinner, 2003), which only bolsters their motivation to learn (Wentzel, Battle, Russell, & Looney, 2010). Feeling a connection to their school and their classroom may be particularly important for ELL newcomers who may miss their home country and perhaps feel isolated culturally and excluded linguistically.

Teachers play an immense role in helping students feel safe, comfortable, and motivated to perform their best academically. Students who report that their teachers provide them with direct academic support, create a safe learning environment, and are emotionally supportive *want* to perform better academically (Wentzel et al., 2010). These implications are huge for ELLs who may be reticent about practicing their English and performing academically with or in front of their peers. Although we believe that, first and foremost, a teacher's mission is to provide excellent instruction that educates all of his or her students, we also know that a teacher who cultivates a responsive and warm classroom environment that integrate both academic *and* social learning tends to have the students who perform better academically (Brock, Nishida, Chiong, Grimm, & Rimm-Kaufman, 2008). Thus, the importance of cultivating a healthy school and classroom environment cannot be minimized. Indeed, Hamre and Pianta (2005) reported that both instructional support (e.g., providing effective reading instruction and feedback, encouraging students to be responsible for their own learning) and emotional support from the classroom teacher moderated students' risk of academic failure. In other words, educators who build warm and welcoming schools and classrooms set the stage for successful RTI programs that make sure *all* students, including ELLs, are academically successful.

Warm and Welcoming Classrooms

We both agree that one of the best online resources for teachers (and parents) of ELLs, particularly Spanish-speaking ELLs, is Colorín Colorado (*www.colorincolorado.org*). Colorín Colorado provides access to a large number of resources for educators addressing ELL-related issues, including components of ELL instruction, academic language issues, professional development resources (including videos), and recommendations for reaching out to ELL students and their families. It describes for parents activities that can be done in the home setting to assist the child in developing additional English language and academic skills, makes recommendations for working with the child's school, and provides multiple reading tips and activities. As an example of available educator resources, one article (*www. colorincolorado.org/educators/reachingout/welcoming*) lists pragmatic strategies teachers can use to create a warm and welcoming classroom environment and ensure that their ELLs feel at ease. We offer an adapted version of this list that describes these strategies in more detail.

1. Learn each student's name and make sure you pronounce it correctly each time you say it. Ask the children to teach you how to pronounce their names correctly. Insist that all students in the class also learn to pronounce other students' names correctly.

2. Assign a peer partner/buddy to your ELL newcomer. Identify a student in the classroom who will be a good mentor and want to help the ELL student experience success (e.g., properly following classroom routines). You may want to assign different buddies for different school activities, such as lunch and recess. Enlist the support of all the students in the class to help the ELL feel comfortable and safe as he or she also develops new friendships.

3. Label classroom objects in the ELL student's native language and in English, and refer to the names in both languages frequently. Enlist the other students in learning the new vocabulary as well. L2 learning can be a venture that *everyone* in the class can enjoy!

4. Help your ELLs follow the established classroom rules by modeling them explicitly and reinforcing behavior that follows the classroom rules. You can't expect the ELL (or any student) to know your expectations if you don't demonstrate them explicitly and in a safe environment where it is OK for students to make mistakes as they learn what is expected of them.

5. Post a visual daily schedule and refer to it at the beginning of class and throughout the day. Posting a daily schedule (with words *and* visuals) helps all students take comfort in your organization of the classroom and expectations for the day's activities.

6. Incorporate reading and instructional materials related to your ELLs' native countries and cultures. Integrate literature, books, and artifacts into your instruction and classroom environment as much as possible. This not only creates a welcoming environment for your ELLs, but it also promotes cultural awareness and acceptance on behalf of all students in the class. Similarly, invite your students' culture(s) into the classroom. Is there a special dish that a student can bring to share with the class? What about a specific song or music genre associated with the child's culture that can be incorporated into music class? Would a parent like to come and do a show-and-tell about his or her home country? Think outside the box!

7. Offer frequent, one-on-one assistance to your ELLs. Excellent classroom instruc-

tion involves a combination of large-group, small-group, and individual teaching as needed. For ELLs, it may be especially important for the classroom teacher (not the assistant or the bilingual aide) to provide as much of the small-group and individual teaching as possible. Interpreters or instructional assistants who speak the language can be helpful, but do not depend on them to provide for your ELLs the instruction *you* should be giving them.

8. Include ELLs in all classroom activities in a nonthreatening manner. In other words, do not put ELLs (or any student) on the spot to answer a question or perform in front of their peers.

9. Involve ELLs in cooperative learning groups and pair them with non-ELL students or ELLs with stronger English proficiency. ELLs need to be included in activities with native English speakers for as much of the day as possible (an appropriate exception would include being pulled out of class for intense ESL instruction). Interacting and socializing with peers who are native English speakers is the best possible way to enhance both social and Academic English by fostering development of pragmatics of the English language in social situations.

In summary, these nine strategies (as well as the many you surely have come up with on your own) for fostering warm and welcoming classroom environments can be expressed in one word: *caring*. Excellent teachers are not only excellent instructors, but they also are attentive to the emotional and social needs of their students and possess a powerful attribute: They care. Caring is one of the core tenets of *culturally responsive teaching* (Gay, 2010), which is a philosophy that embraces culture in all aspects of teacher instruction and student learning, and is vitally important for appropriately addressing the academic needs of ELLs.

Culturally Responsive Teaching

Culturally responsive teachers teach "to and through (their students') personal and cultural strengths, their intellectual capabilities, and their prior accomplishments" (Gay, 2010, p. 26). Moreover, culturally responsive teachers recognize the "close interactions among ethnic identity, cultural background, and student achievement" (p. 27). While culturally responsive teachers recognize and hail ethnic and linguistic diversity, we believe that culturally responsive teaching *also* includes instructional emphasis on learning Academic English, as emphasized in this book. Culturally responsive pedagogy and excellent instruction in English are not mutually exclusive. We believe that one of the most caring, ethical, and instructionally responsible professional activities of the general education classroom teacher is the academic empowerment of each and every ELL students. Teachers can academically empower students by providing them with excellent instruction that prepares them to be successful in and out of school in the United States. In many circumstances, the provision of excellent instruction is dependent on using a sound core curriculum, a subject to which we now turn our attention.

EFFECTIVE INSTRUCTIONAL PRINCIPLES AND SOUND PEDAGOGY

The research base in support of effective classroom modifications for ELLs is relatively limited; however, research suggests that many strategies that work well for general education non-ELLs also improve the English literacy development of ELLs (Goldenberg, 2008). Strategies such as creating motivational learning environments, offering immediate feedback, specifying clear learning goals, and providing a content-rich curriculum benefit all students (Goldenberg, 2008; Kame'enui, & Simmons, 1999). However, there is still limited research examining the specific effects of these strategies with ELLs. The *Report of the National Literacy Panel on Language-Minority Children and Youth* (August & Shanahan, 2006) examined studies that looked at instructional practices in literacy and students' progress based on their language proficiency status. August and Shanahan reported that the instructional strategies employed benefited *all* students regardless of ELL status. However, the effect size for ELLs was smaller than that for non-ELLs (Escamilla, 2009), which suggests that whereas ELLs *can* benefit from common but excellent teaching strategies, they still require additional, targeted classroom modifications to succeed on par with their native English-speaking peers.

Although there are general teaching strategies that should be employed with all students regardless of their language proficiency status, some necessary modifications are specific to the academic and language proficiency needs of ELLs. For example, employing manipulatives or visual aids to break down new or complex words during instruction has been found to be beneficial for teaching ELLs (Mathes, Pollard-Durodola, Cárdenas-Hagan, Linan-Thompson, & Vaughn, 2007). As another example, demonstrating the concept of gravity in a science class is enhanced and becomes more comprehensible if the teacher uses visual aids and real-life examples to demonstrate the concept. Similarly, the use of the students' primary language as a scaffolding tool can be helpful for ELLs learning new material (August & Shanahan, 2006). In this situation, the classroom teacher would allow the student to preview a lesson in the ELLs' native language (e.g., by listening to a podcast in the native language or reading from a text in the native language), which allows students to encounter content in a more comprehensible way (Markham & Gordon, 2007). Another way to use students' primary language is to teach explicit comprehension strategies in the primary language (Goldenberg, 2008). Of course, doing this requires that a teacher or other education professional be fluent in the student's native language and competent to teach in the native language effectively. Last, having ELLs note similarities and differences in English and their native language (e.g., identifying cognates) may help students take an active role in making explicit and meaningful connections between the two languages (Goldenberg, 2008).

In the next section, we review four basic principles of sound instruction for all students that may be particularly salient for teaching ELLs effectively. These include the concepts of (1) opportunity to learn (OTL), (2) differentiation, (3) direct/explicit instruction, and (4) practice and corrective feedback.

Opportunity to Learn

The use of instructional models and learning theories plays a vital role in the way classroom instruction is delivered to all students. Previous learning theories focused intently on the background characteristics that students brought to the educational context. These theories looked at the specific behaviors or traits (e.g., IQ, self-efficacy, cultural capital) students need in order to succeed. The OTL framework shifts the focus off the student and onto the educational context. Therefore, the OTL framework seeks to determine the environmental or extraneous *conditions* needed to promote a positive learning environment for all students (Aguirre-Muñoz & Amabisca, 2010).

Four variables, in particular, influence OTL in schools (Stevens, 1993). The first variable is the amount of content that is covered. Providing more breadth and depth of content necessarily results in more OTLs for students. The second variable, the amount of exposure to the content the students receive, refers to how much time students are given to work with academic material or tasks. The third variable is the way in which content is emphasized for the student and whether lower or higher order skills are required. Educators may sometimes have a misconception that ELLs need lower order cognitive tasks in order to learn English, when, in fact, ELLs need higher order cognitive tasks, so that they can be challenged and motivated to achieve (Aguirre-Muñoz & Amabisca, 2010). The final variable relates to the quality of instructional delivery. Aguirre-Muñoz and Amabisca argue that the OTL framework has great potential for supporting the learning of ELLs. However, we believe the framework needs to include specific cultural features and linguistic components to maximize its effectiveness. For ELLs, we suggest that all of their OTLs must also explicitly aid in strengthening their Academic English. Within this framework, there are multiple techniques to increase OTLs for ELLs. Certain classroom modifications, including the use of differentiation, direct instruction, and practice and corrective feedback, have varying support for their effectiveness with students of diverse linguistic backgrounds.

Differentiation

Another way to support all students, and especially ELLs, is through the use of differentiated instruction, or *differentiation,* which is an indispensible approach to excellent teaching. In differentiation, the teacher differentiates or individualizes the common content for a whole class (i.e., the academic goal or task to be accomplished), both with activities and approaches that allow students to demonstrate what they know and can do, and based on each student's specific needs, academic levels, or language proficiency. Teachers' failure to differentiate students' activities and assessment tasks (i.e., when they teach only to the "middle" of the class) is a surefire way to leave behind both struggling students (including ELLs) and advanced learners (who might also include ELLs!). Consider this: "If you teach the same curriculum, to all students, at the same time, at the same rate, using the same materials, with the same instructional methods, with the same expectations for performance and grade on a curve you have fertile ground for growing special education" (Tilly, 2003, PowerPoint presentation). There is no question that one of the most important foundations of effective teaching is differentiated instruction. When teachers differentiate instruction, they demonstrate a deep awareness of and respect for where individual students currently are and where the teacher knows their students can be as learners. It is important, however, to remember that differentiated tasks must be meaningful and engaging, and respectful of all groups and individual students. One way that teachers uphold their commitment to securing a safe and respectful environment is by planning differentiated tasks and assessments, and providing all students with equally engaging, interesting, and important learning activities (Tomlinson, 1999).

Tomlinson (1999) articulated eight essential tenets of differentiated instruction. These include having the teacher (1) focus on the essentials; (2) modify content, process, and products as appropriate and necessary; (3) consider assessment and instruction as inseparable; (4) attend to student differences; (5) balance group and individual norms; (6) ensure that all students participate in respectful work; (7) ensure that teacher and students work together flexibly; and (8) ensure that teacher and students collaborate in learning. Focusing on the essentials of differentiation anchors instruction so that its premise is based on ensuring that all children get the "big ideas" of a lesson. For example, when teachers plan their lessons, they decide at the front end what those "big ideas" are and modify or differentiate both the *activities* in which students will engage in to practice the big ideas and the *assessments* they are given to demonstrate what they have learned and can do. Authentic, frequent, formative assessment that guides and informs how instruction proceeds next is also a key feature of differentiated instruction. The teacher who differentiates instruction essentially is in a collaborative partnership with his or her students. Both teacher and students are working toward the goal of learning; the teacher is a flexible, engaging, and involved facilitator who fosters motivation and makes sure learning happens for each and every student in his or her classroom.

Differentiated instruction can be tailored to individual small groups of students who have similar difficulties. In the case of ELLs, we recommend that these small groups be determined by their ELP level (Beacher, 2011). As noted earlier, differentiated instruction can be adapted at the levels of content, process, and product. For content-level adaptations, the text to be understood by the student is modified. For example, the teacher might provide visual depictions of the text or even shorten the text or offer a simpler, parallel text (e.g., an abridged version of a book chapter). Process adaptations allow the student multiple opportunities to engage with new content. Teachers who differentiate instruction by process, for example, might allow students to work collaboratively in groups or use instructional aids, such as a Spanish–English dictionary, to help them better understand the material. Product adaptations or differentiation provide unique ways for students to demonstrate what they have learned or understand. For example, after watching a documentary on the life of Abraham Lincoln, the teacher might have most of the class submit a one-page summary, but he or she might allow a particular group of students to demonstrate their understanding in a group essay, in which each student in the group contributes one paragraph or section (Beacher, 2011). Conversely, members of another group in the same class might be expected to demonstrate their understanding by orally retelling what they understood from the documentary, using a mix of their native language (and a peer interpreter) and as much English as they know. According to Martinez (2014), excellent differentiated teaching is no easy task, because teachers are on their toes from the second the bell rings in the morning until it rings again at the end of the day (and usually beyond) as they meticulously and thoughtfully implement an explicit and continuous *teach–assess–differentiate* process that meets the needs of all their students on a daily basis.

Direct/Explicit Instruction

A teacher mindfully provides direct instruction (DI) or explicit instruction so that students can complete a learning task by observing exactly what they are expected to do in order to demonstrate that they have learned a concept or skill. When teachers use DI to teach reading, for example, they focus on three core areas: instructional organization, program design, and teacher presentation techniques (Carnine, Silbert, & Kame'enui, 1997). In DI, students are given step-by-step instructions and receive feedback immediately after completing each step of a particular task (Gersten, Woodward, & Darch, 1986). Nevertheless, there has been much controversy regarding the use of DI with students. For ELLs, in particular, traditional DI may limit opportunities for students to negotiate meaning from the language they are using (Aguirre-Muñoz & Amabisca, 2010). Consequently, DI may be effective for ELLs only at certain junctures within a lesson. Although there are mixed research results regarding the use of DI with students who have particular needs (Gersten et al., 1986) including ELLs, the IES recommends the use of explicit instruction and DI as the primary means of instructional delivery for ELLs (Gersten et al., 2007).

It is important to recognize the distinction between DI as a specific intervention (frequently referred to as "capital DI") and the need for instruction to be explicit (frequently referred to as "small di"), as recommended by the IES. According to the National Institute for Direct Instruction (NIFDI, 2011, para. 1), the DI approach is "a model for teaching that emphasizes well-developed and carefully planned lessons designed around small learning increments and clearly defined and prescribed teaching tasks." The basic philosophy of DI embraces the ideas that (1) all children's academic functioning can be improved, (2) teachers can succeed with adequate resources, (3) low-performing students must be taught at a faster rate in order to catch up to their peers, and (4) instruction *must* be explicit and systematic (i.e., follow a logical order) to eliminate students' misinterpretations and misunderstandings of material that is taught. A specific element of DI that is most applicable for low-performing students, including ELLs, consists of sufficient instructional time of *several* 60- to 90-minute blocks of time in the school day during which an "every second counts" attitude inspires the maximization of instruction time. In this example, students participate in leveled groups with four to six students per teacher or teaching assistant, in which instructors follow lesson scripts, detect and correct students' errors immediately, and reinforce hard work. In DI, there is a focus on students' mastery of material and correct performance, with presentation of only 10–15% new material per lesson (NIFDI, 2011).

Historically, the strategies of DI just outlined have a mixed scientific base for use with low-performing students (regardless of their language status). Part of President Johnson's War on Poverty in the 1960s involved the largest education research project in history, Project Follow Through, which examined numerous strategies to improve education (e.g., DI,

Parent Education, Cognitive Curriculum, Open Education). Results at the conclusion of the study in 1995 indicated that DI was the *only* strategy that yielded the desired outcomes of raising student performance to the 50th percentile (Adams & Engelmann, 1996).

Other research findings indicate mixed results for the extension of DI with ELLs to improve academic outcomes and academic language proficiency. Nonetheless, one specific DI program, Reading Mastery, was reported by the What Works Clearinghouse (U.S. Department of Education, 2006a) to have potentially positive effects on ELLs' English reading achievement for kindergarten through sixth-grade students. This program groups students based on reading ability level, and teachers provide quick-paced, interactive, explicit instruction. Students are continuously monitored and receive immediate feedback on their performance. Early lessons focus on phonemic awareness and sound–letter correspondence; intermediate lessons focus on word and passage reading, vocabulary development, comprehension, and building oral reading fluency; later lessons focus on the continuation of reading fluency, with an emphasis on accuracy and comprehension.

Practice and Corrective Feedback

Giving students' corrective feedback—by repairing or correcting a student's speech—is a helpful teaching strategy. However, it also can be controversial when applied to ELL students. Razfar (2010) discussed the sociocultural context, or implicit consequences, when teachers provide corrective feedback to ELLs and argued that corrective feedback signals implicit (negative) attitudes and beliefs about what the teacher values. Culturally sensitive corrective feedback in an ELL classroom is possible, however. In his case study of a teacher of ELL students, Razfar noted three classroom features that created a safe environment where corrective feedback was not detrimental. In his observations, the teacher (1) was critically aware of corrective feedback and its potential negative consequences if not handled delicately; (2) allowed students to use their native language to demonstrate understanding and make meaning; and (3) created a warm, welcoming, and safe environment, in part through her use of endearing terms to refer to the students (e.g., "my dear one," "my children").

TEACHING STUDENTS TO READ

Learning to read likely is the most important academic skill taught in schools, at least at the elementary school level. Given this significance, we feel that a book describing many best practices when working with ELLs to promote their academic success must include a discussion of reading. Thus, we now turn to a discussion of issues associated with the teaching of reading to ELLs. We begin with an overview of considerations relating to the selection of a sound core reading curriculum, then continue with an examination of the *Five Pillars of Reading Instruction*, consideration of whole-language versus phonics-based approaches to reading instruction, and conclude with considerations associated with reading at the secondary levels.

A Sound Core Reading Curriculum

At the start of this chapter, we briefly mentioned the necessity of choosing "best bets" in core curriculum. Although curricula are available for all K–12 academic subjects (e.g., mathematics, world geography, social studies, biology), most of the literature about core curricula in RTI addresses the core curriculum in early reading, especially in grades K–3. We believe this emphasis on excellent core reading curricula is due to several reasons. First, reading is undoubtedly a *cultural imperative* (Shinn, 1998); thus, teaching reading is perhaps *the* most important and basic responsibility of any elementary school teacher. Second, the largest category served in special education is students with specific learning disabilities (SLD; Snyder & Dillow, 2012) and, specifically SLD in reading. Referrals for special education evaluation are overwhelmingly made for students with reading problems (Machek & Nelson, 2007). Third, reading is the most researched and best remediated of the academic skills; thus, there is no excuse for students to have reading difficulties that stem from poor instruction. We know how to fix the problem for students who struggle in reading (and do not have an endogenous learning or cognitive disability), and it begins, at the most basic level, with selecting a "best bet" sound core curriculum. Given the significance and corresponding knowledge base on reading, our emphasis through this chapter—and throughout the book—is on reading instruction and intervention. Clearly, other academic areas (e.g., writing, mathematics, science, social studies) also are important, but it is almost a certainty that a student with weak reading skills will struggle in these other academic areas to varying degrees.

According to Simmons and Kame'enui (2003), a core reading curriculum is the main or primary tool (i.e., material) used to teach reading. However, supplemental strategies, interventions, and materials *can* and *should* be used in addition to the core curriculum. Simmons and Kame'enui contend that when a core curriculum is adopted, there is an assumption that (1) most teachers are involved in the adoption selection decision and (2) all teachers will use the core curriculum as the foundation for their reading instruction. Thus, selecting and adopting core reading curricula is a critical decision and the foundation for success in your school's RTI program.

Simmons and Kame'enui (2003) describe a two-stage process for identifying and selecting core reading curricula that are "best bets" or have the highest likelihood of being effective with most students, including ELLs. The first stage in this process is the review of multiple curricula *prior* to the adoption decision. During the review process, they recommend that adoption committees consider the following four questions in reference to each reading program under review (p. 3):

1. Does the program have evidence of efficacy established through carefully designed experimental studies?
2. Does the program reflect current and confirmed research in reading?
3. Does the program provide explicit, systematic instruction in the primary grades (K–3) in the following dimensions: phonemic awareness (grades K–1), phonics/decoding, vocabulary, and comprehension (listening and reading)?
4. Was the program tested in schools and classrooms with learner profiles that are similar demographically to those of students enrolled in your school?

Next, Simmons and Kame'enui (2003) delineate a second, more in-depth stage of curriculum review that incorporates analyzing the specific and critical elements of the reading curriculum. According to the authors, research-based core reading curricula contain all grade-level standards (e.g., state or Common Core) with ample quality, breadth, and depth. A rubric and rating scale are provided so the reviewer can scrutinize each element of the curriculum under review by using the following scale: (1) element consistently meets/exceeds| criterion, (2) element partially meets/exceeds criterion, and (3) element does not satisfy the criterion. These elements are as follows:

1. (**w**) = Within a sequence of lessons. A specified element is best analyzed by reviewing a particular lesson or a series of two or three successive lessons.
2. (**ss**) = Scope and sequence. A specified element is best analyzed by reviewing the program's scope and sequence.
3. (**st**) = Skills trace. A specified element is best analyzed by completing a skills trace over a series of 10 consecutive lessons (p. 5).

See Figure 5.8 for sample components from *A Consumer's Guide to Selecting a Core Program* (Simmons & Kame'enui, 2003).

The Five Pillars of Reading Instruction

In the area of early reading, effective curriculum and instruction means explicit and systematic instruction in phonemic awareness, phonics, vocabulary, reading fluency, and reading comprehension (Good, Kame'enui, Simmons, & Chard, 2002). Indeed, both NCLB 2001 and IDEA 2004 actually define these essential components of reading instruction. For example, IDEA 2004 codified the following within special education law:

SEC 1208. (3) The term "essential components of reading instruction" means explicit and systematic instruction in—

(A) phonemic awareness;
(B) phonics;
(C) vocabulary development;
(D) reading fluency, including oral reading skills; and
(E) reading comprehension strategies.

It is noteworthy that federal law does not define essential components of instruction in any other area (e.g., math), only in reading. We believe this to be true because of the plethora of research available to support evidence-based approaches to reading instruction. Quite simply, we are confident that we know what works in reading, and researchers are working as quickly as possible in other academic areas, especially in mathematics (e.g., Clarke, Doabler, & Nelson, 2014; Siegler et al., 2010; Woodward et al., 2012; Zannou, Ketterlin-Geller, & Shivraj, 2014) and writing (Gravois & Nelson, 2014; Malecki, 2014) to reach the level of understanding that we have in reading.

A Consumer's Guide to Selecting a Core Program:
A Critical Elements Analysis

A key assumption of a core program is that it will (a) address all grade-level content standards and (b) ensure that high priority standards are taught in sufficient depth, breadth, and quality that all learners will achieve or exceed expected levels of proficiency. All standards are not equally important. Our critical elements analysis focuses on those skills and strategies essential for early reading.

General Review Process

1. Scope of Review
   Review each critical element for each grade.

2. Type of Review and Sampling Procedure
   To gain a representative sample of the program, we recommend the following strategies:
   (a) Within lesson procedure (w) involves identifying the first day (lesson) in which a critical skill or strategy (e.g., letter–sound correspondence, word reading, identifying main idea) is introduced and following that skill over a sequence of 2–3 days. Then, repeating the process to document evidence at two other points in time (e.g., middle/end of program) where new skills or strategies are introduced. In the evidence columns, document the lesson/unit number to reference the specific information you reviewed.
   (b) Scope and sequence procedure (ss) involves using the scope and sequence to identify the initial instruction in a skill or strategy area (e.g., phonemic awareness, fluency) and analyze how instruction progresses over time. Document progression in the evidence columns by indicating unit, lesson, section numbers you reviewed.
   (c) Skills trace procedure (st) will be used for selected skills and is designed to provide in-depth analysis of the sequence and review schedule of instruction.

3. Documenting Evidence
   On the review forms there is space to document specific information. Example information may include lesson number, particular skill/strategy introduced, etc.

4. Calculating Scores and Summarizing Findings
   Criteria are calculated at the Critical Element level by grade and across Critical Elements by grade level. At the end of each critical element, tally the number of consistently, partially, and does not satisfy criterion scores.

5. Grade Level Design Features Analysis
   At the end of each grade, there are 4–6 overarching items to assess the design, coherence, and systematic nature of instruction across lessons in the program. These items are intended to provide a big picture analysis.

Use the following criteria for each critical element:

● = Element consistently meets/exceeds criterion. Use this rating when the majority of lessons you review meet or exceed the criterion.

◐ = Element partially meets/exceeds criterion. Use this item when instruction meets the criterion in one instance but not in the other or when the instruction only partially satisfied the criterion.

○ = Element does not satisfy criterion.

When evaluating individual elements, slash (/) the respective circle that represents your rating (e.g., ◐) or put an X in the box below the appropriate circle.

Type of Review

1. *(w)* = Within a sequence of lessons. A specified element is best analyzed by reviewing a particular lesson or a series of 2–3 successive lessons.

2. *(ss)* = Scope and sequence. A specified element is best analyzed by reviewing the program's scope and sequence.

3. *(st)* = Skills trace. A specified element is best analyzed by completing a skills trace over a series of 10 consecutive lessons.

(continued)

FIGURE 5.8. Excerpts from *A Consumer's Guide to Selecting a Core Program.* Reprinted with permission from Simmons and Kame'enui (2003).

Program Name: _____   **Date of Publication:** _____

Publisher: _____   **Reviewer Code:** _____

1. _____ The program meets the following criteria for a comprehensive/core program and will be evaluated using the *Consumer's Guide.*

       _____ Includes comprehensive materials for grades K–3.

       _____ Provides instruction in each of the critical elements.

          _____ phonemic awareness

          _____ phonics and word analysis

          _____ fluency

          _____ vocabulary

          _____ comprehension

2. _____ The program does not meet the following criteria for a comprehensive/core program and will be evaluated using the *Consumer's Guide* (select all that apply).

       _____ Includes comprehensive materials for grades K–3.

       _____ Provides instruction in each of the critical elements.

          _____ phonemic awareness

          _____ phonics and word analysis

          _____ fluency

          _____ vocabulary

          _____ comprehension

3. _____ The program meets criteria for a supplemental or intervention program and will be reviewed for that purpose.

       _____ Provides targeted instruction on specific skill (select all that apply).

          _____ phonemic awareness

          _____ phonics

          _____ fluency

          _____ vocabulary

          _____ comprehension

       _____ Specify for which Grade/Age the program is appropriate.

FIGURE 5.8. *(continued)*

The five identified areas—phonemic awareness, phonics, fluency, vocabulary, and reading comprehension—are collectively referred to as the *five pillars of reading instruction* (Good et al., 2002). The origin of the five pillars of reading instruction stems from a specific and important history relevant to our current instruction, in which Congress convened a panel of 14 experts in 1997 and charged them with the onerous task of evaluating the existing reading research in an effort to identify the salient instructional elements that are indispensable for teaching young children to read. The panel produced a report of their findings, *Teaching Children to Read: An Evidence-Based Assessment of the Scientific Research Literature on Reading and Its Implications for Reading Instruction* (National Institute of Child Health and Human Development [NICHD], 2000), which described the features of effective, scientifically based reading instruction. We discuss each of the pillars next.

Phonemic Awareness

One of they key tasks of learning to read is the ability to hear and manipulate the sounds in language, otherwise known as *phonological awareness.* One aspect of phonological awareness, *phonemic awareness,* is the ability to detect and manipulate the *smallest* unit of sound in speech, or the distinct sounds (i.e., phonemes) attributed to individual letters (i.e., graphemes). Phonemic awareness is demonstrated when children can (1) *segment* words into phonemes and (2) *blend* phonemes to make words (Adams, 1990). According to the National Reading Panel report, *Teaching Children to Read* (2000), phonemic awareness is a skill that *can* be taught, and it assists children in learning both to read and to spell. Also, according to the panel, phonemic awareness instruction is most effective when it is explicitly taught and relatively brief (e.g., 25-minute sessions). Phonemic awareness and phonics, which we describe next, are often used interchangeably, although they are different concepts. Phonemic awareness requires only the ability to *hear* the sounds (i.e., phonemes), whereas phonics calls into play *both hearing* the sounds and *seeing*—or mapping—those sounds to letters (i.e., graphemes).

Phonics

Phonics is knowledge of the relationship between letters and their sounds, and this relationship is called the *alphabetic principle.* Knowledge of the alphabetic principle is considered the "linchpin of real reading" (Roberts, 1998, p. 44). According to the National Reading Panel report (NICHD, 2000), teaching phonics is a means to an end—the end being children's ability to apply what they know about phonics to their ability to read and write.

Fluency

Reading *fluency* refers to the speed and accuracy with which a person can read connected text. Fluent readers not only read quickly and accurately, but they also read with good prosody, or expression. Although the best way to foster reading fluency is to practice reading (Snow, Burns, & Griffin, 1998), classroom teachers do not give students enough instructional time to practice and learn how to be good, fluent readers (NICHD, 2000). Nevertheless, reading fluency is critical to students' ability to understand what they read. According to the National Reading Panel report (p. 3-3):

> Teachers need to know that word recognition accuracy is not the end point of reading instruction. Fluency represents a level of expertise beyond word recognition accuracy, and reading comprehension may be aided by fluency. Skilled readers read words accurately, rapidly and efficiently. Children who do not develop reading fluency, no matter how bright they are, will continue to read slowly and with great effort.

Many teachers, especially teachers of students from the middle elementary years through the secondary grades, believe that students who struggle with reading do so because they do not understand what they read (i.e., they have a reading comprehension problem).

These students frequently are referred to as "word callers" in the literature, or students who can decode/read words accurately but fail to understand what they are reading (Stanovich, 1986). Word callers "sound good" when they read, that is, they have good fluency, but they have poor understanding of what they read. The problem with this concept, however, is that word readers actually rarely exist, at least in native English speakers; the extent to which word readers exist in the ELL population is a little less understood at this time. When assessed, teacher-identified word callers are indeed students with poor reading comprehension, but they *also* have poor reading fluency (Hamilton & Shinn, 2003). In general, teachers both overestimate the number of word callers they have in their classrooms (Hamilton & Shinn; Meisinger, Bradley, Schwanenflugel, Kuhn, & Morris, 2009) and do not have a high degree of accuracy in identifying students who actually are work callers (Knight-Teague, Vanderwood, & Knight, 2014). The problem is that good teachers modify their instructional strategies based on the reasons they believe (or, better yet, that the data tell them) a student is struggling. Herein lies the problematic issue concerning word callers; teachers who believe that struggling readers struggle because they do not understand what they read will likely focus on reading comprehension instruction and intervention, when in fact, bolstering reading fluency is the actual area to target, because it will both improve reading fluency *and* reading comprehension. Furthermore, we have many more effective strategies for boosting reading fluency—and it is a skill that is very sensitive to good intervention—than strategies for improving poor reading comprehension. Teachers must be very careful because ELLs may struggle to understand what they read even after being able to decode connected text accurately (Nakamoto, Lindsey, & Manis, 2007; Proctor, Carlo, August, & Snow, 2005). Indeed, recent research suggests that reading fluency and reading comprehension scores relate more strongly for native English speakers than for Spanish-speaking ELLs (Crosson & Lesaux, 2010). In other words, good reading fluency in native English speakers is predictive of good reading comprehension, whereas good reading fluency in ELLs may not be as predictive of their understanding of text.

Vocabulary

Vocabulary, or knowledge of words, significantly contributes to readers' ability to read and understand text. The importance of building ELLs' English vocabulary reservoir cannot be underestimated. A child's oral vocabulary is a critical component in successfully learning to read, and a child's ability to understand the words that he or she encounters in text is essential in comprehending that text (NICHD, 2000). Typically, readers don't need to understand all of the words in the text they read; however, if the ratio of unknown words to known words is too high, comprehension is thwarted (Carver, 1994). In general, ELLs are at a greater disadvantage in their vocabulary knowledge than are native English speakers; this disadvantage is in terms of both breadth (i.e., number of known English vocabulary) and depth (i.e., knowledge of the multiple meanings of terms; August, Carlo, Dressler, & Snow, 2005). All educators who work with ELLs should be familiar with the concept of *cognates,* or words in English and the target language that are orthographically, phonologically, and semantically similar. Interestingly, the Spanish and English languages share approximately

20,000 cognates! For example, note the similarities in the following pairs of English–*Spanish* cognates: president/*presidente*, television/*televisión*, and frequently/*frecuentemente*. One of the most beneficial instructional strategies to bolster English reading comprehension, especially in Spanish–English ELLs, is cognate recognition. Spanish-speaking ELLs who are able to identify cognates when reading text in English gain more meaning from what they read than students who cannot identify cognates (Jiménez, García, & Pearson, 1996). There are many ways to increase ELLs' vocabulary skills, including the use of flashcards and self-graphing procedures (Albers & Hoffman, 2012).

Reading Comprehension

The reason we read is to gain meaning from text. The five pillars of reading presented earlier (i.e., phonemic awareness, phonics, fluency, vocabulary, and reading comprehension) influence the degree to which students are able to gain meaning from the text they read. Klingner and Geisler (2008) suggest that many ELLs actually may understand more than they are able to demonstrate in English and should be allowed to use alternate ways to demonstrate their understanding, including the use of diagrams and drawings. Klingner and Geisler also urge teachers not to focus so much on their students' heavy accents or grammatical errors that might be characteristic of ELLs, and instead to focus on the *content* of their responses in demonstrating what they indeed do understand.

Whole-Language versus Phonics Approaches to Teaching Reading

For what seems like a long time, there have been two core philosophies, at opposite ends of the spectrum, about the most effective way to teach children in school to read. The first is a whole-language approach, which also is known as a *literature-based approach*. Teachers who teach reading using a whole-language approach do so by encouraging young children's interaction with authentic literature, especially children's books. There is an obvious natural appeal to whole-language pedagogy, and more than half of all students learn to read without incident when taught using the whole-language instructional approach (Olson, 2004). These children inadvertently learn to break the code (Adams, 1990) and naturally become successful, independent readers. The remaining students, however, in many of these classrooms simply do not learn to read well or to read at all. Can more intense whole-language instruction help these struggling readers break the code? If we read to them for twice as long, can they learn to read eventually? The answer to the last two questions is a categorical "no." Let us be clear: Students for whom English reading does not come easily (i.e., ELLs and students who do not learn to read in the whole-language tradition) *cannot* and *will not* break the code and become independent readers *unless* they are taught to attend to the relationship between letters and their sounds through *explicit* and *systematic* instruction that focuses on the five pillars of reading instruction. According to Moats (n.d., p. 6):

> For more than three decades, advocates of "whole language" instruction have argued—to the delight of many teachers and public school administrators—that learning to read is a

"natural" process for children. Create reading centers in classrooms; put good, fun books in children's hands and allow them to explore; then encourage them to "read," even if they can't make heads or tails of the words on the page. Eventually, they'll get it. So say the believers.

Struggling readers—including ELLs—*must* be taught explicitly and systematically how to read in English. Yes, we agree that it is magnificent when we expose ELLs (and all students) to authentic literature (e.g., children's books that feature diverse characters from diverse settings to whom they can relate), and we *should* expose them to this beautiful literature; however, explicit instruction in phonemic awareness, phonics, fluency, vocabulary, and comprehension also *must* be a *major* focus of ELLs' and struggling readers' daily reading instruction. If your goal is truly to empower your students so that they can read the authentic literature themselves, you must teach them to break the code. We refer to instruction that focuses on the five pillars of reading instruction as the *scientific way* to teach struggling readers—including ELLs—to read. Critiques of the scientific method for teaching children to read include allegations that it is inauthentic and that it promotes "kill and drill" exercises and stifles teachers' creativity in the classroom. Both of us disagree and have seen excellent, balanced teaching of reading that combines authentic literature and an emphasis on explicit and systematic instruction in the five pillars of reading instruction in classrooms across the country! Excellent teaching, based both on the science of what works and the art of being an exemplary, resourceful, creative, fun, and engaging teacher, is possible and goes on in classrooms where there are ELLs and struggling readers across the country every day!

Considerations for Reading at the Secondary Level

We know that in the elementary years, teaching reading to struggling readers requires a focus on the five pillars of reading instruction. However, at the secondary level, teaching struggling readers and nonreaders is a much more complex issue. Slavin, Chamberlain, and Daniels (2007) noted that at the secondary level,

> it matters a great deal how reading is taught. Secondary reading is different from elementary reading. The students are far more sophisticated in their interest and social skills, and those who are struggling in reading have little patience for methods or materials designed for younger children. Students are likely to have uneven reading skills and gaps, so teaching everyone the same content is both inefficient and demotivating. (p. 1)

Teaching English reading to ELLs in the secondary grades requires special considerations given the increased academic rigor and variations in instructional methods used to teach content at the middle and high school levels. It is critical also to remember that ELLs enter U.S. schools at different grade levels, with varying levels of ELP and native language proficiency, and academic background. The gaps in English proficiency among ELLs at the secondary level are often much larger than the gaps among ELLs at the elementary level, which greatly increases the need for differentiated instruction and frequent formative assessment at the secondary level. In addition, students beginning to learn English for the first time as adolescents may need not only intensive language, content, and literacy instruction but also an introduction to the basics of the U.S. school and classroom culture; this instruction is not always a common practice at the secondary level (Spaulding, Carolino, & Amen, 2004) or even the elementary level.

Perhaps the most imperative idea we wish to convey in this section on effective instruction in teaching ELL students to read in English at the secondary level is that "every secondary teacher is a teacher of reading" (Betts, 1939). This may be a hard sell for many secondary teachers, however, because, professionally, most secondary classroom teachers see themselves as teachers within their disciplines (e.g., biology, literature, world history), and not as reading teachers per se (Shanahan & Shanahan, 2008). Similar to the approaches for effectively instructing elementary-level ELLs, there are various effective approaches to content-area English instruction for secondary-level ELLs. Three of the most common approaches are (1) instruction delivered by teachers trained in L2 instruction only, (2) instruction delivered by a team of L2 and content-area teachers, and (3) modified instruction using sheltered immersion by content-area teachers. Recently, a fourth approach— referred to as *newcomer schools or programs*—has become more popular. Most important, all four approaches show promise as being useful with ELLs, if implemented well (Meltzer & Hamann, 2005).

Currently, research on effective practices with secondary ELLs is relatively limited. For example, out of 309 studies on increasing literacy in ELLs reviewed by the National Literacy Panel on Language-Minority Children and Youth (August & Shanahan, 2006), fewer than 30 studies focused on students at the secondary level. The limited evidence that is available suggests that similar to their native English-speaking peers, adolescent ELLs benefit from instructional strategies such as (1) teacher modeling of explicit learning strategies in context; (2) the use of multiple methods of formative assessment and progress monitoring; (3) an emphasis on not only reading and writing but also speaking, listening, and viewing; (4) an emphasis on critical thinking and metacognitive skills; (5) the use of flexible grouping and learner-centered classrooms; (6) recognizing and analyzing content-area discourse features; (7) understanding text structures within the content areas; and (8) focusing on vocabulary development (Francis et al., 2006a; Meltzer & Hamann, 2005). More specifically, to improve reading in secondary content-area subjects (e.g., history and biology), Torgesen and colleagues (2007) suggested five areas of emphasis for teachers: (1) provide explicit instruction and supportive practice in the use of effective comprehension strategies throughout the school day; (2) increase the amount and quality of open, sustained discussion of reading content; (3) set and maintain high standards for text, conversation, questions, and vocabulary; (4) increase students' motivation and engagement with reading; and (5) teach essential content knowledge, so that all students master critical concepts.

In addition, it is important for ELLs to have access to the same content material as their English-only peers, despite their language barriers (Fu, 2004; National High School Center, 2009). All too often, the language development needs of a student may seem to outweigh the need to gain an understanding of academic content. While emphasizing language to the exclusion of content may seem like a more focused approach toward increasing language and academic success, it actually keeps ELLs perpetually behind their English-only peers. Consequently, differentiated instruction is beneficial for meeting ELLs' needs, in that teachers can assign similar content topics for ELLs, but with materials at the appropriate reading level (Fu, 2004). For example, everyone in a class can learn about the horrors of the Holocaust, but demonstrate this learning through different (but equally meaningful and engaging) classroom activities, tasks, and assessments. One of the main barriers to appropriate differentiation for ELLs at the secondary level is that it can often be difficult to find "high–low" materials (reading material with high interest for a secondary student, but with lower readability), or phonics instructional materials that are appropriate or engaging for use with older ELLs (Alliance for Excellent Education, 2007).

All teachers need to use data to make decisions about instruction and intervention, including teachers at the secondary level (National High School Center, 2009). Tracking academic growth for ELLs at the secondary level is crucial to helping them acquire academic language in English. It also allows educators to understand each student's strengths and assess their progress, understand what teaching strategies are working, and recognize whether instruction needs to be altered (Francis et al., 2006; Fu, 2004).

Finally, encouraging collaboration between content-area teachers and English language development (ELD) teachers is another specific consideration for secondary schools (Fu, 2004). All content areas should address English language and literacy skills needed for academic success in the content area, as well as expose children to the specific academic language (vocabulary, grammar, comprehension) of that particular content area (Francis et al., 2006). As we have mentioned previously, content-area teachers at the secondary level may have limited knowledge and access to strategies that help ELLs acquire content material effectively. Working in collaboration with ESL and ELD teachers allows both groups of educators to provide targeted academic support to ELL students (Fu, 2004). Collaborative professional relationships between and among content area and ESL–ELD teachers can be especially instrumental in ensuring that ELL students continue to improve their Academic English. Martinez, Harris, and McClain (2014) call for educators across the broad spectrum of disciplines (i.e., general education teachers, special education teachers, administrators, counselors, and all related services personnel) to get out of their "silos" and begin working collaboratively in order to be more effective at improving English reading success for ELLs.

WHAT'S NEXT: MOVING ON TO TIER 2 AND TIER 3

Tier 1 instruction clearly needs to be the foundation within any educational setting, and particularly within any RTI model. Not having this strong core foundation will result in a situation in which a school will be have to intervene itself out of poor Tier 1 instruction. Doing so is essentially impossible, as the number of students in need of supplemental services will far outnumber the availability of such services. But for those students who have received strong core instruction yet continue to have a need for supplemental academic services, Tier 2 and Tier 3 services likely are appropriate; we now turn to such services in Chapter 6.

Monitoring Progress, Determining Growth Rates, and Intensifying Instruction for ELLs at Tiers 2 and 3

We believe that most ELLs—*because* they are learning English as a second language—require both frequent progress monitoring and intensified instruction from the get-go (*in addition to* triennial universal screening and exposure to sound core instruction). In other words, you should expect to provide many of your ELLs with Tier 2 (and possibly Tier 3) supports in assessment and intervention immediately. There is no need to wait and see whether they need extra support: *They need extra support.* Thus, our goal in this chapter is to address both general and specific assessment and instruction/intervention principles for student success at Tiers 2 and 3. Regarding assessment at Tiers 2 and 3, we describe in detail how to use your CBM assessments to monitor progress—from documenting the progress being made when interventions are implemented to graphing data and actively using the data to make instructional decisions to modify or intensify the instruction and/or intervention. In this chapter, we also demonstrate how to determine growth rates, set short- and long-term instructional goals, and establish local norms for your school or district. Specific to instruction and intervention at Tiers 2 and 3, we describe broad principles for intensifying core instruction (i.e., rate, dosage, frequency, duration) and illustrate a variety of evidence-based interventions that are appropriate for use at Tiers 2 and 3. Finally, we introduce a series of *RTI program participation worksheets* to help you in your RTI documentation efforts.

ASSESSMENT AT TIERS 2 AND 3

Why and How to Monitor Progress Frequently

As we saw in Chapter 5, the collection of data (through universal screening and progress monitoring procedures) to make decisions is indispensable in an RTI model; in fact, we would describe the collection of data as a "non-negotiable" activity that *must* occur at multiple levels (e.g., district, school, grade, individual) *and* at varying levels of frequency. Given the variability in teacher training for working with ELLs, the wide range of skills displayed by ELLs, and the relative lack of validated, evidence-based interventions for use with ELLs, this data-based approach is even more critical to ensuring that what we do is having a positive impact on students. Nevertheless, there is flexibility in determining what procedures to use in monitoring intervention effectiveness. For example, Albers, Elliott, Kettler, and Roach (2013) identified a number of progress monitoring approaches, including (1) observations, (2) permanent products, (3) rating scales, (4) goal attainment scaling, and (5) curriculum-based measurement (CBM). For reasons described in Chapter 5 (e.g., wide evidence base, strong technical characteristics, ease of administration and use, appropriateness), we specifically recommend CBM procedures for monitoring the effectiveness of academic interventions for ELLs in grades K–8, particularly in the areas of reading, writing, and mathematics. We are hesitant to recommend the use of CBM procedures in high school settings, however, simply because the applicability and utility of using these procedures with high school ELLs have yet to be determined. Additionally, although the use of CBM progress monitoring approaches for non-ELLs has received at least some attention in other content areas such as science (e.g., Johnson, Semmelroth, Allison, & Fritsch, 2013) and social studies (e.g., Beyers, Lembke, & Curs, 2013), similar investigations have not addressed how to conduct progress monitoring with ELLs in these other content areas. Until this validation work occurs, the practitioner should consider incorporating some or all of the other progress monitoring approaches with ELLs as identified earlier by Albers, Elliott, et al. (2013) with the caveat that resulting data should be interpreted with significant caution.

We discussed in Chapter 3 that at Tiers 2 and 3, the frequency of progress monitoring should increase (compared to the frequency of benchmarking at Tier 1, which is two or three times a year). Intensifying instruction and intervention and increasing progress monitoring frequency go hand in hand. Thus, at Tiers 2 and 3, progress monitoring may occur as frequently as several times a week or as infrequently as every other week. We believe the frequency requirement of progress monitoring at Tiers 2 and 3 eliminates lengthier and more in-depth assessments that often are used in schools as progress monitoring tools. Because a student is receiving supplemental interventions at Tier 2 and Tier 3, frequent progress monitoring is essential to determine whether the intervention is improving performance; if progress monitoring is not being conducted frequently, the student may be participating in an intervention that is not resulting in progress (i.e., student success). Clearly, it is preferable to know as soon as possible whether an intervention is working, so that the intervention can be changed, revised, or intensified in an effort to make sure that every student is improving.

Determining what progress monitoring approach or approaches to use is only one of several issues that education professionals need to resolve in the early stages of RTI model implementation and when fine-tuning the model to effectively address the specific needs of ELL students. Additional issues to resolve include determining (1) how often the data will be collected, (2) how long the data will be collected, (3) how the data will be collected, (4) how the data will be analyzed, (5) who will collect the data, and (6) how data will be used to guide the classroom teacher and other educators in making decisions regarding intervention provision. We turn to a description of these issues next. Albers, Elliott, et al. (2013)

identified four time periods within the scope of intervention implementation during which data ought to be collected. Collecting data at these critical junctures is important when working with all students in an RTI model, but it may be especially critical when considering ELLs. These time periods are as follows:

1. At the beginning of an intervention to serve as baseline data and to aid in problem identification and analysis.
2. During the intervention, to determine whether there is progress.
3. At the end of the intervention.
4. During a time period following the end of the intervention (e.g., 1 month later), to determine whether the improvement in performance was maintained (p. 346).

Riley-Tillman and Burns (2009) identified single-case design (SCD) as an ideal methodology to evaluate intervention effectiveness within RTI models. Given the high-quality nature of multiple books examining SCD (e.g., Brown-Chidsey & Steege, 2010; Kazdin, 2010; Riley-Tillman & Burns, 2009), we avoid the more technical details and instead focus on "nonexperimental" A-B designs ("A" phase with no intervention, "B" phase with intervention) that are the most user friendly and frequently used within school settings to evaluate intervention effectiveness. We encourage readers to become familiar with the multiple computer programs (e.g., Microsoft Excel) that are readily available (see Riley-Tillman & Burns, 2009) and the various Internet websites (for multiple examples, see *www.interventioncentral.org*) that can facilitate data collection and evaluation process in SCDs.

To assist the educator who may not be familiar with what progress monitoring looks like at Tiers 2 and 3, we present two examples that demonstrate the utility of using CBM procedures for progress monitoring, the benefit of graphing data in an SCD approach, and how specific ELP levels (recall our examples in Chapter 5) impact the interpretation of data collected during an intervention.

Tier 2 and Tier 3 Progress Monitoring with ELLs

In Chapter 5 we presented several examples demonstrating how appropriate progress monitoring of ELLs requires explicit consideration of their individual ELP levels. As we saw in Figure 5.5 (and again here in Figure 6.1) consideration of these ELP levels allowed the RTI team to speculate that Martín (ELP level 2.0) actually was making progress that exceeded the typical progress displayed by ELLs at a similar level of ELP proficiency. Thus, the RTI team was able to conclude that a *supplemental* English reading intervention (i.e., a more intense intervention) did not appear necessary at that time and that the current progress monitoring frequency of once a month also was adequate.

Now let's consider the case of Ana, a second-grade ELL enrolled at the same school as Martín, and one who also had a composite ELP level of 2.0. However, Ana's ORF performance at the fall universal screening was significantly below the average performance of other ELLs in the district. As indicated in Figure 6.2, Ana's ORF during the fall benchmark was seven words read correctly per minute (WRCM), whereas the 50th percentile rank

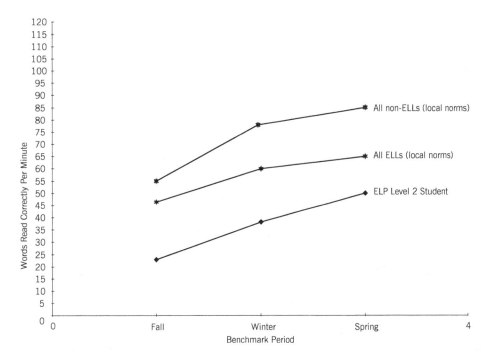

FIGURE 6.1. ORF scores for an ELL during the fall, winter, and spring benchmark periods as compared to the 50th percentile rank (local norms) by specific ELP levels.

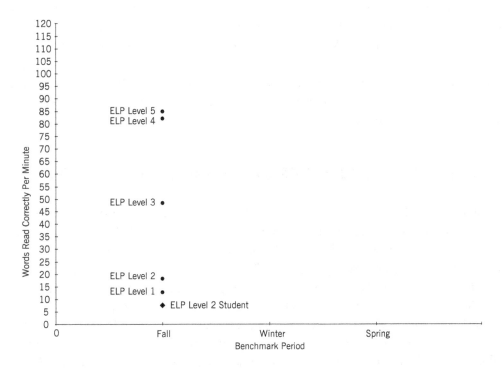

FIGURE 6.2. ORF score for an ELL during the fall benchmark period as compared to the 50th percentile rank (local norms) by specific ELP levels.

for other ELP level 2.0 second-grade ELLs in the local norm group was approximately 19 WRCM.

Owing to Ana's much lower than expected performance relative to other ELLs in the local norm group at the same ELP level, the school RTI team determined that it would be appropriate to implement a more intense English reading intervention (Tier 2) with Ana, in addition to the core instruction already taking place. To monitor progress, the school personnel planned also to increase the frequency of data collected for Ana to every other week. The expected goal was to get her performance up to the average (i.e., at least the 50th percentile) ORF rates for other ELP level 2.0 second-grade ELLs, which means that the end-of-year goal for Ana (as well as the other ELP level 2.0 second-grade ELLs) was 42 WRCM. Because Ana was currently reading 7 WRCM, she needed to improve her WRCM by 35 WRCM (42 WRCM – 7 WRCM = 35 WRCM) by the end of the year; with 28 weeks left in the school year, the rate of improvement needed to reach this goal was an average increase of 1.25 WRCM per week. This was calculated by the following formula: 35 ÷ 28 = 1.25 WRCM per week. Shown in Figure 6.3 are Ana's end-of-year goal and the rate of improvement (ROI) needed to reach that goal. Note that in different circumstances, it might be appropriate to establish a more ambitious goal (i.e., a higher ROI in less time). These decisions should be made by a team familiar with the student and ELL instruction.

Additionally, Figure 6.3 indicates that after collecting four baseline data points,[1] a Tier 2 intervention was implemented. Further evaluation of the data indicated that Ana's ORF performance changed little during this 6-week intervention phase; consequently, a different intervention was implemented to encourage faster gains. The results during this second intervention phase indicated that Ana's performance increased to such a degree that even prior to the spring benchmark, her performance increased to the anticipated goal level, which was the number represented by the average performance of other second-grade ELP level 2.0 ELLs. In this example, we have demonstrated how carefully considering an ELL's ELP levels against a set of local norms, and using current data to modify or intensify intervention, resulted in a very successful outcome for Ana (and her teachers).

DETERMINING PROGRAMMING FOR TIERS 2 AND 3

If a student struggles in Tier 1, despite a sound core curriculum and instructional best practices, it is necessary to increase the intensity of the services provided to that student. In the case of ELLs, we believe that they must be provided with intense academic intervention at Tier 2 and possibly Tier 3 from the get-go. The academic and cognitive demands placed on ELLs to learn English (L2) and academic content simultaneously warrant additional and immediate intense instruction. The RTI model is ideally suited to providing this intense instruction to ELLs. Please understand that provision of services beyond Tier 1 for any student *does not* mean that the student necessarily will be referred for special education evaluation, let alone qualify for special education as a student with a disability. *Participa-*

---

[1] We recommend at least three baseline points, although the number of necessary baseline data points sometimes is determined by the stability of the data; see Kazdin (2010) and Riley-Tillman and Burns (2009) for a more in-depth discussion of this issue.

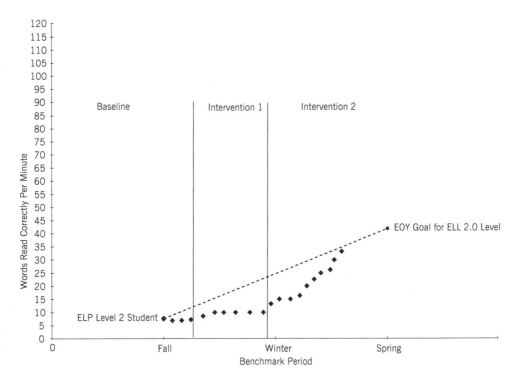

FIGURE 6.3. ORF scores for an ELL (ELP level 2.0) beginning with the fall universal screening benchmark and ongoing progress monitoring during interventions 1 and 2.

tion in Tiers 2 and 3 does not serve as a placeholder for special education for any student. Nevertheless, when services at the intensity of Tiers 2 and 3 do not result in "getting the job done" (i.e., eliciting gain, growth, or achievement), the RTI team may decide whether a special education evaluation might get to the bottom of what may be contributing to the student's difficulties and inform the team of adaptations and accommodations, if appropriate. Because *some* students (i.e., those who persistently do not make progress) who participate in Tiers 2 and 3 *may* be eligible for a special education evaluation, it becomes imperative for the classroom teacher to document very carefully the programming given to and the progress made by all individual students at Tiers 2 and 3. For the few students who *do* go on to special education evaluation, the careful documentation and paper trail collected by their teachers during their participation in Tiers 2 and 3 are necessary—in addition to the full evaluation—to inform the case conference committee whether the student is eligible for special education services as a student with a disability.

INSTRUCTION AT TIERS 2 AND 3

Intensifying Instruction at Tiers 2 and 3

Ideally, at least 80–90% of students in a given population (e.g., a school, a grade level, a classroom) experience academic success in Tier 1. The percentage of students experiencing success at this level indicates that the Tier 1 curriculum is meeting the needs of the majority of students. With such levels of success, then, 10–20% of the population would theoretically require Tier 2 instruction (in addition to Tier 1 instruction) and only the smallest percentage of students—approximately 1–5%—would require the most intense Tier 3 services (in addition to Tier 1 and 2 instruction and intervention; Walker & Shinn, 2002). As we discussed in Chapter 2, because ELLs have the challenging task of learning both English and academic content in English, they need extra academic supports, instruction, and intervention. In addition to participating in excellent core instruction (Tier 1) with their native English-speaking peers for the majority of the day, planning for the appropriate instruction of ELLs using an RTI model *will* include participation in Tier 2 or Tier 2 *and* Tier 3 supplemental instruction and intervention.

One of the more relevant concepts we want to share with you on how to intensify instruction at Tiers 2 and 3 is Faggella-Luby and Deshler's (2008) concept of *instructional dosage*. What we are most fond of regarding this concept is that if you are using an excellent core curriculum and following the instructional strategies outlined in Chapter 5, the likelihood of having to purchase a new or different curriculum to implement Tier 2 and 3 intensive services effectively is significantly reduced. In our work in schools across the country, we have found a great deal of misunderstanding regarding what to do in Tiers 2 and 3. More often than not, that misunderstanding has led to costly and often unnecessary decisions to purchase *stuff* (e.g., extravagant or flashy new curriculum packages). On a good day, these materials get into the hands of the classroom teachers, and perhaps they get used; however, these materials tend not to be used in a systematic, comprehensive, or consistent manner. Furthermore, many of these packages are not even used in the context of the larger RTI efforts that include frequent formative assessment, fluid movement across instructional groups, and explicit use of data to modify and intensify instruction. Thus, money and time are wasted when these packages are purchased and implemented. You may be surprised at the simplicity of what we are going to say, but excellent Tier 2 and Tier 3 supplemented instruction/intervention does not need to cost a penny! What it does require is an astute teacher, who is excellently trained to deliver core instructional principles (from a high-quality core curriculum) at various *instructional dosages* based on student needs.

Instructional Dosage

Faggella-Luby and Deshler's (2008) concept of *instructional dosage* refers to features or dimensions with which a teacher can easily, and without needing to purchase any additional materials, intensify his or her core instruction to meet the needs of all students, including those students who struggle and those in need of enrichment. Thus, the process of intensifying Tier 1 instruction *is*, in effect, Tier 2 and possibly Tier 3 intensive support. Faggella-Luby and Deshler's framework is based on four instructional dimensions: (1) group size, (2) instructional period (session length), (3) frequency (number of sessions per week), (4) and duration (total number of sessions). By manipulating these instructional dimensions, teachers can intensify the degree to which core instruction is delivered to certain groups of students, or individual students, thereby providing Tier 2 or Tier 3 services within the RTI model.

One example of increasing the frequency and intensity of instruction at Tier 2 is that the instruction might be provided to a student (in addition to Tier 1) for 30 minutes a day, 3 to 4 days a week (McCook, 2006). To illustrate, a student would participate in not only the regularly scheduled language arts block but *also* an enrichment language arts block that would be considered Tier 2. In another example of what Tier 2 time might look like, Fuchs's and Fuchs's (2005) delivery of Tier 2 instruction was provided to small groups of no more than three students, three times a week for 30 minutes and delivered by *certified* school personnel (i.e., the licensed classroom teacher, not a paraprofessional). Again, the Tier 2 instruction was provided in addition to the core instructional block in which all students participated.

Another way to differentiate instruction delivery, thus taking advantage of this relatively straightforward instructional dimension, is by reteaching core content to small groups of struggling students. Reducing the teacher–student ratio alone increases the intensity of the instruction by increasing individual students' opportunity to respond (OTR) and teachers' occasion to reteach and provide corrective feedback. When incorporating this instructional dimension in Tier 2 and/or Tier 3, we recommend teaching small groups of no more than three students. Vaughn, Linan-Thompson, and Hickman (2003) demonstrated in their research that it is as effective to teach students in small groups of three as it is to teach students individually; thus, it can be more efficient for teachers to work with small groups of three students experiencing similar difficulties than working with each of those students individually.

According to Faggella-Luby and Deshler (2008), another way to increase the instructional dosage of the core curriculum to achieve desired intensity levels at Tiers 2 and 3 is to provide struggling students, including ELLs, longer instructional periods, delivered with greater frequency and over extended periods of time. So, whereas the majority of students in a class might participate in 35 minutes of math instruction 4 days a week, students struggling with double-digit division would participate in an *additional* 20 minutes of double-digit division instruction, perhaps up to twice a day. In another example, perhaps a main grammar lesson on contractions is scheduled to be delivered to the class over 5 weeks. However, for students who do not master contractions, instruction may need to be extended for an extra 2 weeks. Which dimensions to alter and to what degree are at the discretion of the classroom teacher, informed by student formative assessment data and perhaps in consultation with colleagues, an administrator, or other school professional such as a school psychologist.

SUPPLEMENTING WITH EVIDENCE-BASED STRATEGIES AND INTERVENTIONS TO SUPPORT CORE CURRICULUM AT TIER 2 AND TIER 3

We have found in our collective experience working with teachers across the country that many want creative and fresh new ways to deliver their instruction, especially at Tiers 2 and 3. In this section we discuss the how (i.e., instruction) of intensifying a good core curriculum. Although we already described specific ways to tweak the instructional dosage (Faggella-Luby & Deshler, 2008), in this section we discuss specific instructional strategies and interventions that can be incorporated into your instructional repertoire. We urge you, however, to go back to the section "Effective Instructional Principles and Sound Pedagogy," in Chapter 5, because these concepts (e.g., Opportunity to Learn, Differentiation, Direct Instruction, Practice and Corrective Feedback) are as relevant for Tier 1 as they are for Tiers 2 and 3.

According to Martinez (2014), if teachers are going to use new instructional strategies and activities, these (1) should be easy to set up and implement, (2) should not involve any special training, and (3) should not require costly materials. There are a number of evidence-based strategies meeting these three criteria that classroom teachers can implement in their instructional repertoires. We are excited to introduce you to the Evidence-Based Intervention (EBI) Network (*http://ebi.missouri.edu*) if you are not already familiar with it. The EBI Network, a website that began in 2007 with the East Carolina University Evidence-Based Intervention Project, is now based at the University of Missouri–Columbia. The EBI Network is free of charge, and its sole purpose is to serve the education community in an effort to improve student outcomes. The site is directed by T. Chris Riley-Tillman in collaboration with several colleagues, including Erica Lembke, Rebecca S. Martinez, Sarah Powell, Pamela Seethaler, and Melissa Stormont. The criterion for selecting the resources provided in the EBI Network is that the resources be scientifically based and adhere to a functional approach to understanding academic and social behavior problems. By *functional approaches to solving academic and social behavioral problems,* we mean getting to the bottom of the academic or behavior problem by examining carefully what is happening in the classroom. The functional approach to understanding academic and behavioral problems focuses on the instructional environment and the factors that contribute to maintaining or reducing academic and behavioral problems. This approach is especially appealing for work with ELL students because it allows the educator to identify content-specific functional interventions that have the greatest chance of promoting academic gain.

The good news about focusing on the instructional environment, as we discussed in Chapter 5 in the context of creating warm and welcoming instructional environments for ELLs, is that instructionally related factors are within the control of the classroom teacher (e.g., providing students more opportunities to respond, additional practice in an area of weakness), and can therefore be manipulated and controlled to yield positive outcomes. Based on the original work of Daly, Witt, Martens, and Dool (1997), the EBI Network's framework for understanding why children, including ELLs, struggle academically focuses on five main reasons:

1. The task is too hard for the student.
2. The student has not had adequate or sufficient help doing the task.
3. The student has not spent enough time doing the academic activity.
4. The student has not done the academic task that way before.
5. The student does not want to do the academic task.

For each of these reasons for academic failure (which are very intuitive and appealing in their simplicity), the EBI Network describes a number of evidence-based strategies and interventions that can be implemented to address the problem. Moreover, for each intervention, the EBI Network provides the following resources: (1) *Full Intervention Briefs* (documents that provide a description of the intervention, the common problem the intervention addresses, procedures and materials for implementing the intervention, and citations for the research backing the intervention); (2) *Evidence Briefs* (similar to the Full Intervention Briefs but more "scholarly" in that they provide an introduction to and summaries of the theoretical and empirical research for each intervention); and (c) *Modeling Videos* (various versions of videos demonstrating how to implement the intervention; the Modeling Videos were created primarily by graduate students but include several videos provided by actual teachers implementing the interventions in their classrooms).

Evidence-Based Interventions

In contrast to evidence-based strategies, such as many of the strategies featured in the EBI Network, which can be adopted and implemented very simply and with limited resources, evidence-based interventions are stand-alone packages or programs that can be used in the classroom to supplement the excellent core instruction and that teachers can incorporate into their everyday teaching. All educators, but especially classroom teachers, ought to have access to or knowledge of a host of evidence-based interventions. A necessary starting point in filling this "toolbox" of interventions is determining first whether a strategy or activity is evidence-based (as opposed to adopting interventions simply because they seem fun or appealing, or because other teachers are using them). Indeed, federal law requires that teachers use only scientifically validated practices and interventions. Perhaps the foremost authority and resource for identifying the research base behind a host of educational practices, programs, and interventions is the What Works Clearinghouse (WWC; *www.whatworks.ed.gov*). The WWC is a government agency that has developed a rigorous review protocol for determining the extent of scientific evidence to support educational practices, including specific intervention approaches. The WWC also has special review standards that consider effects on English language development, reading achievement, and mathematics achievement of ELLs in particular.

In the following sections we discuss several of the programs and curricula that have been evaluated and positively rated by the WWC, and with which you are very likely familiar (but perhaps not yet knowledgeable about their research base), including *Read Well*, *Instructional Conversations and Literature Logs*, *Peer-Assisted Learning Strategies* (PALS), *Bilingual Cooperative Integrated Reading and Composition*, *Arthur*, and the *Vocabulary Improvement Program for English Language Learners and Their Classmates*.

Read Well

Read Well is a reading curriculum that targets literacy skills development for kindergarten and first-grade students. This intervention offers opportunities to discuss vocabulary in the context of stories during daily whole-class activities and small-group lessons. It utilizes scaffolded instruction, in which teachers first present models and provide guided practice, then gradually decrease their support and ask students to practice the skill or strategy independently. Although the WWC reported that Read Well had no discernible effects on reading achievement, it was found to have potentially positive effects on English language development for elementary school ELLs, with one randomized controlled trial that met evidence standards (Frasco, 2008; U.S. Department of Education, 2010c).

Instructional Conversations and Literature Logs

Instructional Conversations and Literature Logs is a program that aims to help ELLs develop reading achievement and ELP through "Instructional Conversations," or small-group discussions. Teachers facilitate conversations about stories, key concepts, and related personal experiences that allow students to build on each other's knowledge. "Literature Logs" require ELLs to respond to writing prompts or answer questions related to stories. These responses are then shared in small groups or with a partner. The WWC found that this intervention has potentially positive effects in the areas of reading achievement and English language development. In two studies that met WWC evidence standards and included over 200 ELLs in grades 2 through 5, this intervention had statistically significant positive effects on reading achievement, measures of factual comprehension, and interpretive comprehension (Saunders, 1999; Saunders & Goldenberg, 1999; U.S. Department of Education, 2006b).

Peer-Assisted Learning Strategies

PALS is an intervention strategy for reading proficiency improvement in elementary students with diverse academic needs; it also has been used with ELLs. PALS aims to supplement an existing reading curriculum through peer-tutoring activities in three strategic reading areas: retelling (i.e., sequencing information), paragraph shrinking (i.e., generating main idea statements), and prediction relay (i.e., generating and evaluating predictions). The WWC found potentially positive effects in the area of reading achievement. The one study that met WWC evidence standards found that PALS students outgrew comparison group students on reading comprehension (Sáenz, Fuchs, & Fuchs, 2005; U.S. Department of Education, 2010b).

Bilingual Cooperative Integrated Reading and Composition

Bilingual Cooperative Integrated Reading and Composition (BCIRC) is an adaptation of the Cooperative Integrated Reading and Composition (CIRC) program, which was designed to help Spanish-speaking ELLs succeed in reading Spanish, then make a successful transition to reading English. In the adaptation, students complete tasks that focus on reading, writing, and language activities in Spanish *and* English, while working in small cooperative learning groups. BCIRC was found to have potentially positive effects on reading achievement and English language development. A single quasi-experimental study that included 222 third-grade Spanish-speaking ELLs from Texas met WWC evidence standards with reservations. The size of the effects on reading achievement and English language development were both large enough to be considered substantively important, although statistical significance was not found (Calderón, Hertz-Lazarowitz, & Slavin, 1998; U.S. Department of Education, 2007b).

Arthur

Arthur is a listening comprehension and language development program that has been used to enhance ELLs' listening comprehension and English language development. This educational television program is designed for children ages 4–8 and is based on the Arthur storybooks. Arthur was found to have potentially positive effects on English language development for ELLs. The one study of Arthur that met the WWC evidence standards was a randomized controlled trial that included 108 Spanish-speaking ELL kindergartners from six schools in a large urban school district; the students who viewed three episodes of Arthur per week had greater improvement in narrative skills development than students in a control group, who watched a different television program (Uchikoshi, 2005; U.S. Department of Education, 2010a).

Vocabulary Improvement Program for English Language Learners and Their Classmates

The Vocabulary Improvement Program for English Language Learners and Their Classmates (VIP) was designed for ELLs and native English speakers; the curriculum focuses on vocabulary development of students in grades 4–6. The intervention aims to increase understanding of target vocabulary words included in weekly reading assignments over the course of 15 weeks, and includes whole-class and small-group activities. The WWC reported that VIP has potentially positive effects on reading achievement and English language development. One study of VIP met WWC evidence standards with reservations due to differential attrition. This study analyzed 142 ELLs in 16 classrooms across three states, and results indicated that VIP has substantively important, though not statistically significant, effects on ELLs' reading achievement and English language development (Carlo, et al., 2004; U.S. Department of Education, 2006c).

FRAMEWORK FOR ASSESSMENT AND INSTRUCTION PLANNING AND DOCUMENTATION AT TIER 2 AND TIER 3

The principal framework we adopt for assessment, instruction and intervention planning, and documentation at Tiers 2 and 3 is based on the work of Shapiro (2011). Specifically, we follow a modified process based on his articulated four-step approach for assessing academic skills. The steps in Shapiro's model include the following:

- Step 1: Assess the academic environment.
- Step 2: Assess the instructional placement.
- Step 3: Assess instructional modifications.
- Step 4: Conduct progress monitoring.

Assessment (and documentation) of the academic environment is the first step taken whenever a teacher or other educator begins to document the point at which a student begins to demonstrate difficulty (or, in the case of ELLs, immediately after they matriculate, or at the beginning of the year). We agree with Shapiro (2011) in that "because academic responses occur in the context of an instructional environment, an effective evaluation of academic problems must contain more than just an assessment of academic skills. . . . Academic skills are a function of environmental *and* individual variables" (pp. 67–68; emphasis in original). It may seem odd for a classroom teacher to document portions of his or her own instructional environment, but as you will see later (especially in Chapter 7), a comprehensive assessment of the academic environment is a legally required piece of information in determining eligibility and programming for students who eventually are evaluated for special education (i.e., those students who do not make sufficient progress at Tiers 2 and 3). According to Shapiro, five areas of documentation are necessary to assess the academic environment comprehensively: (1) teacher interview or interviews, (2) direct observation, (3) student interview, (4) permanent product review, and (5) curriculum-based assessment (CBA) of academic skills.

The second step in Shapiro's (2011) model is assessment of the instructional placement, which is done to determine whether the student is being instructed in materials that are at his or her appropriate instructional level. Many times, students in a particular grade level will all be taught using texts and other materials written at that grade level. Students who are learning from materials at their grade level but who are themselves at instructionally frustrational levels (i.e., the material is too difficult) need to be assessed, so that their actual instructional level can be identified and they can receive materials at a more appropriate level, where they will be able to make gains. For example, a fifth-grade student whose instructional level in reading is second-grade level will struggle tremendously in his fifth-grade class if the materials used in class are all at a fifth-grade level (e.g., readers and basals).

A student's instructional level is determined by directly assessing his or her academic skills using curriculum-based assessment (CBA), which consists of utilizing materials that are very similar to CBM probes. The process of using CBA to assess instructional level or academic functioning in a particular academic area (e.g., math computation, reading fluency) is called survey-level or instructional-level assessment (SLA or ILA). The instructional level is the level at which interventions and goals for progress should be targeted, because the classroom teacher can reasonably be certain that the student will demonstrate progress (Hopf & Martinez, 2006). ILA is very easy. First, CBA probes are administered in the area of difficulty (or the target area; e.g., reading fluency or numerical operations) at the child's *current* grade level.

As an example, Mario, who is in the fifth grade, is struggling with reading fluency. Begin by giving Mario a fifth-grade-level reading fluency probe (R-CBM). Next, you administer single reading fluency probes in succession, with each probe one grade level below the previous probe. As the student completes each probe, you score it and use the raw score and norms table (aggregate or local, you decide) to determine at which percentile rank each raw score lies. You want to keep assessing "backward" by grade until the student achieves a score that is at least at the 50th percentile and reads with 90–95% accuracy. For example, on fifth-grade R-CBM passages, Mario read 103 WRCM (2 errors), which is below the 25th percentile for his grade based on aggregate or national norms. He read the fifth-grade passages with 98% accuracy. On fourth-grade passages, Mario read 101 WRCM (5 errors), which is between the 25th and 50th percentiles and with 95% accuracy, indicating that these passages were at Mario's instructional level and just right for him. So Mario is most likely to be successful in intervention and assessment tasks and texts that are at the fourth-grade instructional level. Note that you always continue to benchmark with grade-level probes. Progress monitoring can be done with instructional level probes, however.

The third step in Shapiro's (2011) four-step model is instructional modification, which is followed by the fourth step, progress monitoring. We discussed these two concepts at the beginning of the chapter. In our advanced RTI graduate courses, we have drawn heavily on the Shapiro model. We made modifications to meet our needs and developed our own set of RTI worksheets.

DOCUMENTING TIERS 2 AND 3: RTI PROGRAM PARTICIPATION WORKSHEETS

One of the key areas we have found to be absent from currently published RTI books and manuals involves the lack of precise guidance regarding assessment and instruction/intervention planning and documentation at Tiers 2 and 3. For all struggling students, including ELLs, to be successful, we believe it is absolutely essential that the classroom teacher, as well as other educators (e.g., interventionists and school psychologists), document carefully all of the activities that take place at Tiers 2 and 3. In this section, we provide documentation and recording materials that we feel will be of assistance to you in the day-to-day implementation of Tiers 2 and 3 in RTI. Many of these materials initially were created for use in a graduate practicum on RTI. However, classroom teachers and other educators around the country also have used these materials to help document and organize their RTI efforts.

Although we divide the RTI program participation worksheets (hereafter referred to as RTI worksheets) into those most likely to be used by the classroom teacher and those most likely to be used by assessment specialists, such as school psychologists, we encourage you to determine which ones for both categories might be most beneficial to you, and we encourage you to adapt them for your particular needs (reproducible worksheets are available in Appendices 6.1–6.12 at the end of the chapter). To illustrate, in Table 6.1 we put the *Intervention Progress Notes Worksheet* (Appendix 6.9) in the school psychology section.

However, a classroom teacher may also use this worksheet if she is consulting with, say, the ELL coordinator or ESL teacher. Table 6.1 lists which documents are most likely to be used by teachers versus school psychologists (or school psychology students) or other educators.

The purpose of the RTI worksheets is to help educators document the RTI process and maintain written accountability for individual students at all stages of the problem-solving model, but particularly for students who receive more intense intervention at Tier 2 and Tier 3 (e.g., struggling non-ELLs and ELLs). It is important to keep in mind that *some* students who struggle and receive services at Tiers 2 and 3, including ELLs, *may* eventually be referred for testing and consideration for special education eligibility. One requirement of that eligibility process (IDEA, 2004) includes documentation of past academic history. We created the RTI worksheets in large part to facilitate record keeping for this purpose. We recommend keeping the worksheets in a folder (whether paper or electronic) for each student in your class or caseload who is participating in Tier 2 or Tier 3 supplemental instruction/intervention. We hope that the process of monitoring progress and documenting gains and losses will be facilitated by using the RTI worksheets. We introduce the RTI worksheets in the case study of Susanna, then illustrate how they were used to document Susana's RTI participation.

TABLE 6.1. Worksheets to Be Used by Classroom Teachers and Other Educators

Procedure	Classroom teacher	School psychologist, school psychology students, other educators
Summary of Existing Information and Assessment Data (Appendix 6.1)	X	X
Student Observation (structured setting and unstructured setting) (Appendix 6.2)		X
Review of Student-Generated Products (Appendix 6.3)	X	X
Teacher Interview (Appendix 6.4)		X
Student Interview (Appendix 6.5)	X	X
Parent Interview (Appendix 6.6)	X	X
Determination of Instructional Level and Intervention Goal (Appendix 6.7)	X	X
Comprehensive Intervention Plan (Appendix 6.8)	X	X
Intervention Progress Notes (Appendix 6.9)	X	X
Intervention Fidelity Checklist (Appendix 6.10)	X	X
Parent Data-Share (Appendix 6.11)	X	X
Teacher Data-Share (Appendix 6.12)		X

CASE STUDY: SUSANA

Introduction to the Case Study

Susana is of Mexican descent but was born in the United States and raised in Mexico City, Mexico. Prior to attending fourth grade in Miami, Susana attended public Spanish-only schools in Mexico. Susana's mother is an American who speaks Spanish, but whose native language is English, and her father is Mexican and a native Spanish speaker, although he speaks English. Interestingly, Susana grew up speaking to her mom in English and to her father in Spanish. She speaks both languages perfectly fluently but had never been in a U.S. school until the fourth grade, and she cannot read or write in English. Her school records from Mexico indicate that she was on grade level in Spanish reading, Spanish writing, and mathematics. She is matriculating in fourth grade (the grade she would have started had she stayed in Mexico) with Ms. Beckman, but is pulled out for twice-weekly ESL with Ms. Rodriguez, in addition to receiving Tier 2 services in reading through in-class small-group and individual instruction with Ms. Beckman. Susana makes slow but steady progress in English reading.

RTI Program Participation Worksheets

Summary of Existing Information and Assessment Data

To know where you are going with a student when planning for Tier 2 and Tier 3, it is important to know where the student has been. Often a student's academic data are scattered in different locations (in the cumulative folder in the front office, on the computer in your classroom, in the grade book, etc.). The *Summary of Existing Information and Assessment Data Worksheet* is intended to assist the teacher or other educator in compiling a student's relevant data on one form. Specifically, it is used to document succinctly the instructional techniques and interventions that have been tried (be sure to include by whom, on what dates, and the assessment/progress results) and the overall instructional environment in which the student is learning (e.g., reading is taught 90 minutes a day and the student participated in small-group reading instruction, in addition to the 90 minute large-group instruction). Teachers, parents, and the student are all interviewed, and summaries of those interviews are included on this worksheet. In the "Summary of other existing information" section, be sure to include any relevant academic or psychosocial information. And don't forget to include current grades and benchmark scores. The end-of-chapter appendices include the following worksheets that can be used to facilitate the information-gathering process: (a) *Summary of Existing Information and Assessment Data* (Appendix 6.1), *Student Observation* (Appendix 6.2), *Review of Student-Generated Products* (Appendix 6.3), *Teacher Interview* (Appendix 6.4), *Student Interview* (Appendix 6.5), and *Parent Interview* (Appendix 6.6). Figure 6.4 shows the Summary of Existing Information and Assessment Data worksheet filled out for Susana.

Summary of Existing Information and Assessment Data

Student: Susana   Grade: 4

Instructional strategies and interventions tried:

Since Susana has been enrolled at Bay Harbor Elementary, she has participated in the 60-minute daily reading block in which all students across the 4th grade participate (i.e., Tier 1). However, because Susana is an ELL and this is her first year in a U.S. school, she also has participated in numerous add-on activities and programs to bolster her ELP and English reading skills. Some of these strategies include small-group instruction, individual instruction, 30 additional minutes twice a week with a reading specialist, daily ESL, instructional conversation and literature logs, and the Arthur program.

Instructional environment:

Current environment is print-rich and structured in terms of all classroom routines. The core reading curriculum has been newly adopted and has very strong research support. The classroom climate is warm and inviting; children seem to feel comfortable taking academic risks and asking their teacher for help.

Teacher interview summary:

Ms. Beckman verified that Susana has multiple strengths, including a high motivation to be successful. However, she also expressed some concern with how far behind Susana is in her English academic language and English reading compared to other students in the class and also to other ELLs with whom Ms. Beckman has worked in the past.

Parent interview summary:

Susana is being raised by a single mother and lives with her mother and sister. Ms. Reardon corroborated that Susana is a very hard worker but indeed struggles with English. Ms. Reardon commented that Susana is much more comfortable speaking in Spanish and that she misses her family and friends back in Mexico a great deal.

Student interview summary:

Susana was a bit shy but easy to warm up to. She said she loves animals and that she wants to do well in school. Her favorite subject is science, but she dislikes math.

Student observation:

Susana was observed during reading instruction. She receives small-group instruction and participates in additional blocks of reading time. She is definitely Spanish-language dominant and has an accent when she speaks in English. Susana seems to be making friends and is otherwise adjusting well.

Summary of other existing information:

Susana's grades are B's and C's, and Ms. Beckman says that she has to modify many of the assignments so that Susana can complete them successfully. Susana has not yet taken the statewide achievement test and has been exempt this year because of her ELL status.

Summary of additional assessment data collected:

Susana participated in the schoolwide benchmark assessment in R-CBM. She scored 21 WRCM and had five errors, which places her below the 10th percentile compared to the aggregate norms. (No local norms are available, because there are so few ELLs matriculated at this school.)

FIGURE 6.4. Summary of Existing Information and Assessment Data worksheet for Susana.

Comprehensive Intervention Plan Worksheet

The Comprehensive Intervention Plan (CIP) worksheet facilitates the process of determining who will do what, when, and how at Tiers 2 and 3. The first part asks you to identify briefly the data that support the selection of a particular intervention. Be specific and make sure that the intervention selected directly matches the assessment data collected. Intervention selection is not a random act; it should be purposeful and driven *by* the assessment information available. For example, if the student's data point to difficulties in phonological processing, the interventions selected should focus on phonological processing (e.g., word-segmenting games) and so should the progress monitoring assessment task (e.g., phoneme segmentation fluency and/or nonsense word fluency). Students often struggle in more than one academic area. It is essential to focus on an area and a goal that is Specific, Measurable, Attainable, Routines-based, and Tied to a functional priority (SMART; Jung & Grisham-Brown, 2006). The CIP worksheet allows for a description of the intervention, but the reader may also wish to attach a more comprehensive description to the form. For example, Jim Wright (Intervention Central; *www.interventioncentral.org*) offers many PDFs of evidence-based interventions that can be printed and affixed to the CIP worksheet. Another resource for downloadable descriptions of interventions, which we described previously, is the EBI Network (*http://ebi.missouri.edu*). The section on the CIP worksheet about research support for the intervention has been a requirement for graduate students who have used these forms in their RTI class, but we encourage you to fill out this section as well. Jim Wright has done much of the work for you in his handouts.

We have received feedback from practitioners that the sections in the CIP worksheet for documenting the intervention schedule and progress monitoring plan are perhaps the most important, yet often overlooked, part of the Tier 2 and Tier 3 intervention planning and implementation process. We urge you to be specific: Identify where, when, and who is responsible for the intervention and for monitoring student progress. Also, how will responsiveness be determined? In other words, how will you know that progress is being made at an acceptable rate? Finally, you need to document that an intervention was implemented with fidelity or as it was intended to be implemented (and we have a worksheet, the *RTI Program Participation Worksheet: Intervention Fidelity Checklist* [Appendix 6.10] just for that purpose).

We should also mention that in our presentations around the country about topics related to RTI for ELLs, we have encountered a lot of confusion about whether related services personnel (e.g., speech–language pathologists, school psychologists) can and should be able to work with students who have not been identified as eligible for special education services (e.g., ELLs). We urge you to make maximum use of your existing resources (i.e., time, people, and money) and if you have, say, a school psychologist with experience in conducting interventions, we believe there is no reason why he or she should not run an academic intervention group for struggling students. Maximize the resources you have! Figure 6.5 illustrates the CIP worksheet completed for Susana.

Comprehensive Intervention Plan

Student: Susana _____   Grade: 4 _____

Teacher: Ms. Beckman _____

Summary of assessment data to support selection of this particular intervention:

Susana's Survey Level Assessment, as well as teacher observation, indicates that she is reading well below the expected level compared to other fourth graders (although local ELL norms were not available). Susana's reading fluency is at approximately a first-grade level.

Intervention areas to target:

Reading fluency and Academic English vocabulary

Intervention description (include description of each component, if relevant):

For the first 6 weeks of the Tier 2 intervention period, Susana will participate in a specific reading fluency intervention called Repeated Readings with Error Correction. In addition, Susana will participate in Incremental Rehearsal to boost English reading and vocabulary.

Research support:

Reading Fluency: Daly, E. J., Chafouleas, S., & Skinner, H. (2005). Producing measurable increases in reading fluency. Interventions for Reading Problems: Designing and Evaluating Effective Strategies (pp. 89–94). New York: Guilford Press.

Vocabulary: Joseph, L. M. (2006). Incremental rehearsal: A flashcard drill technique for increasing retention of reading words. The Reading Teacher, 59, 803–807.

Intervention schedule (day/time):

Three days a week (Monday, Wednesday, Friday) from 9:30 A.M. to 10:00 A.M. for the Repeated Reading and until 10:10 A.M. for the Incremental Rehearsal.

Progress monitoring plan (include skill/s to be monitored for progress and goal):

Monitor progress each Friday with an R-CBM probe before the start of the intervention. Will use the flashcards in the Incremental Rehearsal portion of the intervention to determine percent correct.

Method of determining responsiveness:

Two-stage process articulated in Riley-Tillman & Burns (2009). Step 1: Was there change; Step 2: Was the documented change functionally related to the intervention?

Implementation fidelity checks:

Intervention fidelity will be checked in the second week and again 2 weeks later.

Home–school link:

Susana will be provided with books on tape as well as a set of vocabulary flashcards to practice at home.

FIGURE 6.5. CIP worksheet for Susana.

RTI Participation Worksheet: Determination of Instructional Level and Intervention Goal

Prior to selecting a specific intervention it is important to determine the student's instructional level. The instructional level is the reading level that is just right for students (not too easy and not too difficult). Hasbrouck and Tindall (2006) suggest that students who are reading within ten points above or below the 50th percentile are making adequate progress in reading fluency. Figure 6.6 illustrates the determination of instructional level and goal intervention worksheet completed for Susana.

Determination of Instructional Level

Student: *Susana*   Grade: *4*

Step 1: Determine the Student's Instructional Level.

Select three passages for each grade level beginning with the grade in which the student is currently enrolled and then do the same working backward by grade until the student reads within the 25th-to-50th percentile.

Passage Grade Level	Passage 1 WRC/E	Passage 2 WRC/E	Passage 3 WRC/E	Median WRC/E[1]
4th	34/5	44/4	46/6	44/5
3rd	47/3	45/3	41/2	45/3
2nd	53/2	54/1	56/1	54/1
1st	—	—	—	

Step 2: Identify the Student's Instructional Level.

The Instructional Level is the grade level at which the student successfully reads within the 25th-to-50th percentile, as determined by the assessment above.

AIMSweb Aggregate Norms
Year 2014–2015[2] R-CBM

Grade level	WRC for 25th–50th Percentile Range
First	6–13
Second	35–62
Third	59–87
Fourth	84–107
Fifth	94–121
Sixth	116–141
Seventh	119–144
Eighth	123–146

Instructional Grade Level: *2nd Grade*

(continued)

[1]Be sure to calculate WRC and Error medians *separately.*

[2]Update norms as necessary.

FIGURE 6.6. Determination of Instructional Level and Goal Intervention worksheet for Susanna.

Step 3: Decide whether a realistic or an ambitious growth rate is more appropriate for the student.

Realistic and Ambitious Growth Rates (Fuchs, Fuchs, Hamlett, Walz, & Germann, 1993)

Grade level	Realistic Goals (words per week)	Ambitious Goals (words per week)
1	2.0	3.0
2	1.5	2.0
3	1.0	1.5
4	.85	1.1
5	.5	.85

Realistic (typical) Growth Rate: <u>1.5</u>

Ambitious (accelerated) Growth Rate: <u>2</u>

Step 4: Determine how many weeks the intervention (and concurrent progress monitoring) will be implemented. This information should crosscheck with information provided in Appendix 6.8, RTI Program Participation Worksheet: Comprehensive Intervention Plan.

Number of Weeks of Intervention and Progress Monitoring: <u>8</u>

Step 5: Calculate Intervention Goal.

weeks <u>8</u> × growth rate <u>2</u> + median instructional level <u>54</u> =

Reading Fluency Goal <u>70 WRC</u>

FIGURE 6.6. *(continued)*

Intervention Fidelity Checklist

It is important to implement the steps of an intervention in the way that they were intended to be implemented. This is intervention fidelity, which is actually relatively easy to document, although we have found that many educators express a lot of anxiety and trepidation about determining intervention integrity. We adapted a checklist from Brown-Chidsey and Steege (2010) to create the Intervention Fidelity Checklist included here. In the left column, list the individual steps of the intervention. An independent observer (colleague or supervisor) observes the intervention session and checks Yes or No after each step to indicate whether he or she observed you implement the intervention following each step on the form. In the right column, the observer jots down notes (e.g., encouragement or a reminder). Divide the number of NO checks by the number of YES checks and you have your fidelity percentage. We suggest that you strive for an ambitious 90% or above observer reliability rate. Figure 6.7 contains the completed Intervention Fidelity Checklist for Susana's intervention.

Student Observation Worksheet

It is important for someone other than the classroom teacher to observe the student in the instructional setting. School psychologists who conduct psychoeducational evaluations almost always conduct a student observation in the natural setting. We recommend two relatively brief observations of the student (15–20 minutes each): one in a structured set-

Intervention Fidelity Checklist

Student: Susana   Grade: 4

Intervention Components	Completed	
	Yes	No
Passage at instructional level placed in front of student.	X	
Interventionist reads passage aloud and student follows along.	X	
Student then reads same passage aloud.	X	
Interventionist records errors.	X	
At end of 3 minutes, interventionist reports WRC and number of errors to student.	X	
Show student missed words. Have student read whole sentence containing missed words three times.	X	
Ask student to "beat first score." Student reads passage again and score is recorded and reported after 3 minutes.	X	

FIGURE 6.7. Intervention Fidelity Checklist for Susana.

ting (preferably in the area of instruction in which the child is experiencing difficulty) and the other in an unstructured setting (e.g., playground, recess, lunch). The purpose of the unstructured setting observation is to consider the child's behavior in a nonacademic setting to get a good picture of how the child is doing socially and to corroborate any additional concerns raised by teachers, parents, or guardians. Figure 6.8 shows a completed Student Observation worksheet for Susana.

Student Interview Worksheet

We also recommend conducting a student interview. The classroom teacher or another educator can conduct the interview. We feel it is important to hear from Susana herself and ask her what she likes and dislikes about school, what is hard and easy for her, and what she does when she experiences trouble in a particular academic area or a specific assignment. Figure 6.9 illustrates a completed Student Interview worksheet for Susana.

Review of Student-Generated Products Worksheet

Student-generated products, or permanent products, refer to the classroom activities and assignments the child has completed that illustrate without question the difficulty, or lack of difficulty, the child is having. For example, for a student who is struggling with written expression, the review of student-generated products might include the student's daily reflection journal, an essay he or she wrote on riding horses, and last week's spelling test.

The classroom teacher already should be quite familiar with the relevant student-generated products. The teacher can select exemplars to describe on the form or have a colleague review them and document his or her observations on the form. Figure 6.10 includes Susana's Review of Student-Generated Products worksheet.

Parent Interview Worksheet

Parents are an integral part of their child's education and cannot be excluded from the process of helping their struggling child succeed in school. We hope that teachers will have had numerous contacts with all of their students' parents and that the parent interview is by no means the first contact a school professional has with that particular parent or guardian, especially for students who require Tier 2 and 3 intervention. The Parent Interview form is intended to record parents' specific concerns about their child, as well as document what, if any, interventions have been attempted at home. Figure 6.11 is a completed Parent Interview worksheet for Susana.

Student Observation

Student: Susana _____   Grade: 4 _____

Structured setting observation

Time:	9:30 A.M.	Date: 2/3/12
Location:	Ms. Beckman's class	Subject: Reading

The examiner observed Susana during the regular Tier 1 core reading instruction time in Ms. Beckman's class. The reading curriculum used is a research-based program that was selected and implemented 2 years ago. The lesson observed was echo reading activity using a reader from the core curriculum. In this activity, Susana was paired with another student, a native English speaker. The student read a paragraph from the reader, modeling fluent reading with good prosody. Susana followed along in her book but did not do any reading aloud. When discussing the observation with the teacher at a later time in the day, Ms. Beckman commented that Susana can understand English but is not able to read any English text, so she is not required to do so in the echo reading activities.

Unstructured setting observation

Time:	11:30 A.M.	Date: 2/4/12
Location:	Lunchroom	

The examiner observed Susana in the cafeteria during lunchtime. Susana seemed very excited and full of energy as she entered the cafeteria. She stood and talked with a group of girls in line and smiled and laughed frequently. After receiving her tray, Susana quickly walked to get a seat next to another girl. She turned sideways often while eating her sandwich to take part in the conversations going on next to her. Susana talked to the peers next to her and across the table throughout the lunch period. After she finished eating, Susanna cleared her tray and walked toward the recess line. She stopped to wait for a friend, and they lined up together. Susana sat on the floor quietly as instructed until her line was permitted to leave the cafeteria and go outside for recess.

FIGURE 6.8. Student Observation worksheet for Susana.

Student Interview

Student: Susana _____ Grade: 4 _____

What do you like most about school? What is your favorite subject?

Susana indicated that she really likes school. She wants to be a pediatric organ transplant surgeon or an ice skater when she grows up. Her favorite subject is science.

What do you like least about school? What is your least favorite subject?

Susana likes everything about school; however, she misses her friends and family back in Mexico. Her least favorite subject is math, followed by social studies.

What are some of the things you're learning in your classes?

Susana told the examiner that the main thing she is learning in her classes is how to write better in English and how to read hard words in English. Susana reminded the examiner that she feels more comfortable reading, writing, and speaking in Spanish, but she is not too shy about speaking in English (though she hates to read aloud in English because she can't read many of the words and she is aware of her accent).

What are some of the things you like to do for fun?

Susana had a hard time telling the examiner what she likes to do for fun. She did mention that she loves animals and wants to be able to save the harp seals from becoming extinct. She loves music and is starting to be invited to go places with the new friends she is meeting.

Do you have a lot of friends in your classes?

She is making many new friends, but Susana told the examiner that she is most comfortable around other Spanish-speaking students.

Do you enjoy working with other students when you are having trouble with assignments?

Susana said she prefers getting help from her teacher rather than from her classmates because she doesn't like to feel that she is bothering anybody.

What do you do when you are unable to solve a problem or answer a question in your subjects?

When Susana experiences difficulty, she either doesn't tell anybody or she tries really hard to figure it out on her own. She admitted that she often gets frustrated when this happens (which happens a lot because she has such difficulty with reading). When she is very frustrated, she asks Ms. Beckman for help. When she is frustrated at home, she asks her mom for help or, at times, has called the homework hotline that is run by the local library.

FIGURE 6.9. Student Interview worksheet for Susana.

Review of Student-Generated Products

Student: _Susana_   Grade: _4_

Product 1
What did you revview?
In-class daily journal.
What did you observe?
Susana had a daily journal with entries nearly every day, starting in September when the class first began to use daily journals. Many of the entries actually were written in Spanish, indicating that Susana expresses herself in writing better in Spanish than in English. In a few of the entries, she also had drawn pictures to illustrate the stories she had written in Spanish. On a few occasions (presumably when Ms. Beckman asked her to try to write in English), the words she did write in English were spelled phonetically, and it appeared she struggled greatly because the stories in English were very short.
Product 2
What did you review?
Numerous spelling tests taken over the last 2 months.
What did you observe?
Susana has a very difficult time with writing spelling words. When she writes words in English, she uses phonetic spellings exclusively. Even when the spelling lists were shortened to 10 words (from 20), Susana struggled greatly. Her highest grade was a D–.

FIGURE 6.10. Review of Student-Generated Products worksheet for Susana.

Parent Interview

Student: <u>Susana</u>   Grade: <u>4</u>

Teacher: <u>Ms. Beckman</u>   Parent: <u>Pam Reardon</u>

Child's strengths:

Ms. Reardon was quick to point out many of Susana's strengths, including her compassion for animals and children less fortunate than herself. With regard to academic strengths, Ms. Reardon noted that Susana is a very hardworking child and that she is exceptionally motivated to succeed in school. She also commented that Susana was very upset when they moved to the United States from Mexico, and that her biggest fear was that her school in the United States would retain her (have her repeat third grade) because of her lack of reading and writing skills in English.

Areas of concern:

Ms. Reardon, like Ms. Beckman, is very concerned about Susana's reading ability in English. She believes that if Susana can't learn to read well in English, she is always going to struggle in school. Furthermore, she is concerned about Susana's self-esteem, because Susana was a great student in Mexico and now in the United States perceives herself to be a terrible student and is often very self-conscious. Ms. Reardon wants the school to do everything it can to help Susana get up to where she needs to be, so she can be successful in all her classes now and in the future.

Interventions tried at home:

Ms. Reardon works full-time and is a single mother. She tries to help Susana with her homework most evenings but admits that she is usually too tired to help Susana. She did help Susana get a library card, and Susana likes to go to the library on Saturdays and check out books about animals.

Learning environment at home:

Susana lives in a one-bedroom apartment with her mother and younger sister. She does not have a separate study area, and it is difficult to concentrate on her homework when the television is on in the background. Ms. Reardon is very supportive of education and definitely wants Susana to be successful in school.

Parent interview summary:

Ms. Reardon reported many of Susana's strengths, including her daughter's motivation and work ethic. Ms. Reardon is very supportive of her daughter's education and worries that Susana will continue to struggle in school if she doesn't catch up in English reading and writing. Ms. Reardon is involved and willing to help Susana at home.

FIGURE 6.11. Parent Interview worksheet for Susana.

CONCLUDING REMARKS

In this chapter we have discussed several important concepts to consider when providing ELLs Tier 2 and Tier 3 instructional supports. We have described frequent formative assessment as a "non-negotiable" activity for monitoring student growth at Tiers 2 and 3. Notably, we presented the four time periods—at a minimum—during Tier 2 and Tier 3 when data ought to be collected. According to Albers, Elliott, and colleagues (2013), data should be gathered before an intervention is implemented, during an intervention, when the intervention is over, and again at some point following the end of the intervention (e.g., 1 month later) to determine whether the improvement in performance was maintained. Frequent data collection and concomitant tweaking of instruction are indeed hallmarks of RTI models, and particularly at Tiers 2 and 3. Although frequent formative assessment is indicated for all students participating in Tiers 2 and 3 RTI programming, there are unique issues to consider for ELLs who receive intense RTI services at these tiers. We introduced the concept of local norms and the importance of comparing individual ELL's intervention gains based on comparing their ELP levels to non-ELLs (1) with the same ELP level, (2) in the same grade, and (3) in the same district or building. One of the primary take-home messages we hope to get across to the reader is that *participation in Tiers 2 and 3 does not serve as a placeholder for special education for any student,* and especially not for ELLs who should receive Tier 2 and Tier 3 intensive services from the get-go. In this chapter, we also discussed the concept of instructional dosage and how manipulating four simple instructional features (e.g., group size, instructional period, frequency, and duration; Faggella-Luby & Deshler, 2008) can be incorporated into the instructional day to intensify existing core instruction for struggling students, including ELLs. We reviewed several reading intervention programs and curricula that may be used in addition to good core Tier 1 instruction. We also revisited the concept of ecological factors and the critical role they play in instructional planning for ELLs. Finally, we introduced a series of RTI worksheets that may be incorporated into an RTI model. To demonstrate how these worksheets might be used, we introduced Susana and presented her filled-out RTI worksheets.

RTI Program Participation Worksheet:
Summary of Existing Information and Assessment Data

Student: _____ Grade: _____

Instructional strategies and interventions tried:

Instructional environment:

Teacher interview summary:

Parent interview summary:

(continued)

Student interview summary:

Student observation:

Summary of other existing information:

Summary of additional assessment data collected:

RTI Program Participation Worksheet: Student Observation

Student: _____ Grade: _____

Structured setting observation
(preferably in area related to area in which the student is struggling)

Time: _____ Date: _____

Location: _____ Subject: _____

Unstructured setting observation

Time: _____ Date: _____

Location: _____

RTI Program Participation Worksheet:
Review of Student-Generated Products

Student: _____   Grade: _____

Be sure to review student-generated work (e.g., essays, tests) in the area of difficulty.

Product 1
What did you revview?
What did you observe?

Product 2
What did you review?
What did you observe?

Product 3
What did you review?
What did you observe?

RTI Program Participation Worksheet: Teacher Interview

Student: _____ Grade: _____

Teacher: _____

Child's strengths:

Areas of concern:

Interventions tried by the teacher:

Learning environment (e.g., where child sits, services he or she receives):

Teacher interview summary:

RTI Program Participation Worksheet: Student Interview

Student: _____ Grade: _____

What do you like most about school? What is your favorite subject?

What do you like least about school? What is your least favorite subject?

What are some of the things you're learning in your classes?

What do you find particularly hard in your subjects? Easy?

(continued)

What are some of the things you like to do for fun?

Do you have a lot of friends in your classes?

Do you enjoy working with other students when you are having trouble with assignments?

What do you do when you are unable to solve a problem or answer a question in your subjects?

RTI Program Participation Worksheet: Parent Interview

Student: _____ Grade: _____

Teacher: _____ Parent: _____

Child's strengths:

Areas of concern:

Interventions tried at home:

Learning environment at home:

Parent interview summary:

APPENDIX 6.7

RTI Program Participation Worksheet:
Determination of Instructional Level and Intervention Goal

Student: _____ Grade: _____

Step 1: Determine the Student's Instructional Level.

Select three passages for each grade level beginning with the grade in which the student is currently enrolled and then do the same working backward by grade until the student reads within the 25th-to-50th percentile.

Passage Grade Level	Passage 1 WRC/E	Passage 2 WRC/E	Passage 3 WRC/E	Median WRC/E[1]

Step 2: Identify the Student's Instructional Level.

The Instructional Level is the grade level at which the student successfully reads within the 25th-to-50th percentile, as determined by the assessment above.

AIMSweb Aggregate Norms
Year 2014– 2015[1] R-CBM

Grade level	WRC for 25th–50th Percentile Range
First	6–13
Second	35–62
Third	59–87
Fourth	84–107
Fifth	94–121
Sixth	116–141
Seventh	119–144
Eighth	123–146

Instructional Grade Level: _____

(continued)

[1]Update norms as necessary.

Step 3: Decide whether a realistic or an ambitious growth rate is more appropriate for the student.

Realistic and Ambitious Growth Rates (Fuchs, Fuchs, Hamlett, Walz, & Germann, 1993)

Grade level	Realistic Goals (words per week)	Ambitious Goals (words per week)
1	2.0	3.0
2	1.5	2.0
3	1.0	1.5
4	.85	1.1
5	.5	.85

Realistic (typical) Growth Rate: _____

Ambitious (accelerated) Growth Rate: _____

Step 4: Determine how many weeks the intervention (and concurrent progress monitoring) will be implemented. This information should crosscheck with information provided in Appendix 6.8, RTI Program Participation Worksheet: Comprehensive Intervention Plan.

Number of Weeks of Intervention and Progress Monitoring: _____

Step 5: Calculate Intervention Goal.

weeks _____ × growth rate _____ + median instructional level _____ =
Reading Fluency Goal _____

RTI Program Participation Worksheet:
Comprehensive Intervention Plan

Student: _____ Grade: _____

Teacher: _____

Summary of assessment data to support selection of this particular intervention:

Intervention areas to target:

Intervention description (include description of each component if relevant):

Research support:

Intervention schedule (day/time):

(continued)

Progress monitoring plan (include skill/s to be monitored for progress and goal):

Method of determining responsiveness:

Implementation integrity checks:

Home–school link:

RTI Program Participation Worksheet: Intervention Progress Notes

Student: _____   Grade: _____

Interventionist: _____   Teacher: _____

Date of intervention session: _____

Is student getting closer to goal (based on progress monitoring data)?   YES   NO

Summary of session: **What went well:**   **What did not go well:**   **What to remember or change for next time:**

RTI Program Participation Worksheet:
Intervention Fidelity Checklist

Student: _____ Grade: _____

Date: _____ Time: _____ Intervention name: _____

Evaluator: _____

Directions: After observing the intervention session, the evaluator is to complete this form regarding how the interventionist implemented the intervention during *that* day.

Intervention implemented by: _____

Intervention Components	Completed		Comments
	Yes	No	

Adapted from Brown-Chidsey and Steege (2010). Copyright 2010 by The Guilford Press. Adapted by permission.

RTI Program Participation Worksheet: Parent Data-Share

Student: _____ Grade: _____

Teacher: _____

Data-share session:

                         1   2   3   4   5

Summary of sessions so far:

Report of student progress in classroom (based on teacher data-shares):

What is going well:

What may need improvement:

Questions or concerns raised by parent:

Items to follow up with before next data-share:

RTI Program Participation Worksheet: Teacher Data-Share

Student: _____   Grade: _____

Data-share session:

1   2   3   4   5

Data shared with the teacher:
Teacher's report of student progress in classroom:
What went well:
What did not go well:
Questions or concerns raised by teacher:
Items to follow up with before next data-share:

CHAPTER 7

Special Education Referral and Evaluation Considerations for ELLs Who Have Not Responded to Instruction and Intervention

ELLs who have participated in excellent core instruction during which the general education classroom teacher has differentiated that instruction as needed and provided supplemental and intense intervention (i.e., Tiers 2 and 3) *still* may not make adequate progress. In such cases, it may be appropriate to refer the student to a prereferral team, if one exists. The prereferral team should include at least one member who is knowledgeable about L2 acquisition and familiar with ELLs. The names of prereferral teams vary (e.g., RTI team, child study team), but the goal is the same, which is for a school panel to review extant data, evaluate the instructional environment, and recommend and/or implement additional strategies and interventions to be tried *before* the student is formally referred for special education evaluation. In many cases, the interventions implemented during the prereferral process represent Tier 3 in the RTI model, but the intervention tier used can vary by state and district. Prereferral intervention strategies should include a rigorous sequence of *assessments* followed by targeted, intense *intervention*, as has been described in the previous chapters, especially Chapter 6. But what if intense intervention is implemented and the student *still* struggles? At this point, then, it may very well be appropriate to refer the student for a comprehensive special education evaluation. In this chapter, we discuss the process of deciding *when* to refer an ELL for special education evaluation and the responsibilities of the general education classroom teacher, as well as other educators, before and during this process. Finally, we address best practices in psychoeducational report writing in general, and those for ELLs in particular. The discussion in the latter part of the chapter on psychoeducational reports is geared primarily toward school psychologists and educational diagnosticians, but teachers and other educators also may also benefit from reviewing this information.

BEFORE THE REFERRAL OCCURS

Teachers need to be judicious in their referral practices. Failure to identify and refer persistently struggling students and overreferral of ELL students for special education evaluation are *both* problematic practices. One systemic consequence of under- and overidentifying ELL students, as discussed in Chapter 2, is that it may result in a disproportionate representation of ELL students in (or out) of special education. Alas, there is a long-standing history of *educational disproportionality*—the over- or underrepresentation of students in a particular disability category—concerning racial and ethnic/minority children. Much of the literature on disproportionality has focused on the overrepresentation of student groups in the categories of specific learning disabilities, cognitive impairment, and emotional disabilities. The majority of this research has also addressed the disproportionate representation of specific student groups, namely, African American males. Research examining disproportionality based on language status has pointed to both underrepresentation (Zehler et al., 2003) and overrepresentation of ELLs in special education (Artiles et al., 2005; Linn & Hemmer, 2011). Both over- and underrepresentation of any student group represent an endemic problem within our educational system that is intended to meet the needs of all students by providing equal access and opportunity to high-quality educational opportunities and services.

What to Document

We noted earlier that in an ideal RTI model, a tremendous amount of work (on the part of the teacher, other educators, *and* the student) transpires before a referral is even considered. We believe that there are two distinct types of activities that take place prereferral. The first comprises the actual teaching, reteaching, assessment, and intervention that we have discussed as standard practice at Tiers 1, 2, and 3. The second refers to the classroom teacher's careful documentation of these activities and how students responded to them. We realize that paperwork or documentation is often treated with derision; however, to make appropriate decisions about programming for struggling students and, for some, eventually determine special education eligibility (at least within the RTI model), thorough documentation of the assessment and intervention activities that transpired *before* the referral is made is absolutely obligatory. Although such documentation is laid out in the law, we are not aware of any published resources that provide reproducible worksheets for educators and school psychologists to document RTI intervention activities at Tiers 2 and 3. Thus, we created our own. We presented in Chapter 6 a series of forms (RTI Program Participation worksheets) for you to use as a starting point in developing your own forms for documenting the procedures in *your* RTI program.

Within the RTI model, particularly as described in this book, any student who demonstrates the first sign of difficulty based on poor performance on a universal screening measure or other formative assessment tool (plus classroom observation) must be provided with a series of increasingly intense, data-informed, evidence-based interventions in the general education setting in a direct and targeted attempt to ameliorate the difficulty. Thus, one of the hallmarks of an appropriate ELL referral (or any referral for that matter) is that *everything* that is within a school's and a teacher's resources and power has been attempted in an effort to help the struggling student (and these efforts have been documented carefully). In other words, all relevant ecological factors (as discussed in Chapter 3) should be considered, and corresponding instructional and intervention efforts should be applied in an attempt to remedy the difficulties to ensure that the student has not become an "ecological casualty." Too often, teachers refer a student for special education testing prematurely, *before* making every effort to remedy the problem. Illustrating this error in judgment, Rodriguez and Carrasquillo (1997) reported that very few ELL students who were referred for special education evaluation had received *any* type of intervention prior to referral, even though more than half of their sample had been in the United States for less than 3 years! Although the study was conducted over 15 years ago, before RTI as we view it today was widely recognized as a potential service delivery model, it is quite possible (and we are hopeful) that a replication of the study today would reveal different results.

Making the Referral

Teachers may deliberate, even agonize, over the decision to refer or not to refer a student (any student) for a special education evaluation. Unfortunately, there is a relative lack of research on ELLs with special education needs (Klingner et al., 2006), including knowledge about when it is most appropriate to make a special education evaluation referral or decide that a student has had sufficient Tier 2 and 3 instruction and intervention. One of the most important questions for researchers and practitioners alike is how to distinguish validly and reliably between ELLs' academic difficulties that stem from an underlying or endogenous disability (e.g., specific learning disability, cognitive impairment) and those related to the L2 acquisition process.

Recall from Chapter 4 that the ESL process is lengthy and for many children can take up to 10 years or more. In addition, many of the common linguistic patterns exhibited by L2 learners are indistinguishable from the common linguistic errors made by native English speakers who have a language-based disability. For example, students with a true SLD in reading may struggle with reading connected text fluently, and/or have a difficult time sounding out new and unfamiliar words (i.e., decoding). Their reading is often slow, choppy, laborious, and lacking in prosody. These students may have a limited vocabulary and may not read fluently or understand much of what they read. These students also perform at the lowest percentiles in formative assessment tasks such as R-CBM, and they do poorly on most of the reading tasks required in the regular classroom. ELLs, particularly those at the earlier ELP levels, are very likely *also* to struggle reading connected text in English and sounding out new vocabulary. ELLs usually have a limited English vocabulary, especially a limited academic language vocabulary. Thus, both the non-ELL student with a learning disability and the typical ELL student frequently perform very similarly in the classroom and struggle in the same areas; consequently, it may *seem* logical to the classroom teacher that the ELL student has an endogenous learning difficulty or disability, *but this conclusion is erroneous in many cases.* Indeed, "there is no reason why English learners' bilingual development should be diagnosed as a specific learning disability" (Figueroa & Newsome, 2006, p. 213). In many but, of course, not all cases, ELLs' low achievement in English can be explained by ecological factors. Recall that the primary goal of RTI is to *prevent* and/or *intervene early* to thwart learning difficulties that otherwise look like true disabilities but are actually the direct result of ineffective teaching and learning environments.

So, what if you *still* believe (based on existing data and careful observation) that one of your ELLs has a *true* disability, such as a learning disability? How can you be sure? Unfortunately, there are no magic answers or explicit rules of thumb to guide you; however, there are a number of critical issues to consider carefully when trying to make the best, most informed decision about whether to refer an ELL student for special education evaluation. We urge you to reflect carefully on your answers to each of the following questions *prior* to making a referral. It may be especially helpful to discuss these questions with a colleague. We recommend consulting with another teacher who has had the same or more experience than you working with ELLs, an administrator who is familiar with the district's overall referral rates for ELLs, or a school psychologist or speech–language pathologist who can help you think through some of the more complex questions that follow:

1. Are multiple sources (e.g., other teachers, including past teachers, parents) persistently corroborating your concern(s) about the ELL in question? For example, if you are concerned about a student's reading skill, do you know if last year's teacher also had similar concerns? Have other teachers this year noted problems with the student's English reading performance? Do the student's parents or guardians have concerns about the student's reading in either English or the family's native language? Given your past experience teaching ELLs and native English speakers, does the student under consideration perform like other struggling students you have taught? If so, in what ways? How do they differ?

2. For students whose dominant language is Spanish or French, and if your school uses Spanish or French language screening tools in addition to the English language assessments, do the results show the same trajectory of poor academic gain in Spanish or French as that in English?[1]

3. Has the student participated in a sound core curriculum (e.g., the focus in reading has been on the five pillars of reading instruction [see Chapter 5] consistently (e.g., the student was not repeatedly pulled out; excessive absences have not been a problem) that used the sound pedagogical practices described in Chapter 5 (e.g., explicit

---

[1] At the time of writing this book, we were aware of Spanish-language and French-language curriculum-based measurement tools; DIBELS/AIMSweb and i-STEEP, respectively. It is entirely possible that formative assessment tools in other languages have been published since that time.

instruction, differentiation, small groups, frequent progress monitoring)? Was the dosage of the curriculum content for this student appropriately increased (e.g., with more time spent per session and/or for longer periods)?

4. Were additional *research-based* interventions provided by either the general education teacher or another educator or interventionist and implemented with fidelity (i.e., Tier 2 of the RTI model)? Has the teacher done an excellent job of documenting what was done, how long it was done, and what results were achieved?

5. When core instruction plus Tier 2 instruction did not yield acceptable academic gains, was instruction intensified *even further* with additional intervention provision (and correspondingly more frequent progress monitoring; i.e., Tier 3 services)? Has the teacher done an excellent job of documenting what was done, how long it was done, and what results were achieved?

If the answer is "yes" to all or most of these questions, it is very likely that the student you have considered for referral for special education evaluation is a good candidate for a more in-depth evaluation to determine eligibility for special education services.

ONCE THE REFERRAL OCCURS

After students are referred for a special education evaluation, the school psychologist, speech–language pathologist, educational diagnostician, or other education professional with assessment knowledge generally conducts most of the formal assessments and other evaluation procedures, which we discuss in a later section in this chapter. We wish to emphasize, however, that *a teacher's job in the referral and evaluation process does not stop (or start) simply when he or she fills out the referral paperwork*. In the best-case scenario, *prior* to making a referral, a huge amount of work on the part of the student, the teacher, and other educators has transpired in the general education classroom, and the classroom teacher has carefully documented all of these efforts *and* their outcomes (i.e., progress monitoring results and behavioral observations). In the case of a student who is referred for special education evaluation, the prereferral activities themselves, and the corresponding documentation of those efforts, are critical components of the special education evaluation process, including the final decision to identify (or not identify) the student as eligible for special education services. We believe that an excellent ELL evaluation for special education (or any education evaluation for that matter), to a large extent, is only as strong as were the prereferral interventions and the corresponding documentation gathered by the teacher *prior* to the referral.

Referral procedures and paperwork requirements vary by local school district, perhaps even by school building. However, there are general documentation requirements (as required by federal and state law) that all general education teachers can and should actively collect (especially during a student's participation in Tiers 2 and 3) to facilitate the special education evaluation and identification process. Careful documentation of the observations, assessments, instructional adaptations, accommodations, and interventions implemented in the general education classroom *prior* to the referral are collectively a significant component of special education evaluation for those students who eventually are referred. These pieces of information appropriately inform the case conference committee, allowing the group to make the best possible decision about eligibility and programming. Federal criteria in IDEA 2004 specify what documentation is necessary for determining whether a student is entitled to special education services as a student with a disability. We strongly encourage you to become familiar with your state's special education law, which is an interpretation of IDEA 2004 (or, as is the case in some states, adopted verbatim from the federal language). Pay close attention to nuances in the language and terminology used in your state's special education regulations. If you have never read your state's special education law, we encourage you to find the webpage for your state's Department of Education and do a key word search (e.g., in Indiana you can search for *special education laws, rules and interpretation*). Once you locate the regulations, print the document and keep it on your desk; refer to it often. As you go through the regulations, we encourage you to pay particular attention to the sections pertaining to identification and evaluation, eligibility criteria, and determination of special education services. We consider a state's special education regulations to be mandatory reading for all educators in that state—not the least of which include general education teachers.[2]

Consideration of Exclusionary Factors

We now return to the concept of ecological factors (i.e., lack of appropriate instruction, curriculum factors; school and classroom, cultural, economic, and environmental factors) that we originally introduced and discussed in Chapter 3. As we indicated in that discussion, the true value of implementing an RTI model with ELLs—particularly a model that utilizes a problem-solving approach—is that the RTI process should facilitate the consideration of multiple ecological variables associated with academic underachievement and encourage minimizing the impact of these ecological variables in the school setting. Now that we have moved to a full evaluation of an ELL student, the terminology associated with the concept of *ecological factors* changes to consideration of *exclusionary factors*. If the classroom teacher and other members of the RTI team have been collecting and documenting data and intervention efforts, the special education evaluation team will be able to address more confidently the impact of multiple exclusionary factors and be able to indicate whether the presence of these exclusionary factors is the determining factor in the child's difficulties. Thus, the concept underlying exclusionary factors (i.e., ecological factors) requires that these factors be considered from the beginning (when the student enrolls in the school or

---

[2] In our courses, we have used the "talk to the text (T4)" reading strategy to introduce our graduate students to our state's special education law. In this in-class activity, the students read the legal text, line by line, and jot down their thoughts and questions about what they are reading *as* they read it. They use pens and highlighters in various colors to highlight and annotate as they read. We pause periodically to review what they have learned and discuss any questions they have. You also may find this strategy useful when reading your state's special education law.

when the initial indicators of academic difficulties arise), during an official special education evaluation (as discussed here), and also at the conclusion of a comprehensive evaluation. This three-prong approach to considering these ecological factors is illustrated in Figure 7.1.

Legal Foundations of Exclusionary Factors

The Individuals with Disabilities Education and Improvement Act (IDEA, 2004) specifies that the classification SLD "does not include learning problems that are primarily the result of *visual, hearing, or motor disabilities, of mental retardation, of emotional disturbance, or of environmental, cultural, or economic disadvantage*" (emphasis added). This clause contains what has come to be known as exclusionary criteria for SLD, in that children who meet any of these criteria should not, according to federal law, be classified as having an SLD. The logic applied is that if a child meets any or all of these criteria, he or she does not have a true learning disability, but an "external" or environmental problem (e.g., poor curriculum and/or instruction) that is influencing academic difficulties and giving the student academic trouble such that the student may "look" like he or she has an SLD. This clause has caused confusion among school practitioners and researchers that has led to a great deal of variability in both research standards and school diagnostic/classification decisions (Barrera, 2006; Katsiyannis, 1990; Speece & Case, 2001) and, unfortunately, may have perpetuated an increasing number of students' inappropriate referral and placement in special education (Fletcher & Navarrete, 2003).

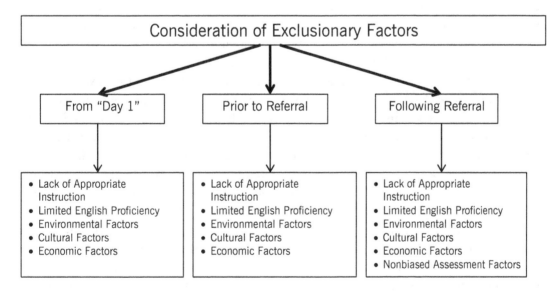

FIGURE 7.1. An overview illustrating that exclusionary factors should be considered throughout a student's educational experience, as compared to considering these factors only during special education eligibility meetings.

In addition to the exclusionary clause concerning SLD, IDEA 2004 contains exclusionary criteria that apply to all disability categories. The determinant factor for establishing *any* disability (e.g., cognitive impairment, speech–language impairment) may not be a "lack of appropriate instruction in reading, including the essential components of reading instruction, lack of instruction in math, or limited English proficiency; [or] if the child does not otherwise meet the eligibility criteria" (§ 300.306). This incredibly important and highly relevant statement for all educators speaks directly to the issue of considering the academic environment first and foremost when trying to understand a student's academic difficulties. The federal guidelines define *appropriate reading instruction* as consisting of explicit, systematic instruction in phonemic awareness, phonics, fluency, vocabulary, and comprehension (i.e., the five pillars of reading instruction). That is, for struggling students, whole-language curricular and instructional approaches that fail to incorporate the five pillars of reading instruction typically are not considered to be appropriate instruction in reading.

Furthermore, given the language in this federal statute, it is important to examine the variability in language regarding exclusionary criteria used as state standards. All 50 states use the eight criteria specified in IDEA 2004, but some states specify autism (California, Michigan, Vermont, and Wisconsin), emotional stress, difficulty adjusting to home or school (Louisiana and Vermont), lack of motivation (Louisiana and Tennessee), and temporary crisis situation (Louisiana, Tennessee, and Vermont) as *additional* criteria that can exclude a child from receiving an SLD classification (Reschly & Hosp, 2004). Apart from these additional criteria, researchers and state departments of education have noted criteria that align with but differ semantically from those specified in IDEA 2004. For example, mental retardation (MR) has been referred to as *low general intelligence, mental deficiency,* and *mental impairment.* While each of these terms suggests impaired cognitive functioning, they do not necessarily include the legal requirement for impaired adaptive functioning (i.e., standard score below 70 in addition to a standard score below 70 on a measure of intellectual ability) that is required for a diagnosis of mental retardation. In another example, emotional disturbance (ED) has been equated with emotional disorder, emotional behavioral disorders, and behavior disorder. What is most significant in this case is the tendency for researchers and state education departments frequently to interchange the terms *emotion* and *behavior.* Likewise, environmental, cultural, or economic factors can be described as socioeconomic impoverishment; socioeconomic disadvantage; cultural, social, or economic conditions; environmental, cultural, or economic influences; and racial or ethnic factors. Once again, overlap is inevitable among the environmental, cultural, economic, and social aspects of a child's life. However, schools may be neglecting aspects of a child's culture that are incongruent with the dominant culture—and possibly detrimental to that child's academic success—if culture is not specified in the language chosen for publication (i.e., state guidelines). These publications ideally guide the practices of school professionals, inform future research, and have the potential to influence legal standards. Here, IDEA 2004 is therefore used as a comparison to the literature rather than an absolute model for best practice. Moreover, given the confusion that exists in the field as to how these criteria should be applied, some researchers have suggested that semantic agreement must first exist before practical consensus can be reached.

Exclusionary criteria exist to rule out external factors as possible contributors to a child's low achievement. A number of conceptual difficulties arise with this assertion, as the nature of exclusionary criteria focuses on what children are *not* rather than providing a descriptive representation of, say, a child with an SLD. That is, classifying a child as having an SLD traditionally has entailed demonstrating a significant discrepancy (as defined by the state) between scores on an IQ test and a standardized measure of achievement. A criticism of this model is that a learning disability entails much more than simply a difference between two scores, and that demonstrating this discrepancy neither describes the specific nature of the academic difficulty nor informs appropriate intervention targets (Lyon, 2005; Speece & Case, 2001). The idea is that a child meeting any of the exclusionary criteria would be *expected* to underachieve and therefore does not have a *true* learning disability. The crux of the issue, however, is whether a child has had the *opportunity* to learn and achieve to an expected degree. If a child who has cerebral palsy has difficulty writing as the result of an associated motor impairment, he or she may likely display a significant discrepancy between scores. However, a learning disability specific to written expression is not likely warranted in this case, because this child would meet the exclusionary criterion for motor disability (and more likely be identified as meeting eligibility as a student with an orthopedic impairment). Some students may in fact have an SLD if the individualized education plan (IEP) team concludes that the student would exhibit significant discrepancy even if the exclusionary factor(s) were not present. If provided proper accommodations (i.e., adaptive pencils, deemphasis on time, closed-circuit television), it may be easier to determine a child's level of achievement and ability to learn in the absence of the exclusionary criterion. However, this is not always possible, because one cannot correct the negative effects of economic disadvantage and assess a child as if economic disadvantage were never present. Indeed, objectivity is noticeably absent when applying exclusionary criteria, because what is perceived as disadvantaged in one neighborhood could be easily regarded as typical in another (or within the same school by different professionals). But perhaps a misperception among many within the field is that exclusionary criteria exist to exclude a child from necessary services. More accurately, exclusionary criteria, as they pertain to SLD, for example, exist to exclude a child from receiving services for an SLD when, in fact, *no learning disability exists*. Procedures for identifying students with a disability should result in placing only those students who truly need special education, and not those students who would benefit from a different form of instruction, accommodation, or related service.

We must consider whether applying exclusionary criteria can reliably distinguish between low achievers who do meet exclusionary criteria and low achievers who do not. While the goal of exclusionary criteria is to rule out learning difficulties that are explained by environmental variables, almost all learning is unavoidably explained by environmental variables, such as exposure to academic materials, having adequately trained teachers, experience with relevant cognitive tasks, and so forth. Low socioeconomic status (SES) has been linked to poor educational outcomes through factors such as low birthweight, poor nutrition, poor housing quality, lack of access to health care, perinatal complications, increased exposure to lead, elevated exposure to acute and chronic stressors, growth retardation, maternal substance abuse, truancy, and homelessness (e.g., Arnold & Doctoroff, 2003; Black & Krishnakumar, 1998; Bradley & Corwyn, 2002; McLoyd, 1998). Each of these factors has the potential to affect brain development in such a way that a child's capacity to learn may be impeded. A paradox therefore arises as a child with such developmental conditions who performs poorly in school may be excluded from an SLD category on the basis of economic or environmental disadvantage, whereas a child with an identical cognitive and academic presentation may be included in this category. Poverty could serve as an exclusionary factor for a child who learns at a normal rate and demonstrates academic growth but has missed school frequently because of homelessness. This assessment of academic growth rate is therefore imperative in determining a child's capacity to learn, rather than a single assessment of academic material that a child has *already* learned. Regardless of the assessment method, under current regulations, it is difficult to determine whether a child would still show a pattern of academic strengths and weakness if such pervasive negative circumstances had not been present. This issue further highlights the idea that exclusionary criteria are not intended to prevent students from receiving services, but rather to prevent them from receiving services that are misdirected.

A primary reason for examining these issues as they relate to exclusionary criteria is the current disproportionate representation of minority groups in special education, as we discussed at the beginning of the chapter. Approximately 69% of African American and 64% of Latino children show reading skills deficits (Arnold & Doctoroff, 2003), and the high proportion of racial and ethnic/minority groups living in poverty has caused many to assume that disproportionality in special education is an artifact of poverty (Skiba, Poloni-Staudinger, Simmons, Feggins-Azziz, & Chung, 2005). Skiba et al. have suggested that poverty makes a weak and inconsistent contribution to the prediction of disproportionality across a number of disability categories, but the overlap of minority groups, poverty, and disproportionality in special education cannot be overlooked. Artiles (2003) has discussed how the educational policies of the dominant culture maintain the status quo of a minority group conforming to the dominant group's practices. Practices of institutional racism, including availability of bilingual programs, district size, and ELLs taught by unqualified teachers, exemplify how schools can construct differences to justify and enforce exclusions. Exclusions in this sense, however, are not exclusion from an SLD category, but rather the physical exclusion from a mainstream, adequate, and appropriate education. Thus, if an educational system is committed to inclusion and equality for all students, including ELLs, it must acknowledge current problems with educational categorization and realize the contexts that may contribute to students' learning problems. Governmental systems define educational policy, and these policies and standards are designed to fit a particular system. It is crucial to recognize that children within a disadvantaged group are forced to conform to a set system; the system generally will not change to accommodate a disadvantaged group. Conversely, RTI implementation emphasizes that schools must adapt to the needs of their students, including ELLs, who are the focus of this book.

Unfortunately minimal information is available for professionals to accurately and genuinely apply exclusionary criteria in a manner that is in the best educational interest of the children they serve. Categorical placement may currently be unreliable because inclusionary and exclusionary criteria are not applied consistently among professionals (Jankowski & Heartland Area Education Agency 11, 2003). Harris, Gray, Davis, Zaremba, and Argulewicz (1988) analyzed surveys of 74 school psychologists practicing across the United States and found that 37% reported that they routinely ignored or attempted to circumvent the exclusionary clause. However, this finding concerned compliance with the Education for All Handicapped Children Act of 1975, and since the survey was conducted in 1984, the finding may not reflect the current practices of school psychologists. On the contrary, the Wisconsin Department of Public Instruction (2005) reviewed 213 records of students across Wisconsin who were classified as learning disabled and found that exclusionary factors were applied and well documented in 83% of the cases. This higher percentage of compliance with the law is encouraging, but under current state and federal standards, exclusionary factors must be considered in the assessment of all children considered for special education programming.

Kavale (2005) provided a flowchart for SLD decision making in which exclusionary criteria are considered as a fifth tier of assessment activities that are completed after documenting skills deficits and determining whether there was insufficient learning efficiency and whether process deficits were present. Although exclusionary criteria appear to be given due consideration in this model, it may be more beneficial to consider exclusionary factors *before* and *while* making other determinations about a student's academic performance, rather than conceptualizing these factors *after* all other aspects of an assessment have been completed.

Exclusionary Factors Worksheets

In Chapter 3, we provided ecological factors worksheets to enable educators and RTI teams to document their attempts to address ecological factors affecting a child's academic performance. Once an official referral is made for a comprehensive and individualized evaluation, the terminology changes to *exclusionary factors*. To assist the evaluation team, we have provided exclusionary factors worksheets in Appendices 7.1–7.7 at the end of the chapter.

Concluding Comments Regarding Exclusionary Factors

Special education exclusionary factors should be considered with the following in mind:

1. Exclusionary factors are intended to make educators aware of the environmental variables (e.g., inappropriate curriculum and/or instruction) that can negatively affect a student's academic performance. When these environmental variables are identified and recognized as being detrimental, educators should then attempt to minimize their influence. Thus, exclusionary factors are intended to contribute to

the appropriate level of academic services for all students, whether through feder-
ally mandated special education services or locally based (i.e., school-level) intervention services. Although consideration of exclusionary factors was driven by legal
and ethical requirements for providing appropriate services to non-ELL students
with disabilities through special education placements, it is important to recognize
that *the placement of students without disabilities (i.e., ELLs without disabilities)
in special education programs is detrimental to the student and is an inappropriate
allocation of resources.* Thus, the presence of exclusionary factors should serve as a
motivator for the development of locally based universal and selected intervention
options to provide services more appropriately to students without disabilities who
still have significant educational and developmental needs.

2. Exclusionary factors should not be recognized as being only a special education
   issue. Instead, regular education also has to be connected to exclusionary factors
   in recognition of regular education and special education services being provided
   along a continuum and not as distinct and separate entities.

3. Although exclusionary factors should be considered for all students, they are
   indirectly connected to the issue of disproportionate representation of racially-,
   culturally-, ethnically-, economically-disadvantaged, and language-diverse students
   in special education.

4. Exclusionary factors can be considered a double-edged sword. While they are
   intended to prevent inappropriate placement of students in special education (i.e.,
   overrepresentation), concern exists that exclusionary factors can be misinterpreted
   and misused, resulting in students with disabilities being excluded from receiving
   legally entitled and mandated services (i.e., underrepresentation).

5. Exclusionary factors should be considered and interpreted in such a way that they
   increase understanding of the school-based and individual differences of the student.

6. Exclusionary factors' effects should be considered at pre- and postreferral time
   points.

Although many issues are connected to the inappropriate placement of students in special education programs, and many factors contribute to the overrepresentation of racially-,
culturally-, ethnically-, economically-disadvantaged, and language-diverse students, the
appropriate use of exclusionary factors and consideration of these factors will enhance
appropriate placement and service provision.

To illustrate these principles, we revisit Susana, who was introduced in Chapter 6,
in which we showed you her RTI program participation worksheets. In this chapter, Figures 7.2–7.8 present Susana's exclusionary factors worksheets. Even though Susana was not
referred for special education consideration, we are illustrating how these worksheets can
be exceptionally useful documentation tools for all ELLs, not just ELLs who are being considered for special education eligibility.

Exclusionary Factor 1 Worksheet: Learner Domain

Possible contributing factor	Example	Evidence source(s)	Is this factor present?
☒ Physical condition impacting learning	Student records, teacher/parent/guardian/ student report indicate: ☐ Visual impairment ☐ Hearing impairment ☐ Motor impairment ☐ Chronic health condition ☐ Transient health condition ☐ Medication side effects ☐ Other	There is no concern for physical conditions negatively affecting learning; however, according to the mother, Susana has recently been prescribed glasses for nearsightedness. It is important that the classroom teacher ensure that Susana wears her glasses as prescribed.	(NO) YES
☐ Existing disability (e.g., autism)	Student records, teacher/parent/ guardian/student report indicate presence of existing disability ☐ Other	N/A	(NO) YES
☐ Impaired cognitive functioning	Student records, teacher/parent/ guardian report indicate presence of impaired cognitive functioning ☐ Other	N/A	(NO) YES
☒ Emotional difficulties	Student records, teacher/parent/guardian/ student report indicate symptoms of: ☐ Anxiety ☐ Depression ☐ Stress ☐ Emotional withdrawal ☐ Other	There is no significant concern for emotional difficulties; however, it is important for teachers to monitor that Susana is adjusting well to being in the United States and leaving most of her family behind in Mexico. Also, Susana is being raised by a single mother (her father stayed in Mexico), so it is important to make sure there are no adverse effects on her academic functioning.	(NO) YES

(continued)

FIGURE 7.2. Exclusionary Factor 1 Worksheet: Learner Domain for Susana.

189

Possible contributing factor	Example	Evidence source(s)	Is this factor present?
☐ Behavioral difficulties	Student records, teacher/parent/guardian/ student report indicate: ☐ Office disciplinary referrals ☐ Disciplinary actions within classroom/ school setting ☐ Other	N/A	(NO) YES
☒ School adjustment difficulties	☐ Teacher/parent/guardian/student report indicating school adjustment difficulties ☐ Other	According to a student observation, it seems Susana is making friends. In a student interview, Susana noted that her best friend is Laura, another student from Mexico. The teacher also noted that Susana is making friends in her class.	(NO) YES
☒ Existence of transient or chronic crisis	☐ Death of parent/ guardian/ family member/relative/friend ☐ Parent/guardian/family member/relative/ friend illness (chronic or transient) ☒ Parental/guardian marital difficulties ☐ Other	Possible parental marital difficulties. The mother did not disclose this; however, she is separated physically from her husband, who stayed in Mexico.	(NO) YES
☐ Drug/alcohol use	☐ Teacher/parent/guardian/student report and/or records indicating possible drug/ alcohol use ☐ Other	N/A	(NO) YES

FIGURE 7.2. (continued)

190

Exclusionary Factor 2 Worksheet: Lack of Appropriate Instruction

Possible contributing factor	Example	Evidence source(s)	Is this factor present?
☒ Good attendance	☒ Full-day absences ☒ Partial-day absences ☐ Tardies ☐ In-school suspension days ☐ Other absences	Susana has missed 4 days so far, all excused due to illness. The classroom teacher spoke with her mother, Mrs. Reardon, who shared that Susana gets frequent throat infections, including strep throat.	(NO) YES
☒ Frequent mobility	☒ Number of moves ☒ Number of schools in which the student was enrolled ☒ Inconsistent academic standards at grade levels in different schools in which the student was enrolled ☐ Other	Frequent mobility is not a significant concern, but it is notable that we have very little information about her schooling in Mexico. We have no records and are not aware of what or how she was taught.	(NO) YES
☐ Use of non-scientifically based curricula	☐ Review by independent organization (e.g., What Works Clearinghouse) documenting effectiveness ☒ District/school-level data indicating curriculum effectiveness ☐ Other	Susana has participated in very high-quality, research-supported instruction since matriculating at Bay Harbor Elementary. We have adopted the Diamond RTI model and incorporate universal screening and other preventive measures to identify and address any issues early. Susana has participated in 60-minute Tier 1 core reading, as well as numerous add-on activities and programs to bolster her English language proficiency and English reading skills, including small-group instruction, individual instruction, 30 additional minutes twice a week with a reading specialist, daily ESL, instructional conversation and literature logs, and the Arthur program.	(NO) YES
☐ Academic match between grade-level curricula and student's skill level	☐ Reading ☐ Math ☐ Writing		(NO) YES

(continued)

FIGURE 7.3. Exclusionary Factor 2 Worksheet: Lack of Appropriate Instruction for Susana.

Possible contributing factor	Example	Evidence source(s)	Is this factor present?
☐ Academic mismatch between grade-level curricula and student's skill level	☒ ELP scores and instructional implications ☐ Progress monitoring data not used to determine student progress and instructional/intervention needs ☐ Reading ☐ Math ☐ Writing ☐ Other	*Not a concern; we use benchmark data to identify student academic needs and provide intervention accordingly. The classroom teacher uses her ELP scores to assist in identifying instructional materials appropriate for her ELP level.*	(NO) YES
☐ Inappropriate match between ELP level and instruction	☐ Failure to use ELP scores in considering instructional implications ☐ Use of old ELP scores in determining services ☐ Progress monitoring data not used to determine student progress and instructional/intervention needs ☐ Other	*Our instructional modifications appear to be appropriately matched to Susana's ELP based on scores from the ACCESS for ELLs.*	(NO) YES
☐ Progress monitoring procedures present	☐ Reading ☐ Math ☐ Writing		(NO) YES
☐ Quality instructional planning	☐ Reading ☐ Math ☐ Writing		(NO) YES
☐ Student behavior is not a deterrent to learning	☐ Office disciplinary referrals ☐ Suspensions from school ☐ Observations regarding time-on–off task		(NO) YES

FIGURE 7.3. *(continued)*

(continued)

Possible contributing factor	Example	Evidence source(s)	Is this factor present?
☐ Goals and objectives are aligned with student's skill level	☐ Appropriate instructional grouping ☐ Use of differentiation		(NO) YES
☒ Lack of prerequisite skills necessary to complete assigned tasks	☒ Performance in prior grade levels/courses ☒ Necessary skills identified through skills analysis ☒ Consideration of instructional ratios ☐ Other	Records and corresponding data suggest that Susana has the necessary prerequisite skills to complete assigned tasks and progress within the existing curriculum. Teacher records and report indicate that instructional ratios are appropriate.	(NO) YES
☐ Lack of progress monitoring procedures	☐ Reading ☐ Math ☐ Writing ☐ Other	Formal progress monitoring in reading, math, and writing occurs a minimum of three times per year.	(NO) YES
☐ Lack of quality instructional planning	☐ Reading ☐ Math ☐ Writing ☐ Other	Staff members meet weekly in grade-level teams to plan for instruction and monthly as a schoolwide staff.	(NO) YES
☐ Student behavior is deterrent to learning	☐ Office disciplinary referrals ☐ Suspensions from school ☐ Observations regarding time on or off task ☐ Other	There is no evidence of any behavior difficulties. Informal observations indicated that Susana is on-task most of the time.	(NO) YES
☐ Goals and objectives not aligned with student's skill level	☐ Appropriate instructional grouping ☐ Use of differentiation ☐ Other	We use local norms initially to set intervention goals; however, we strive for having all of our students eventually reach non-ELL students' (i.e., aggregate) norms so that the gap can be closed. The classroom teacher is very skilled in differentiation to meet the needs of her students.	(NO) YES

(continued)

FIGURE 7.3. *(continued)*

Possible contributing factor	Example	Evidence source(s)	Is this factor present?
Tasks relevant to the student's background and experience not utilized	☒ Instructional materials ☐ Classroom materials ☒ Assignments ☐ Other	*Some concerns were mentioned that there are a relative lack of materials available that are reflective of Susana's background and heritage.*	NO (YES)
Lack of opportunities for active responding	☐ Reading ☒ Math ☒ Writing ☐ Other	*Susana participates in several small instructional groups during which she is given ample opportunity to respond.*	(NO) YES

If you circled YES in column 4 identifying that a factor is of significant concern, continue below:

Lack of appropriate instruction domain factors present	Specific examples in which this factor is of concern	For how long has this factor been/not been present?[a]	Is this factor contributing to the student's difficulties?[b]	Would this student's difficulties continue to exist if this factor was addressed/remedied?[c]	How will this be addressed/remedied?
Tasks relevant to the student's background and experience not utilized	*Instructional materials and assignments*	1 (2) 3 4	1 (2) 3	1 (2) 3 4 5	*Ms. Beckman has begun to incorporate more materials and tasks that are relevant to Susana's experience as a Mexican student attending a U.S. school for the first time. However, Ms. Beckman acknowledged that she would like to collaborate with Ms. Rodriguez, another fourth-grade teacher, to give Susana more ideas for how to do this more frequently and with ease.*

[a]1—From the beginning of the student's educational experiences; 2—For more than one academic year but not the entire time of the student's educational experiences; 3—For only the current academic year; 4—Recently (not present at beginning of academic year but began at some point after the beginning of the year).

[b]1—Yes; 2—Partially; 3—No.

[c]1—Yes, definitely; 2—Yes, the student's difficulties would decrease as a result but would still remain significant; 3—The student's difficulties would decrease, but it is unknown to what degree the difficulties would still be present; 4—No, the removal of this factor would make a significant difference in the child's difficulties; 5—No, the removal of this factor would result in the student's difficulties no longer being present.

FIGURE 7.3. *(continued)*

Exclusionary Factor 3 Worksheet: Core Curriculum

Possible contributing factor	Examples	Evidence source(s)	Is this factor a significant concern?
☐ Use of non-scientifically based curriculum	☒ Review by independent organization (e.g., What Works Clearinghouse) documenting effectiveness ☒ District/school-level data indicating curriculum effectiveness ☐ Other	Core curriculum is research-based, focusing on the Big Five. Additionally, Susana participated in Tier 2 interventions that included repeated readings with error correction and incremental rehearsal (for English vocabulary).	(NO) YES
☐ Lack of data-based process to document ongoing effectiveness of curriculum	☒ Percentage of students at proficient/nonproficient categories ☒ Performance of student subgroups ☐ Other	District-level data suggest that all student groups appear to be making adequate progress.	(NO) YES
☐ Lack of consistency in curriculum between grade levels	☐ Reading ☐ Math ☐ Writing ☐ Other	Current district curricula are vertically aligned. However, Susana's educational records from some of her prior schools have not been located, so it is possible that there was not consistency in the past.	(NO) YES
☐ Insufficient opportunity to respond	☐ Reading ☐ Math ☐ Writing ☐ Other	Informal observations and teacher report indicate that Susana is given opportunities to respond throughout the day. Her teacher is making a concerted effort to give her extra opportunities.	(NO) YES

(continued)

FIGURE 7.4. Exclusionary Factor 3 Worksheet: Core Curriculum for Susana.

Possible contributing factor	Examples	Evidence source(s)	Is this factor a significant concern?
☐ Lack of frequent formative assessment and progress monitoring	☐ Reading ☐ Math ☐ Writing ☐ Other	In reading, progress is monitored each Friday with an R-CBM probe before the start of the intervention. Flashcards in the Incremental Rehearsal portion of the intervention are used to determine percent correct. Math and writing are monitored in multiple ways during the week.	(NO) YES
☐ Lack of multi-tiered intervention opportunities	☐ Reading ☐ Math ☐ Writing ☐ Other	Throughout the current academic year, Susana has received multiple supplemental and tiered interventions.	(NO) YES
☐ Failure to use accommodations when appropriate	☐ Reading ☐ Math ☐ Writing ☐ Other	Accommodations do not appear to be necessary.	(NO) YES
☐ Student's language skills (first vs. second language) do not allow for adequate comprehension of content	☐ Reading ☐ Math ☐ Writing ☐ Other	Based on teacher report and student ACCESS for ELL scores, Susana appears to have strong English listening and speaking skills. Her English skills in reading and writing are relatively lower than her oral English skills.	(NO) YES
☐ Lack of evidence regarding language instructional model effectiveness	☐ Reading ☐ Math ☐ Writing ☐ Other	District-level data suggest that ELL students are making adequate progress as a group. Susana's ACCESS for ELLs data show that she has been making progress each year toward English language proficiency.	(NO) YES

FIGURE 7.4. (continued)

Exclusionary Factor 4 Worksheet: Classroom/School Disadvantage

Possible contributing factor	Example	Evidence source(s)	Is this factor a significant concern?
☐ Use of non-scientifically based curriculum	☐ Review by independent organization (e.g., What Works Clearinghouse) documenting effectiveness ☐ District/school-level data indicating curriculum effectiveness	Core curriculum is research-based, focusing on the Big Five. Additionally, Susana participated in Tier 2 interventions that included repeated readings with error correction and incremental rehearsal (for English vocabulary).	(NO) YES
☐ Lack of appropriately trained teachers	☐ Evidence of teacher certifications, including bilingual staff	Susana's classroom teacher is certified by the state and is known as a great teacher.	(NO) YES
☐ Lack of bilingual programs/quality	☐ Language instructional model ☐ District/school-level data regarding effectiveness of language instructional model	District-level data suggest that the programs in place are effective, as most ELLs make adequate progress each year.	(NO) YES
☐ Large class sizes	☐ District/school records	The school's class sizes meet the state's recommendations.	(NO) YES
☐ Lack of technology use in classroom	☐ District/school records ☐ Teacher report	Susana's classroom has significant amount of technology available in it, including computers, a smartboard, and high speed internet access. She is able to access numerous educational software programs when the schedule allows.	(NO) YES
☐ Lack of schoolwide behavior program	☐ Schoolwide and classroom behavioral data	The school has been implementing PBIS for the past 4 years. Ongoing review of schoolwide data show a low level of behavioral difficulties.	(NO) YES
☐ Lack of clear classroom rules and routines	☐ Schoolwide and classroom behavioral data	Data do not show any pattern of students with behavioral difficulties. There is no evidence that Susana has any behavior difficulties. Informal observations indicated that Susana is on-task most of the time, as are the majority of her classmates.	(NO) YES

FIGURE 7.5. Exclusionary Factor 4 Worksheet: Classroom/School Disadvantage for Susana.

Exclusionary Factor 5 Worksheet: Cultural Factors

Possible contributing factor	Example	Evidence source(s)	Is this factor a significant concern?
☐ Conflicting educational and behavioral expectations between students and/or parents/guardians and school	☐ School reports apparent lack of parental interest in student's educational performance ☐ Parents/guardians report lack of understanding on part of school ☐ Other	*Susana's mother indicated that she is very supportive of the procedures and policies in place at the school.*	(NO) YES
☐ Lack of communication or miscommunication between parents and school	☐ School reports limited follow-up from student's parents/guardians ☐ Parents/guardians report lack of communication from school from school ☐ Other	*Susana's school records, as well as parent and teacher report, indicate that communication occurs frequently between home and school. Susana's mother indicated that she is pleased with the communication between her and the teacher.*	(NO) YES
☐ Limited parental involvement in school due to cultural and communication barriers	☐ Parents/guardians indicate importance of other expectations in place of or in addition to education ☐ Parents/guardians indicate limited desire to be involved in school activities ☐ Parents/guardians indicate barriers to being involved with school activities ☐ School indicates limited success in actively involving parents/guardians ☐ Other	*Susana's mother has attended all parent–teacher conferences and also has attended a number of the academic academies that occur during the evening.*	(NO) YES

(continued)

FIGURE 7.6. Exclusionary Factor 5 Worksheet: Cultural Factors for Susana.

Possible contributing factor	Example	Evidence source(s)	Is this factor a significant concern?
☐ Limited exposure and opportunities to learn in previous educational settings	☐ Student records indicate a lack of quality educational experiences in other schools and/or countries ☐ Student's prior educational experiences were in a foreign country where education system is not strong ☐ Other	*Little is known about previous educational setting; however, Susana comes to us able to read and write in Spanish, so there was some sound instruction in the native country.*	(NO) YES
☒ Use of assessments not validated for use with student characteristics (e.g., language)	☐ Use of inadequate or outdated scores to determine instruction, intervention, and/or services ☒ Assessment of achievement in language other than student's first language ☐ Record of prior evaluations with inadequate consideration of language/cultural factors ☐ Other	*A number of informal and formal assessments are used within Susana's classroom. The ongoing progress monitoring procedures appear to be appropriate for use with ELLs.*	(NO) YES

FIGURE 7.6. *(continued)*

199

Exclusionary Factor 6 Worksheet: Economic Factors

Possible contributing factor	Example	Evidence source(s)	Is this factor a significant concern?
☒ Single-parent/ guardian household	☐ Parent/guardian/student report suggests difficulties with parent/guardian assisting with homework activities due to limited time availability ☐ Other	Mother and father separated (father remains in Mexico while mother is raising Susana and her sister on her own).	NO (YES)
☒ Parent(s) work multiple jobs/work during times when student is at home	☐ Parent/guardian/student report suggests difficulties with parent/guardian assisting with homework activities due to limited time availability ☐ Other	Mother works very long hours to make ends meet. Susana participates in before and after school child care at the local park.	NO (YES)
☐ Exposure to community violence/crime	☐ Parent/guardian/student report that access to community resources is limited due to concerns regarding violence/crime ☐ Other	No indicators of being exposed to violence/crime	(NO) YES
☐ Homelessness and/or frequent mobility	☐ Parent/guardian/student report and/or records suggest lack of stability in prior educational experiences ☐ Other	Although Susana has attended a number of different schools, her mobility is not extremely high. No evidence of not having housing.	(NO) YES
☐ Lack of health care and other health-related services	☐ Lack of insurance ☐ Limited access to community health resources (e.g., physical, mental health) ☐ Other	Susana and her family are reported to have appropriate health and dental insurance and a history of accessing these services.	(NO) YES
☐ Possible lack of appropriate nutrition	☐ Lack of nutrition leading to increased illness ☐ Lack of nutrition leading to student difficulties in maintaining attention	There is no evidence that Susana does not have access to appropriate nutrition.	(NO) YES

(continued)

FIGURE 7.7. Exclusionary Factor 6 Worksheet: Economic Factors for Susana.

Possible contributing factor	Example	Evidence source(s)	Is this factor a significant concern?
□ Limited community resources or limited access to community resources	□ Parent/guardian/student report that access to community resources (e.g., library, afterschool programs, YMCA) is limited □ Other	Susana has access to school and local libraries and is reported to access these services. She also attends before school and afterschool activities.	(NO) YES
□ Student employment	□ Parent/guardian/student report that student works on evenings and/or weekends	N/A	(NO) YES

If you circled YES in column 4 identifying that a factor is of significant concern, continue below:

Economic domain factors present	Specific examples in which this factor is of concern	For how long has this factor not been present?[a]	Is this factor contributing to the student's difficulties?[b]	Would this student's difficulties continue to exist if this factor was addressed/ remedied?[c]	How will this be addressed/remedied?
Single-parent/ guardian household	Because of the single parent status of the household, Susana's mother has to work long hours.	1 (2) 3 4	1 (2) 3	1 (2) 3 4 5	The district social worker will make periodic contact with Susana's mother to ascertain possible community resource needs.
Parent(s) work multiple jobs/work during times when student is at home	Susana's mother has to work long hours, so there are periods where Susana and her sister are home alone.	1 (2) 3 4	1 (2) 3	1 (2) 3 4 5	The district social worker will make periodic contact with Susana's mother to ascertain possible community resource needs.

[a]1—From the beginning of the student's educational experiences; 2—For more than one academic year but not the entire time of the student's educational experiences; 3—For only the current academic year; 4—Recently (not present at beginning of academic year, but began at some point after the beginning of the year).

[b]1—Yes; 2—Partially; 3—No.

[c]1—Yes, definitely; 2—Yes, the student's difficulties would decrease as a result but still remain significant; 3—The student's difficulties would decrease, but it is unknown to what degree the difficulties would still be present; 4—No, the removal of this factor would make a significant difference in the child's difficulties; 5—No, the removal of this factor would result in the student's difficulties no longer being present.

FIGURE 7.7. (*continued*)

Exclusionary Factor 7 Worksheet: Environmental Factors

Possible contributing factor	Example	Evidence source(s)	Is this factor a significant concern?
☐ Difficulties in parents/guardians being actively engaged in student's education	☐ Attendance at parent–teacher conferences ☐ Attendance at school activities (e.g., math night, science night) ☐ Responsiveness to school notes, messages, etc. ☐ Communication from school to home and from home to school ☐ Evidence of parental monitoring of home work assignments	Multiple indicators suggest that Susana's mother is highly engaged with the school.	(NO) YES
☐ Student has significant responsibilities at home that detract from school performance	☐ Single-parent household ☐ Existence of household member with chronic illness, disability, etc. ☐ Presence of younger siblings whose care requires student's assistance ☐ Other	Parent and student report indicate that Susana has plenty of time to complete homework, practice her reading and writing, etc.	(NO) YES
☐ Limited access to books, games, computers, and other resources at home	☐ Limited access to educational materials at home	Family does not have a computer at home, but they do have a library card and can access the computers (and Internet) that is provided free of charge.	(NO) YES
☐ Limited community resources or limited access to community resources	☐ Limited access to educational materials in community ☐ Limited access to libraries, afterschool programs, YMCA, etc. ☐ Other	Susana has access to school and local libraries and is reported to access these services. She also attends before and after school activities.	(NO) YES
☐ Student employment	☐ Parent/guardian/student report that student works on evenings and/or weekends	N/A	(NO) YES

FIGURE 7.8. Exclusionary Factor 7 Worksheet: Environmental Factors for Susana.

FORMAL EVALUATION CONSIDERATIONS

Parental Consent and Explaining the Evaluation Process to Parents

When a student has been referred for a special education evaluation, written consent from the parent or guardian is necessary. Please remember that consent for evaluation does not constitute consent for services, which requires a separate consent. Parents who are unfamiliar with the education system in the United States and/or speak little English may have a difficult time understanding what is being asked of them in the permission form. Since the student has participated in a prereferral process as part of the RTI program, securing written consent for the special education evaluation should certainly not be the first contact education professionals have with the parents or guardians. In this book, we urge education professionals to offer ELLs intense educational services at Tiers 2 and 3, because ELLs can benefit from all the additional instructional support available in a school. Moreover, frequent progress monitoring and parent progress reports should have been provided before the request for referral for special education evaluation. Nevertheless, the process and purpose of special education evaluation should be carefully and fully explained to the parents prior to obtaining their consent. A set of translated forms should be readily available. When possible and necessary, an interpreter can help in this process as well.

Nondiscriminatory Assessment of ELL Students

In addition to the documentation (e.g., observations, interviews, response-to-intervention data) collected using the worksheets presented in Chapter 6, students who are referred for special education evaluation are assessed further in an attempt to pinpoint the origin of their difficulties. Federal law is clear: Assessment instruments and methods used with ELLs must be nonbiased and nondiscriminatory. However, this is no easy task, particularly given the shortage of education professionals who are neither proficient in a language other than English nor have the appropriate professional training to conduct nondiscriminatory assessments (Chabon, Esparza-Brown & Gildersleeve-Neumann, 2010). Assessments at this level are generally administered, scored, and interpreted by evaluation specialists, including school psychologists, speech–language pathologists, and occupational therapists. However, it is imperative to make clear that evaluation is a multidisciplinary team process, of which the evaluation specialist is only a part. Additionally, the multidisciplinary team includes the parent or guardian. Here, we focus primarily on the assessments and procedures for which a school psychologist most likely would be responsible.

Administering Standardized Tests, Including Cognitive Tests, to ELLs

IDEA (2004) requires that students referred for a special education evaluation be assessed "in all areas related to the suspected disability, including, if appropriate, health, vision, hearing, social and emotional status, general intelligence, academic performance, communicative status, and motor abilities" (34 CFR Sec. 300.304). Most school psychologists include intelligence test and standardized achievement test scores in their evaluation reports of ELLs being considered for special education eligibility (Figueroa & Newsome, 2006). However, it is *not* a legal requirement (IDEA, 2004) to assess cognitive functioning, or IQ, in order to determine whether a student meets eligibility for an SLD. Unfortunately, we have encountered great confusion in the field about this important legal fact. Thus, let us reiterate: Unless indicated otherwise by your state's special education laws, you do *not* need to administer an IQ test to *any* student in order to make an eligibility decision about presence of an SLD. However, it is at the discretion of the school psychologist to determine which assessments are appropriate for individual students and which ones will yield the most useful information.

Developmental History and Educational Chronicle from Birth to Present

Thorough evaluation for special education consideration must include a comprehensive developmental history. For many ELLs, especially newcomers and those who have lived outside of the United States prior to attending a U.S. school, it is imperative to make every effort to obtain a detailed educational chronicle for that student. We recommend using the questions provided by Rhodes et al. (2005) as a springboard for gaining this information.

TABLE 7.1. General Educational Background History

1. Did child start his or her formal schooling in the United States? If no, proceed to the following questions.

2. How many years did the child attend school in his or her native country?

3. How is school structured in the child's native country? Ask parents to describe a typical school day in their native country.

4. Are there differences between the school in the native country and that in the United States? If yes, describe these differences and consider how these differences might affect the student's performance.

5. What do we know about the language system used in the native country? For example, does it have a written form and is it read from left to right, or vice versa?

6. Was the school that the child attended in his or her native country located in an urban or a rural area?

7. Did the child regularly attend school in his or her native country?

8. Did the student evidence any academic difficulties/problems while attending school in his or her native country?

9. Do parents have written documentation about their child's school performance in their native country? Have these been translated and reviewed?

Note. Adapted from Rhodes, Ochoa, and Ortiz (2005). Copyright 2005 by The Guilford Press. Adapted by permission.

This information can be obtained by review of the student's educational records and/or interview with the parent/guardian. Table 7.1 lists these questions.

Translators and Interpreters

In many cases, inclusion of interpreters (i.e., people who interpret orally) and translators (i.e., people who translate written text) is an essential component for ensuring that your materials and procedures at all stages of the RTI model, including the evaluation, are culturally appropriate and sensitive. Whenever possible, documents that are sent home to parents (e.g., progress monitoring reports) should be provided in the language in which the parents are proficient. Likewise, qualified interpreters should be chosen to assist in parent data-shares and other parent–teacher meetings and conversations. Selecting appropriate and qualified interpreters and translators can be a tricky issue. First and foremost, we recommend *not* using children (e.g., older child in the family or other children in the school) as interpreters or translators. The potential for miscommunication is great, and the confidential nature of the evaluation and assessment process simply makes it inappropriate to consider using a student as the interpreter. Furthermore, according to Rhodes et al. (2005), interpreters must be able to stay neutral and adhere to ethical guidelines concerning confidentiality sensitivity.

BEST PRACTICES IN WRITING PSYCHOEDUCATIONAL REPORTS

This section is geared primarily for the school psychologist, speech–language pathologist, or educational diagnostician who typically conducts the formal (and to a large extent the informal) assessment and data-gathering procedures *during* the special education evaluation. One of the last activities in the special education evaluation process is writing a report with all the information, including additional assessment information, which has been gathered both *prior* to the referral *and during* the evaluation process. Although shifts in the role of school psychologists have helped the profession move away from the traditional "test and place" role, writing evaluation reports continues to be an important aspect of what school psychologists do; nonetheless, there are few definitive sources providing guidelines for good report writing and there are no national standards for writing or evaluating psychoeducational reports (Brown-Chidsey & Steege, 2005). One criterion on which all education professionals can agree, however, is that psychoeducational reports ought to be "readily understood by the intended recipient," and that school psychologists who write reports should "adequately interpret information so that the recipient can better help the child or other clients" (Jacob & Hartshorne, 2003, p. 97). Indeed, teachers appreciate reports that (1) contain a variety of recommendations specific to the child who is being evaluated, (2) do not make liberal use of psychological jargon, and (3) unmistakably answer the referral question in plain language (D'Amato & Dean, 1987). Whenever possible, we recommend professionally translating reports so parents who are not native English speakers can understand their child's evaluation report.

Writing Psychoeducational Reports for ELLs

In addition to adhering to ethical and legal best practices in writing a psychoeducational report for any student, Páez (2004) also recommends that school psychologists and others plan for a more expansive evaluation process for ELLs than that used for evaluating native English-speaking students. Páez suggests three areas specifically that need to be considered so the evaluations of ELLs are deemed culturally appropriate: (1) allow more time, (2) include alternative procedures, and (3) include additional interpretation questions. According to Páez, and based our own experience, it simply takes longer to do a thorough evaluation of ELL students. In addition to assessing language proficiency, it is essential to document very thoroughly an educational timetable from birth to the present, especially for students who have attended school in another country and those who have moved in and out of schools in the United States. The educational chronology included in a report can be critical in arriving at the eventual conclusions to identify or not identify a student with a disability. Evaluations of ELLs also may very likely involve alternative, authentic, nonverbal, and informal assessment methods that require more time than does administration of traditional standardized assessments. Finally, Páez, suggests including a discussion in the report on language acquisition and the roles of language in the student's past and current educational standing, and the role of cultural issues (e.g., acculturative stress, level of acculturation) in the student's current academic difficulties. School psychologists and other evaluation specialists need to be very careful that they are following federal and state legal guidelines in their evaluations of ELL students. Roseberry-McKibbin and O'Hanlon (2005) succinctly summarize legal considerations for evaluating ELLs in a nondiscriminatory manner (p. 180):

1. Testing and evaluation materials and procedures must be selected and administered in a nondiscriminatory manner.
2. Testing and evaluation materials must be provided and administered in the language or other mode of communication in which the child is most proficient.
3. Tests must be administered to a child with a motor, speech, hearing, visual, or other communication disability, or to a bilingual child, so as to reflect accurately the child's ability in the area tested rather than the child's impaired communication skill or limited English language skill.
4. Accommodations may include alternative forms of assessment and evaluation.

Figueroa and Newsome (2006) examined 19 psychological reports of ELLs across five different school districts in California that were written for the purpose of determining special education eligibility. The authors carefully examined the report writers' (all school psychologists) explicit application of professional and legal specifications within their reports.

Figueroa and Newsome developed and used a checklist to determine the extent of the use of these professional and legal directives. The checklist focuses on ensuring that report writers include information about the impact of past and current instructional programs, family background, and adaptive behavior on a student's current academic functioning. Perhaps not surprisingly, Figueroa and Newsome found that school psychologists *rarely* adhered to the legal and professional guidelines for writing ELL reports for special education consideration. This is a very disturbing finding, and we strongly urge you to make sure you familiarize yourself with your state's guidelines for conducting special education evaluations and writing reports for ELLs.

APPENDIX 7.1

Exclusionary Factor 1 Worksheet: Learner Domain

Possible contributing factor	Example	Evidence source(s)	Is this factor present?
☐ Physical condition impacting learning	Student records, teacher/parent/guardian/ student report indicate: ☐ Visual impairment ☐ Hearing impairment ☐ Motor impairment ☐ Chronic health condition ☐ Transient health condition ☐ Medication side effects ☐ Other		NO YES
☐ Existing disability (e.g., autism)	☐ Student records, teacher/parent/ guardian/student report indicate presence of existing disability ☐ Other		NO YES
☐ Impaired cognitive functioning	☐ Student records, teacher/parent/ guardian report indicate presence of impaired cognitive functioning ☐ Other		NO YES

(continued)

Exclusionary Factor 1 Worksheet: Learner Domain *(page 2 of 3)*

Possible contributing factor	Example	Evidence source(s)	Is this factor present?
☐ Emotional difficulties	Student records, teacher/parent/guardian/student report indicate symptoms of: ☐ Anxiety ☐ Depression ☐ Stress ☐ Emotional withdrawal ☐ Other		NO YES
☐ Behavioral difficulties	Student records, teacher/parent/guardian/student report indicate: ☐ Office disciplinary referrals ☐ Disciplinary actions within classroom/school setting ☐ Other		NO YES
☐ School adjustment difficulties	Teacher/parent/guardian/student report indicating school adjustment difficulties ☐ Other		NO YES
☐ Existence of transient or chronic crisis	☐ Death of parent/ guardian/ family member/relative/friend ☐ Parent/guardian/family member/relative/friend illness (chronic or transient) ☐ Parental/guardian marital difficulties ☐ Other		NO YES
☐ Drug/alcohol use	☐ Teacher/parent/guardian/student report and/or records indicating possible drug/alcohol use ☐ Other		NO YES

(continued)

209

Exclusionary Factor 1 Worksheet: Learner Domain *(page 3 of 3)*

If you circled YES in column 4 identifying that a factor is of significant concern, continue below:

Learner domain factors present	Specific examples in which this factor is of concern	For how long has this factor been present?[a]	Is this factor contributing to the student's difficulties?[b]	Would this student's difficulties continue to exist if this factor was addressed/remedied?[c]	How will this be addressed/remedied?
		1 2 3 4	1 2 3	1 2 3 4 5	
		1 2 3 4	1 2 3	1 2 3 4 5	
		1 2 3 4	1 2 3	1 2 3 4 5	
		1 2 3 4	1 2 3	1 2 3 4 5	
		1 2 3 4	1 2 3	1 2 3 4 5	
		1 2 3 4	1 2 3	1 2 3 4 5	
		1 2 3 4	1 2 3	1 2 3 4 5	
		1 2 3 4	1 2 3	1 2 3 4 5	

[a]1—From the beginning of the student's educational experiences; 2—For more than one academic year, but not the entire time of the student's educational experiences; 3—For only the current academic year; 4—Recently (not present at beginning of academic year, but began at some point after the beginning of the year).

[b]1—Yes; 2—Partially; 3—No.

[c]1—Yes, definitely; 2—Yes, the student's difficulties would decrease as a result, but would still remain significant; 3—The student's difficulties would decrease, but it is unknown to what degree the difficulties would still be present; 4—No, the removal of this factor would make a significant difference in the child's difficulties; 5—No, the removal of this factor would result in the student's difficulties no longer being present.

APPENDIX 7.2

Exclusionary Factor 2 Worksheet: Lack of Appropriate Instruction

Possible contributing factor	Example	Evidence source(s)	Is this factor present?
☐ Good attendance	☐ Full-day absences ☐ Partial-day absences ☐ Tardies ☐ In-school suspension days ☐ Other absences		NO YES
☐ Frequent mobility	☐ Number of moves ☐ Number of schools in which the student was enrolled ☐ Inconsistent academic standards at grade levels in different schools in which the student was enrolled ☐ Other		NO YES
☐ Use of non-scientifically based curricula	☐ Review by independent organization (e.g., What Works Clearinghouse) documenting effectiveness ☐ District/school-level data indicating curriculum effectiveness ☐ Other		NO YES

(continued)

211

Exclusionary Factor 2 Worksheet: Lack of Appropriate Instruction *(page 2 of 5)*

Possible contributing factor	Example	Evidence source(s)	Is this factor present?
☐ Academic match between grade-level curricula and student's skill level	☐ Reading ☐ Math ☐ Writing		NO YES
☐ Academic mismatch between grade-level curricula and student's skill level	☐ ELP scores and instructional implications ☐ Progress monitoring data not used to determine student progress and instructional/intervention needs ☐ Reading ☐ Math ☐ Writing ☐ Other		NO YES
☐ Inappropriate match between ELP level and instruction	☐ Failure to use ELP scores in considering instructional implications ☐ Use of old ELP scores in determining services ☐ Progress monitoring data not used to determine student progress and instructional/intervention needs ☐ Other		NO YES
☐ Progress monitoring procedures present	☐ Reading ☐ Math ☐ Writing		NO YES

(continued)

Exclusionary Factor 2 Worksheet: Lack of Appropriate Instruction *(page 3 of 5)*

Possible contributing factor	Example	Evidence source(s)	Is this factor present?
□ Quality instructional planning	□ Reading □ Math □ Writing		NO YES
□ Student behavior is not a deterrent to learning	□ Office disciplinary referrals □ Suspensions from school □ Observations regarding time–on–off task		NO YES
□ Goals and objectives are aligned with student's skill level	□ Appropriate instructional grouping □ Use of differentiation		NO YES
□ Lack of prerequisite skills necessary to complete assigned tasks	□ Performance in prior grade levels/ courses □ Necessary skills identified through skills analysis □ Consideration of instructional ratios □ Other		NO YES
□ Lack of progress monitoring procedures	□ Reading □ Math □ Writing □ Other		NO YES

(continued)

Exclusionary Factor 2 Worksheet: Lack of Appropriate Instruction *(page 4 of 5)*

Possible contributing factor	Example	Evidence source(s)	Is this factor present?
☐ Lack of quality instructional planning	☐ Reading ☐ Math ☐ Writing ☐ Other		NO YES
☐ Student behavior is deterrent to learning	☐ Office disciplinary referrals ☐ Suspensions from school ☐ Observations regarding time on or off task ☐ Other		NO YES
☐ Goals and objectives not aligned with student's skill level	☐ Appropriate instructional grouping ☐ Use of differentiation ☐ Other		NO YES
☐ Tasks relevant to the student's background and experience not utilized	☐ Instructional materials ☐ Classroom materials ☐ Assignments ☐ Other		NO YES
☐ Lack of opportunities for active responding	☐ Reading ☐ Math ☐ Writing ☐ Other		NO YES

(continued)

Exclusionary Factor 2 Worksheet: Lack of Appropriate Instruction *(page 5 of 5)*

If you circled YES in column 4 identifying that a factor is of significant concern, continue below:

Lack of appropriate instruction domain factors present	Specific examples in which this factor is of concern	For how long has this factor been/not been present?[a]	Is this factor contributing to the student's difficulties?[b]	Would this student's difficulties continue to exist if this factor was addressed/remedied?[c]	How will this be addressed/remedied?
		1 2 3 4	1 2 3	1 2 3 4 5	
		1 2 3 4	1 2 3	1 2 3 4 5	
		1 2 3 4	1 2 3	1 2 3 4 5	
		1 2 3 4	1 2 3	1 2 3 4 5	
		1 2 3 4	1 2 3	1 2 3 4 5	
		1 2 3 4	1 2 3	1 2 3 4 5	
		1 2 3 4	1 2 3	1 2 3 4 5	

[a]1—From the beginning of the student's educational experiences; 2—For more than one academic year but not the entire time of the student's educational experiences; 3—For only the current academic year; 4—Recently (not present at beginning of academic year but began at some point after the beginning of the year).

[b]1—Yes; 2—Partially; 3—No.

[c]1—Yes, definitely; 2—Yes, the student's difficulties would decrease as a result but would still remain significant; 3—The student's difficulties would decrease, but it is unknown to what degree the difficulties would still be present; 4—No, the removal of this factor would make a significant difference in the child's difficulties; 5—No, the removal of this factor would result in the student's difficulties no longer being present.

Exclusionary Factor 3 Worksheet: Core Curriculum

Possible contributing factor	Examples	Evidence source(s)	Is this factor a significant concern?
☐ Use of non-scientifically based curriculum	☐ Review by independent organization (e.g., What Works Clearinghouse) documenting effectiveness ☐ District/school-level data indicating curriculum effectiveness ☐ Other		NO YES
☐ Lack of data-based process to document ongoing effectiveness of curriculum	☐ Percentage of students at proficient/nonproficient categories ☐ Performance of student subgroups ☐ Other		NO YES
☐ Lack of consistency in curriculum between grade levels	☐ Reading ☐ Math ☐ Writing ☐ Other		NO YES
☐ Insufficient opportunity to respond	☐ Reading ☐ Math ☐ Writing ☐ Other		NO YES

(continued)

Exclusionary Factor 3 Worksheet: Core Curriculum *(page 2 of 3)*

Possible contributing factor	Examples	Evidence source(s)	Is this factor a significant concern?
☐ Lack of frequent formative assessment and progress monitoring	☐ Reading ☐ Math ☐ Writing ☐ Other		NO YES
☐ Lack of multi-tiered intervention opportunities	☐ Reading ☐ Math ☐ Writing ☐ Other		NO YES
☐ Failure to use accommodations when appropriate	☐ Reading ☐ Math ☐ Writing ☐ Other		NO YES
☐ Student's language skills (first vs. second language) do not allow for adequate comprehension of content	☐ Reading ☐ Math ☐ Writing ☐ Other		NO YES
☐ Lack of evidence regarding language instructional model effectiveness	☐ Reading ☐ Math ☐ Writing ☐ Other		NO YES

(continued)

Exclusionary Factor 3 Worksheet: Core Curriculum *(page 3 of 3)*

If you circled YES in column 4 identifying that a factor is of significant concern, continue below:

Core curriculum domain factors present	Specific examples in which this factor is of concern	For how long has this factor been/not been present?[a]	Is this factor contributing to the student's difficulties?[b]	Would this student's difficulties continue to exist if this factor was addressed/remedied?[c]	How will this be addressed/remedied?
		1 2 3 4	1 2 3	1 2 3 4 5	
		1 2 3 4	1 2 3	1 2 3 4 5	
		1 2 3 4	1 2 3	1 2 3 4 5	
		1 2 3 4	1 2 3	1 2 3 4 5	
		1 2 3 4	1 2 3	1 2 3 4 5	
		1 2 3 4	1 2 3	1 2 3 4 5	
		1 2 3 4	1 2 3	1 2 3 4 5	
		1 2 3 4	1 2 3	1 2 3 4 5	
		1 2 3 4	1 2 3	1 2 3 4 5	

[a]1—From the beginning of the student's educational experiences; 2—For more than one academic year but not the entire time of the student's educational experiences; 3—For only the current academic year; 4—Recently (not present at beginning of academic year but began at some point after the beginning of the year).

[b]1—Yes; 2—Partially; 3—No.

[c]1—Yes, definitely; 2—Yes, the student's difficulties would decrease as a result but still remain significant; 3—The student's difficulties would decrease, but it is unknown to what degree the difficulties would still be present; 4—No, the removal of this factor would still be present; 4—No, the removal of this factor would make a significant difference in the child's difficulties; 5—No, the removal of this factor would result in the student's difficulties no longer being present.

Exclusionary Factor 4 Worksheet: Classroom/School Disadvantage

Possible contributing factor	Example	Evidence source(s)	Is this factor a significant concern?
☐ Use of non-scientifically based curriculum	☐ Review by independent organization (e.g., What Works Clearinghouse) documenting effectiveness ☐ District/school-level data indicating curriculum effectiveness		NO YES
☐ Lack of appropriately trained teachers	☐ Evidence of teacher certifications, including bilingual staff		NO YES
☐ Lack of bilingual programs/quality	☐ Language instructional model ☐ District/school-level data regarding effectiveness of language instructional model		NO YES

(continued)

Exclusionary Factor 4 Worksheet: Classroom/School Disadvantage *(page 2 of 3)*

Possible contributing factor	Example	Evidence source(s)	Is this factor a significant concern?
□ Large class sizes	□ District/school records		NO YES
□ Lack of technology use in classroom	□ District/school records □ Teacher report		NO YES
□ Lack of schoolwide behavior program	□ Schoolwide and classroom behavioral data		NO YES
□ Lack of clear classroom rules and routines	□ Schoolwide and classroom behavioral data		NO YES

(continued)

Exclusionary Factor 4 Worksheet: Classroom/School Disadvantage (*page 3 of 3*)

If you circled YES in column 4 identifying that a factor is of significant concern, continue below:

School/classroom domain factors present	Specific examples in which this factor is of concern	For how long has this factor not been present?[a]	Is this factor contributing to the student's difficulties?[b]	Would this student's difficulties continue to exist if this factor was addressed/remedied?[c]	How will this be addressed/remedied?
		1 2 3 4	1 2 3	1 2 3 4 5	
		1 2 3 4	1 2 3	1 2 3 4 5	
		1 2 3 4	1 2 3	1 2 3 4 5	
		1 2 3 4	1 2 3	1 2 3 4 5	
		1 2 3 4	1 2 3	1 2 3 4 5	
		1 2 3 4	1 2 3	1 2 3 4 5	
		1 2 3 4	1 2 3	1 2 3 4 5	

[a]—From the beginning of the student's educational experiences; 2—For more than one academic year but not the entire time of the student's educational experiences; 3—For only the current academic year; 4—Recently (not present at beginning of academic year, but began at some point after the beginning of the year).

[b]—Yes; 2—Partially; 3—No.

[c]—Yes, definitely; 2—Yes, the student's difficulties would decrease as a result but still remain significant; 3—The student's difficulties would decrease, but it is unknown to what degree the difficulties would still be present; 4—No, the removal of this factor would make a significant difference in the child's difficulties; 5—No, the removal of this factor would result in the student's difficulties no longer being present.

221

Exclusionary Factor 5 Worksheet: Cultural Factors

Possible contributing factor	Example	Evidence source(s)	Is this factor a significant concern?
☐ Conflicting educational and behavioral expectations between students and/or parents/ guardians and school	☐ School reports apparent lack of parental interest in student's educational performance ☐ Parents/guardians report lack of understanding on part of school ☐ Other		NO YES
☐ Lack of communication or miscommunication between parents and school	☐ School reports limited follow-up from student's parents/guardians ☐ Parents/guardians report lack of communication from school from school ☐ Other		NO YES

(continued)

Possible contributing factor	Example	Evidence source(s)	Is this factor a significant concern?
☐ Limited parental involvement in school due to cultural and communication barriers	☐ Parents/guardians indicate importance of other expectations in place of or in addition to education ☐ Parents/guardians indicate limited desire to be involved in school activities ☐ Parents/guardians indicate barriers to being involved with school activities ☐ School indicates limited success in actively involving parents/guardians ☐ Other		NO YES
☐ Limited exposure and opportunities to learn in previous educational settings	☐ Student records indicate a lack of quality educational experiences in other schools and/or countries ☐ Student's prior educational experiences were in a foreign country where education system is not strong ☐ Other		NO YES
☐ Use of assessments not validated for use with student characteristics (e.g., language)	☐ Use of inadequate or outdated scores to determine instruction, intervention, and/or services ☐ Assessment of achievement in language other than student's first language ☐ Record of prior evaluations with inadequate consideration of language/cultural factors ☐ Other		NO YES

(continued)

Exclusionary Factor 5 Worksheet: Cultural Factors *(page 3 of 3)*

If you circled YES in column 4 identifying that a factor is of significant concern, continue below:

Cultural domain factors present	Specific examples in which this factor is of concern	For how long has this factor been/not been present?[a]	Is this factor contributing to the student's difficulties?[b]	Would this student's difficulties continue to exist if this factor was addressed/remedied?[c]	How will this be addressed/remedied?
		1 2 3 4	1 2 3	1 2 3 4 5	
		1 2 3 4	1 2 3	1 2 3 4 5	
		1 2 3 4	1 2 3	1 2 3 4 5	
		1 2 3 4	1 2 3	1 2 3 4 5	
		1 2 3 4	1 2 3	1 2 3 4 5	

[a]1—From the beginning of the student's educational experiences; 2—For more than one academic year but not the entire time of the student's educational experiences; 3—For only the current academic year; 4—Recently (not present at beginning of academic year, but began at some point after the beginning of the year).

[b]1—Yes; 2—Partially; 3—No.

[c]1—Yes, definitely; 2—Yes, the student's difficulties would decrease as a result but still remain significant; 3—The student's difficulties would decrease, but it is unknown to what degree the difficulties would still be present; 4—No, the removal of this factor would make a significant difference in the child's difficulties; 5—No, the removal of this factor would result in the student's difficulties no longer being present.

Exclusionary Factor 6 Worksheet: Economic Factors

Possible contributing factor	Example	Evidence source(s)	Is this factor a significant concern?
☐ Single-parent/guardian household	☐ Parent/guardian/student report suggests difficulties with parent/guardian assisting with homework activities due to limited time availability ☐ Other		NO YES
☐ Parent(s) work multiple jobs/work during times when student is at home	☐ Parent/guardian/student report suggests difficulties with parent/guardian assisting with homework activities due to limited time availability ☐ Other		NO YES
☐ Exposure to community violence/crime	☐ Parent/guardian/student report that access to community resources is limited due to concerns regarding violence/crime ☐ Other		NO YES
☐ Homelessness and/or frequent mobility	☐ Parent/guardian/student report and/or records suggest lack of stability in prior educational experiences ☐ Other		NO YES

(continued)

Exclusionary Factor 6 Worksheet: Economic Factors *(page 2 of 3)*

Possible contributing factor	Example	Evidence source(s)	Is this factor a significant concern?
☐ Lack of health care and other health-related services	☐ Lack of insurance ☐ Limited access to community health resources (e.g., physical, mental health) ☐ Other		NO YES
☐ Possible lack of appropriate nutrition	☐ Lack of nutrition leading to increased illness ☐ Lack of nutrition leading to student difficulties in maintaining attention		NO YES
☐ Limited community resources or limited access to community resources	☐ Parent/guardian/student report that access to community resources (e.g., library, afterschool programs, YMCA) is limited ☐ Other		NO YES
☐ Student employment	☐ Parent/guardian/student report that student works on evenings and/or weekends		NO YES

(continued)

226

Exclusionary Factor 6 Worksheet: Economic Factors *(page 3 of 3)*

If you circled YES in column 4 identifying that a factor is of significant concern, continue below:

Economic domain factors present	Specific examples in which this factor is of concern	For how long has this factor not been present?[a]	Is this factor contributing to the student's difficulties?[b]	Would this student's difficulties continue to exist if this factor was addressed/remedied?[c]	How will this be addressed/remedied?
		1 2 3 4	1 2 3	1 2 3 4 5	
		1 2 3 4	1 2 3	1 2 3 4 5	
		1 2 3 4	1 2 3	1 2 3 4 5	
		1 2 3 4	1 2 3	1 2 3 4 5	
		1 2 3 4	1 2 3	1 2 3 4 5	
		1 2 3 4	1 2 3	1 2 3 4 5	
		1 2 3 4	1 2 3	1 2 3 4 5	
		1 2 3 4	1 2 3	1 2 3 4 5	

[a]1—From the beginning of the student's educational experiences; 2—For more than one academic year but not the entire time of the student's educational experiences; 3—For only the current academic year; 4—Recently (not present at beginning of academic year, but began at some point after the beginning of the year).

[b]1—Yes; 2—Partially; 3—No.

[c]1—Yes, definitely; 2—Yes, the student's difficulties would decrease as a result but still remain significant; 3—The student's difficulties would decrease, but it is unknown to what degree the difficulties would still be present; 4—No, the removal of this factor would make a significant difference in the child's difficulties; 5—No, the removal of this factor would result in the student's difficulties no longer being present.

Exclusionary Factor 7 Worksheet: Environmental Factors

Possible contributing factor	Example	Evidence source(s)	Is this factor a significant concern?
☐ Difficulties in parents/ guardians being actively engaged in student's education	☐ Attendance at parent–teacher conferences ☐ Attendance at school activities (e.g., math night, science night) ☐ Responsiveness to school notes, messages, etc. ☐ Communication from school to home and from home to school ☐ Evidence of parental monitoring of home work assignments		NO YES
☐ Student has significant responsibilities at home that detract from school performance	☐ Single-parent household ☐ Existence of household member with chronic illness, disability, etc. ☐ Presence of younger siblings whose care requires student's assistance ☐ Other		NO YES

(continued)

Exclusionary Factor 7 Worksheet: Environmental Factors *(page 2 of 3)*

Possible contributing factor	Example	Evidence source(s)	Is this factor a significant concern?
☐ Limited access to books, games, computers, and other resources at home	☐ Limited access to educational materials at home		NO YES
☐ Limited community resources or limited access to community resources	☐ Limited access to educational materials in community ☐ Limited access to libraries, afterschool programs, YMCA, etc. ☐ Other		NO YES
☐ Student employment	☐ Parent/guardian/student report that student works on evenings and/or weekends		NO YES

(continued)

Exclusionary Factor 7 Worksheet: Environmental Factors *(page 3 of 3)*

If you circled YES in column 4 identifying that a factor is of significant concern, continue below:

Environmental domain factors present	Specific examples in which this factor is of concern	For how long has this factor not been present?[a]	Is this factor contributing to the student's difficulties?[b]	Would this student's difficulties continue to exist if this factor was addressed/remedied?[c]	How will this be addressed/remedied?
		1 2 3 4	1 2 3	1 2 3 4 5	
		1 2 3 4	1 2 3	1 2 3 4 5	
		1 2 3 4	1 2 3	1 2 3 4 5	
		1 2 3 4	1 2 3	1 2 3 4 5	
		1 2 3 4	1 2 3	1 2 3 4 5	

[a]—From the beginning of the student's educational experiences; 2—For more than one academic year but not the entire time of the student's educational experiences; 3—For only the current academic year; 4—Recently (not present at beginning of academic year, but began at some point after the beginning of the year).

[b]1—Yes; 2—Partially; 3—No.

[c]1—Yes, definitely; 2—Yes, the student's difficulties would decrease as a result but still remain significant; 3—The student's difficulties would decrease, but it is unknown to what degree the difficulties would still be present; 4—No, the removal of this factor would make a significant difference in the child's difficulties; 5—No, the removal of this factor would result in the student's difficulties no longer being present.

CHAPTER 8

Next Steps

Conclusions and Directions for the Future

We began this book by articulating our belief that to be successful in the prototypical American, English-dominant public school, ELLs must not only learn communicative (i.e., social) English but they also must become proficient in English academic language. Furthermore, becoming fluent in English alone is not sufficient, as the primary goal of schooling is to enhance both short- and long-term academic success. Thus, the emphasis throughout our book has been on identifying best practices in facilitating the development of ELP *and* English language academic outcomes of ELL students. As authors of this book, our responsibility was to examine what we know about educating ELLs and attempt to identify areas in which there are sufficient data and consensus in the research to make useful and viable recommendations for practice.

Use of the scientific process to enhance knowledge is often slow, incremental, and sometimes frustrating. Results from varying studies rarely are definitive and often are contradictory (e.g., think of conflicting research regarding dietary issues!), leading to a lack of consensus regarding how best to move forward. To further complicate matters, political and economic conditions frequently muddle our understanding of issues, creating circumstances in which personal biases may influence how we interpret evidence. Even though throughout this book, we have identified what we consider to be best practices, based on research, we recognize that as the science of educating ELLs progresses, these best practices may become dated and need revision to reflect advances in our understanding of these topics. Although progress has been made since the landmark 2006 *Report of the National Literacy Panel on Language-Minority Children and Youth* (August & Shanahan, 2006), there continues to be a lack of high-quality research that addresses many of the topics of interest to the education of ELLs, and even the high-quality research that does exist is sparse compared to what we know regarding the education of native English speakers.

Thus, a concluding chapter is the natural place to ask, "Where are we now?" The answer to this question isn't easy; however, if we envision knowledge as occurring along a continuum in which "no knowledge" is to the left of the continuum and "all knowledge" is to the right, the reality is that evidence on how best to educate linguistically diverse students is likely somewhere in between the extremes of "no knowledge" and "all knowledge." We have made great strides, but there is much more progress to be made. For example, we know that strong L1 skills benefit L2 development, but we do not necessarily know what this means or the implications regarding how best to facilitate L2 development in students of differing ages who come from different environmental backgrounds and have different levels of proficiency in both L1 and L2. Similarly, we clearly have knowledge demonstrating that, for the majority of students (regardless of language status), high-quality core instruction is essential, but we do not have sufficient knowledge regarding all of the variables that actually constitute high-quality core instruction (and especially in areas outside of basic reading skills).

In the remainder of this chapter, we summarize what we have emphasized in previous chapters, including what we know so far (or at least what we think we know) about best practices for including ELLs in RTI models and what aspects of our knowledge need further development. We start with areas about which we have significant confidence based on what research and data have indicated, then follow up with questions to guide future work—both in research and in practice.

WHAT WE KNOW (OR AT LEAST WHAT WE THINK WE KNOW)

One of the areas in which we have the most comprehensive knowledge about the education of ELLs relates to their demographics. For example:

• The increasing number of ELLs in the public school system has resulted in more classroom teachers serving ELLs, thus requiring *all* educators to have skills in working with students with varying ELP levels.

• Spanish is the language spoken by approximately 70–80% of ELL students enrolled in public schools; however, this percentage varies by region and even school districts. More than 400 languages are represented in schools throughout the United States.

• Lower levels of academic achievement are associated with a wide range of adverse outcomes, including poor health, mental illness, increased incarceration rates, and decreased vocational opportunities. These outcomes, coupled with increasing matriculation of ELLs, warrants urgently that both researchers and practitioners learn what works to strengthen ELLs' achievement in school.

• There is a significant academic achievement gap between ELLs as a *group of students* and non-ELLs as a *group of students*; however, this achievement gap is based on the average performance of both groups of students. Consequently, this *group* achievement gap does not mean that every ELL student is underperforming academically.

- The use of RTI models appears to have significant potential in addressing the achievement gap issue, because RTI models facilitate the use of data to pinpoint *individual* student needs and how to meet those needs accordingly.

- Many education professionals report that they received little or insufficient training in how best to educate ELLs, leading many teachers to feel unprepared in how to teach ELLs.

  o Thus, a critical issue that *must* be addressed at the preservice level is the notion that *all* teacher education students ought to have specific training in addressing the needs of struggling readers, in using data to identify individual student needs, and in ways to apply this knowledge and these skills to working effectively with ELLs.

Our understanding of RTI, particularly with non-ELLs, continues to grow. We know that:

- Some RTI models are being implemented successfully (and others not as successfully) throughout the country. RTI is not a new concept, and like similar previous efforts rolled out in education, it focuses predominantly on a series of steps that can broadly be conceptualized as (a) problem identification, (b) problem definition, (c) selection and design of intervention plans, and (d) intervention implementation and progress monitoring (e.g., Brown-Chidsey & Steege, 2010).

- Although we have described in detail many of the components of RTI in this book, it is essential for the reader to understand that RTI is a schoolwide framework that requires an overhaul in thinking and practice if real change and sustained success are to be expected. Although we present features that can be implemented immediately (e.g., sound instructional practices, specific research-based interventions, ways to document progress), we acknowledge that all components must (eventually) be put into place so that RTI *as a holistic model* can work the way it is intended to prevent academic risk and be ameliorated at the first signs of academic struggle, especially concerning ELLs.

- Research examining the effectiveness of RTI models (i.e., program evaluation research; see Chapter 3 for exceptions) is relatively new; however, there are multiple reports of encouraging outcomes, including positive outcomes for ELLs.

- There seems to be a relatively strong consensus regarding the necessary, non-negotiable aspects of successful RTI models (see Table 3.2), and we can only reasonably presume that these aspects are the same for the successful implementation of RTI models where ELLs are concerned.

Our understanding of ELP, especially academic language proficiency, is rapidly increasing given the extensive attention that researchers, public policymakers, and a wide range of education professionals are giving to this critical variable. We know that:

• Learning Academic English is imperative for ELLs to be successful in school. Promoting Academic English in ELLs is the responsibility of *all* educators, including—and perhaps most importantly—the general education teacher.

  o We again point out that although we know that L1 bolsters gains in L2, our primary goal as educators in schools in the United States is to make sure all students, including ELLs, attain mastery of *English* academic language. It is the best hope we have for ensuring ELLs' success in and beyond school.

• There are multiple instructional English language models being implemented in schools across the country; no single model is best for all students in all academic settings.

Providing Tier 1, Tier 2, and Tier 3 Services to ELLs

The term *Tier 1* in the RTI model refers to frequent formative assessment activities and high-quality instruction for *all* students, regardless of their language status. We recognize that ELLs whose L1 is stronger have a skills set that facilitates L2 acquisition more easily than ELLs whose L1 is not well developed. Nevertheless, a discussion of how to promote and reinforce L1 is outside the scope of this book. There are many fine references available to the reader who is interested in learning more about promoting L1. Our focus in *Promoting Academic Success with English Language Learners* has been on best practices in assessment and instruction across RTI models in English, and for ELLs in particular. We know, for example that:

• Universal screening and progress monitoring are important data collection activities to be conducted with all students; however, doing so with ELLs requires special considerations (e.g., Albers & Mission, 2014).

  o It is essential to consider specific ELP levels and language of instruction when examining ELL universal screening and progress monitoring data.
  o There is an extensive research base supporting the use of CBM with non-ELLs; our knowledge regarding the use of CBM (in English) with ELLs is increasing and appears quite promising.

• High-quality core instructional practices at Tier 1 are essential for *all* students.

• A sound core curriculum in early reading instruction includes the five pillars of reading and multiple opportunities to be actively engaged in reading activities.

• There is a relative lack of research on what works for teaching ELLs to read in English, especially in comparison to what is known about teaching reading to non-ELLs. Consequently, in multiple areas, it is necessary to start with "best bets," because we have evidence that they work with non-ELLs and are therefore an optimal place to start as potential "best bets" for ELLs, too.

• Opportunity to learn, differentiation, direct instruction, and practice and corrective feedback are critical features of excellent instruction; we have evidence that they are "best bets" for instructing ELLs. Again, although these principles apply to general excellence pedagogy, we emphasize how they might be particularly important for meeting the English language and academic learning needs of ELLs.

Tiers 2 and 3 within an RTI model, in addition to the Tier 1 components of universal screening, progress monitoring, and high-quality core instruction, include more frequent progress monitoring, instructional modifications (including increased dosage), and implementation of evidence-based interventions. However, given the relative lack of research examining more intensive intervention options for ELLs, a data-based approach to service delivery, such as that used in problem-solving RTI models, is especially important when implementing RTI with ELLs. We know that the provision of Tier 2 and Tier 3 services to ELLs should:

- Increase the number of opportunities to learn and practice English language skills and English academic skills.

- Emphasize increased instructional dosage (e.g., group size, session length, number of sessions per week, and total number of sessions) based on student needs.

- Be structured around evidence-based strategies and interventions; however, given the relative lack of research in this area, determining whether a strategy or intervention is evidence based often depends on data collection to demonstrate growth or the lack thereof.

WHAT WE DON'T KNOW (YET) AND AREAS WHERE WE NEED ANSWERS

A lack of conclusive evidence in many areas leads to many questions about where we should go from here—and where more answers are needed. Again, this leads us to emphasize that this lack of evidence makes ongoing research and data collection on both individual students and groups of students (i.e., ELLs) absolutely critical. We cannot emphasize enough the importance of collecting and examining data frequently as a way to provide (at minimum) local evidence regarding the effectiveness of various instructional approaches and attempts to enhance the academic success of ELLs. Some of the unanswered questions that remain include:

- How can we expand our knowledge to have more confidence in what we know regarding characteristics of typical L2 development and what type of variation should be expected among and between ELLs?

- What specific risk factors are most relevant for ELLs, and what are the implications of these risk factors for language and academic development? How predictive are these risk factors of future difficulties (e.g., academic, psychosocial, emotional)? If these risk factors are predictive of future difficulties, how should education intervene to minimize the risk?

- How do we conduct frequent and ongoing progress monitoring of ELP? Whereas we have multiple ways to progress monitor academic areas such as reading and math, how can we conduct a similar process with regard to the ever-important concept of ELP?

- Despite our increased knowledge of BICS, CALP, and academic language, and the proliferation in the literature regarding these topics during the past couple of decades, how can we move beyond the theory of these concepts and actually use them to inform decision making (e.g., assessment and programming) in RTI models?

- How do we expand our knowledge about what sound core curricula in English look like for ELLs?

- What needs to be done to expand our knowledge regarding appropriate supplemental interventions in English for ELLs? What impact does ELP level have on the effectiveness of these interventions?

- How do we best train educators (e.g., classroom teachers, classroom assistants, student service providers [school psychologists, speech–language pathologists, social workers], and school and district administrators) to meet the language, academic, social, emotional, and behavioral needs of ELLs? What is the best way to do this at the preservice and inservice levels?

As discussed earlier, advancing knowledge via research often is a slow, incremental, and sometimes frustrating process, particularly when you, as a teacher, are the one who is expected to implement scientifically sound, evidence-based practices in the classroom. This expectation becomes even more frustrating when a limited number of such procedures is available. One of our sincere hopes in writing this book is that you will come to appreciate the implementation of RTI with ELLs as an opportunity—as compared to a mandate of some type—to enhance the services you provide your ELL students. We wholeheartedly believe that the RTI model is a teacher empowerment model. Knowledge is power, right? Well, RTI models and their various components are, by design, set up to provide you with clear information about how your students are performing, which in turn gives you clear information about how *you* are doing in your efforts at teaching your students (ELLs and non-ELLs). We truly believe that all children, and particularly ELLs, can learn and be successful when educators apply the concepts we have outlined in this book with earnestness. As our knowledge of how best to educate ELLs expands as time goes by, we will be back in touch. Until then, we wish you the best.

References

Adams, G. L., & Engelmann, S. (1996). *Research on Direct Instruction: 25 years beyond DISTAR*. Seattle, WA: Educational Achievement Systems.

Adams, M. (1990). *Beginning to read*. Cambridge, MA: MIT Press.

Aguirre-Muñoz, Z., & Amabisca, A. A. (2010). Defining opportunity to learn for English language learners: Linguistic and cultural dimensions of ELLs' instructional contexts. *Journal of Education for Students Placed at Risk, 15*, 259–278.

Albers, C. A., Elliott, S. N., Kettler, R. J., & Roach, A. T. (2013). Evaluating intervention outcomes. In R. Brown-Chidsey & K. J. Andren (Eds.), *Assessment for intervention: A problem-solving approach* (2nd ed., pp. 344–360). New York: Guilford Press.

Albers, C. A., Glover, T. A., & Kratochwill, T. R. (2007). How can universal screening enhance educational and mental health outcomes? *Journal of School Psychology, 45*, 113–116.

Albers, C. A., & Hoffman, A. (2012). Using flashcard drill methods and self-graphing procedures to improve the reading performance of ELL students. *Journal of Applied School Psychology, 28*, 367–388.

Albers, C. A., Kenyon, D. M., & Boals, T. J. (2009). Measures for determining English language proficiency and the resulting implications for instructional provision and intervention. *Assessment for Effective Intervention, 34*, 74–85.

Albers, C. A., & Kettler, R. J. (2014). Best practices in universal screening. In P. Harrison & A. Thomas (Eds.), *Best practices in school psychology: Data-based and collaborative decision making* (pp. 121–131). Bethesda, MD: National Association of School Psychologists.

Albers, C. A., & Mission, P. (2014). Universal screening of English language learners: Language proficiency and literacy. In R. J. Kettler, T. A. Glover, C. A. Albers, & K. A. Feeney-Kettler (Eds.), *Universal screening in educational settings: Evidence-based decision making for schools* (pp. 275–304). Washington, DC: American Psychological Association.

Albers, C. A., Mission, P. L., & Bice-Urbach, B. J. (2013). Considering diverse learner characteristics in problem-solving assessment. In R. Brown-Chidsey & K. J. Andren (Eds.), *Assessment for intervention: A problem-solving approach* (2nd ed., pp. 101–122). New York: Guilford Press.

Alliance for Excellent Education. (2007, February). *Urgent but overlooked: The literacy crisis among adolescent English language learners*. Washington, DC: Author.

Anstrom, K., DiCerbo, P., Butler, F., Katz, A., Millet, J., & Rivera, C. (2010). *A review of the lit-*

erature on academic English: Implications for K–12 English language learners. Arlington, VA: George Washington University Center for Equity and Excellence in Education.

Arnold, D. H., & Doctoroff, G. L. (2003). The early education of socioeconomically disadvantaged children. *Annual Review of Psychology, 54,* 517–545.

Artiles, A. J. (2003). Special education's changing identity: Paradoxes and dilemmas in views of culture and space. *Harvard Educational Review, 73*(2), 164–202.

Artiles, A. J., Rueda, R., Salazar, J., & Higareda, I. (2005). Within-group diversity in minority disproportionate representation: English language learners in urban school districts. *Exceptional Children, 71,* 283–300.

Artiles, A. J., & Trent, S. C. (1994). Overrepresentation of minority students in special education: A continuing debate. *Journal of Special Education, 27,* 410–437.

August, D., Carlo, M., Dressler, C., & Snow, C. (2005). The critical role of vocabulary development for English language learners. *Learning Disabilities Research and Practice, 20,* 50–57.

August, D., & Hakuta, K. (Eds.). (1997). *Improving schooling for language-minority children: A research agenda.* Washington, DC: National Academy Press.

August, D., & Shanahan, T. (Eds.). (2006). *Developing literacy in second-language learners: Report of the National Literacy Panel on language-minority children and youth.* Mahwah, NJ: Erlbaum.

Baker, S., Lesaux, N., Jayanthi, M., Dimino, J., Proctor, C. P., Morris, J., et al. (2014). *Teaching academic content and literacy to English learners in elementary and middle school* (NCEE 2014-4012). Washington, DC: National Center for Education Evaluation and Regional Assistance, Institute of Education Sciences, U.S. Department of Education.

Baker, S. K., & Good, R. (1995). Curriculum-based measurement of English reading with bilingual Hispanic students: A validation study with second grade students. *School Psychology Review, 24,* 561–578.

Baker, S. K., Kame'enui, E. J., & Simmons, D. C. (2002). Characteristics of students with diverse learning and curricular needs. In E. J. Kameenui, D. W. Carnine, R. C. Dixon, D. C. Simmons, & M. D. Coyne (Eds.), *Effective teaching strategies that accommodate diverse learners* (2nd ed., pp. 23–52). Upper Saddle River, NJ: Merrill/Prentice Hall.

Barnett, W. S., Yarosz, D. J., Thomas, J., Jung, K., & Blanco, D. (2007). Two-way and monolingual English immersion in preschool education: An experimental comparison. *Early Childhood Research Quarterly, 22,* 277–293.

Barrera, M. (2006). Assessment models in the identification of new or second language learners of English for special education. *Journal of Learning Disabilities, 39,* 142–156.

Batalova, J., & McHugh, M. (2010). *Number and growth of students in U.S. schools in need of English instruction.* Washington, DC: Migration Policy Institute.

Beacher, L. (2011). Differentiated instruction for English language learners: Strategies for the secondary English teacher. *Wisconsin English Journal, 53*(2), 64–73.

Begeny, J. C., Schulte, A. C., & Johnson, K. (2012). *Enhancing instructional problem solving: An efficient system for assisting struggling learners.* New York: Guilford Press.

Betts, E. A. (1939). Elements in a remedial-reading program. *American School Board Journal, 99,* 29–45.

Beyers, S., Lembke, E., & Curs, B. (2013). Social studies progress monitoring and intervention for middle school students. *Assessment for Effective Intervention, 38,* 224–235.

Black, M., & Krishnakumar, A. (1998). Children in low-income, urban settings: Interventions to promote mental health and well-being. *American Psychologist, 53,* 635–646.

Bradley, R., & Corwyn, R. (2002). Socioeconomic status and child development. *Annual Review of Psychology, 53,* 371–399.

Brock, L., Nishida, T., Chiong, C., Grimm, K., & Rimm-Kaufman, S. (2008). Children's perceptions of the classroom environment and social and academic performance: A longitudinal analysis of the contribution of the "Responsive Classroom" approach. *Journal of School Psychology, 46,* 129–149.

Brown-Chidsey, R. (2005). Academic skills are basic (to) children's personal wellness. *The Trainer's Forum, 25*(1), 4–10.

Brown-Chidsey, R., & Steege, M. W. (2005). Solution-focused psychoeducational reports. In R. Brown-Chidsey (Ed.), *Assessment for intervention: A problem-solving approach* (pp. 267–290). New York: Guilford Press.

Brown-Chidsey, R. M., & Steege, M. W. (2010). *Response to intervention: Principles and strategies for effective practice* (2nd ed.). New York: Guilford Press.

Broxterman, K., & Whalen, A. J. (2013). *RTI team building: Effective collaboration and data-based decision making.* New York: Guilford Press.

Bunch, G. C. (2013). Pedagogical language knowledge: Preparing mainstream teachers for English learners in the new standards area. *Review of Research in Education, 37,* 298–341.

Burns, M. K., Appleton, J. J., & Stehouwer, J. D. (2005). Meta-analytic review of responsiveness-to-intervention research: Examining field-based and research-implemented models. *Journal of Psychoeducational Assessment, 23,* 381–394.

Burns, M. K., & Gibbons, K. A. (2008). *Implementing response-to-intervention in elementary and secondary schools: Procedures to assure scientific-based practices.* New York: Routledge.

Burns, M. K., Haegele, K., & Petersen-Brown, S. (2014). Screening for early reading skills: Using data to guide resources and instruction. In R. J. Kettler, T. A. Glover, C. A. Albers, & K. A. Feeney-Kettler (Eds.), *Universal screening in educational Settings: Evidence-based decision making for schools* (pp. 171–197). Washington, DC: American Psychological Association.

Burns, M. K., Riley-Tillman, T. C., & VanDerHeyden, A. M. (2012). *RTI applications: Vol. 1. Academic and behavioral interventions.* New York: Guilford Press.

Calderón, M., Hertz-Lazarowitz, R., & Slavin, R. (1998). Effects of Bilingual Cooperative Integrated Reading and Composition on students making the transition from Spanish to English reading. *Elementary School Journal, 99,* 153–165.

Carlo, M. S., August, D., McLaughlin, B., Snow, C. E., Dressler, C., Lippman, D. N., et al. (2004). Closing the gap: Addressing the vocabulary needs of English-language learners in bilingual and mainstream classrooms. *Reading Research Quarterly, 39,* 188–215.

Carnine, D. W., Silbert, J., & Kame'enui, E. J. (1997). *Direct instruction reading.* Upper Saddle River, NJ: Prentice Hall.

Carver, R. P. (1994). Percentage of unknown vocabulary words in text as a function of the relative difficulty of the text: Implications for instruction. *Journal of Reading Behavior, 26,* 413–437.

Carvalho, C., Dennison, A., & Estrella, I. (2014). Best practices in the assessment of English language learners. In P. Harrison & A. Thomas (Eds.), *Best practices in school psychology: Foundations* (pp. 75–87). Bethesda, MD: National Association of School Psychologists.

Centers for Disease Control and Prevention (CDC). (2005). *Healthy people 2010.* Atlanta, GA: Author.

Chabon, S., Esparza-Brown, J., & Gildersleeve-Neumann, C. (2010). Ethics, equity, and English language learners: A decision-making framework. *ASHA Leader, 15*(9), 10–13.

Chicago Public Schools. (2012). *Chicago Public Schools amended budget 2012–13.* Chicago: Author.

Chinn, P. C., & Hughes, S. (1987). Representation of minority students in special education classes. *Remedial and Special Education, 8,* 41–46.

Clarke, B., Doabler, C. T., & Nelson, N. J. (2014). Best practices in mathematics assessment and intervention with elementary students. In P. Harrison & A. Thomas (Eds.), *Best practices in school psychology: Data-based and collaborative decision making* (pp. 219–232). Bethesda, MD: National Association of School Psychologists.

Clarke, B., Haymond, K., & Gersten, R. (2014). Mathematics screening measures for the primary grades. In R. J. Kettler, T. A. Glover, C. A. Albers, & K. A. Feeney-Kettler (Eds.), *Universal screening in educational settings: Evidence-based decision making for schools* (pp. 199–221). Washington, DC: American Psychological Association.

Coleman, R., & Goldenberg, C. (2012). The Common Core challenge for ELLs. *Principal Leadership, 12*(6), 46–51.

Collier, V. P., & Thomas, W. P. (2004). The astounding effectiveness of dual language education for all. *NABE Journal of Research and Practice, 2*(1), 1–20.

Crosson, A. C., & Lesaux, N. K. (2010). Revisiting assumptions about the relationship of fluent reading to comprehension: Spanish speakers' text-reading fluency in English. *Reading and Writing, 23*, 475–494.

Cummins, J. (1984). *Bilingual education and special education: Issues in assessment and pedagogy.* San Diego: College Hill.

Cummins, J. (2000). *Language, power and pedagogy: Bilingual children in the crossfire.* Tonawanda, NY: Multilingual Matters.

Daly, E. J., III, Chafouleas, S., & Skinner, C. H. (2004). *Interventions for reading problems: Designing and evaluating effective strategies.* New York: Guilford Press.

Daly, E. J., Witt, J. C., Martens, B. K., & Dool, E. J. (1997). A model for conducting a functional analysis of academic performance problems. *School Psychology Review, 26*, 554–574.

D'Amato, R. C., & Dean, R. S. (1987). Psychological reports, individual education programs, and daily lesson plans: Are they related? *Professional School Psychology, 2*, 93–101.

Deno, S. L. (2013). Problem-solving assessment. In R. Brown-Chidsey & K. J. Andren (Eds.), *Assessment for intervention: A problem-solving approach* (2nd ed., pp. 10–36). New York: Guilford Press.

Dixon, L. Q., Zhao, J., Shin, J. Y., Wu, S., Su, J. H., Burgess-Brigham, R., et al. (2012). What we know about second language acquisition: A synthesis from four perspectives. *Review of Educational Research, 82*, 5–60.

Donovan, M. S., & Cross, C. T. (2002). *Minority students in special and gifted education.* Washington, DC: National Academy Press.

Durlack, J. A., & DuPre, E. P. (2008). Implementation matters: A review on the influence of implementation on program outcomes and the factors affecting implementation. *American Journal of Community Psychology, 41*, 327–350.

Echevarria, J., Vogt, M. E., & Short, D. (2008). *Making content comprehensible for English language learners: The SIOP® Model* (3rd ed.). Boston: Allyn & Bacon.

Escamilla, K. (2009). English language learners: Developing literacy in second-language learners— Report of the National Literacy Panel on language-minority children and youth. *Journal of Literacy Research, 41*, 432–452.

Esquivel, G. B., & Keitel, M. A. (1990). Counseling immigrant children in the schools. *Elementary School Guidance and Counseling, 24*, 213–221.

Fagella-Luby, M. N., & Deshler, D. D. (2008). Reading comprehension in adolescents with LD: What we know; what we *need* to learn. *Learning Disabilities Research and Practice, 23*(2), 70–78.

Federal Interagency Forum on Child and Family Statistics. (2012). *America's children in brief: Key national indicators of well-being, 2012.* Washington, DC: U.S. Government Printing Office.

Federal Interagency Forum on Child and Family Statistics. (2013). *America's children: Key national indicators of well-being.* Washington, DC: U.S. Government Printing Office.

Figueroa, R. A., & Newsome, P. (2006). The diagnosis of LD in English learners: Is it nondiscriminatory? *Journal of Learning Disabilities, 39*, 206–214.

Fletcher, T. V., & Navarrete, L. A. (2003). Learning disabilities or difference: A critical look at issues associated with misidentification and placement of Hispanic students in special education programs. *Rural Special Education Quarterly, 22*(4), 37–46.

Foorman, B. R. (2007). Primary prevention in classroom reading. *Teaching Exceptional Children, 39*(5), 25–30.

Ford, D. Y. (1998). The underrepresentation of minority students in gifted education: Problems and promises in recruitment and retention. *Journal of Special Education, 32,* 4–14.

Francis, D., Rivera, M., Lesaux, N., Kieffer, M., & Rivera, H. (2006a). *Practical guidelines for the education of English language learners: Research-based recommendations for instruction and academic interventions.* Portsmouth, NH: RMC Research Corporation, Center on Instruction.

Francis, D., Rivera, M., Lesaux, N., Kieffer, M., & Rivera, H. (2006b). *Practical guidelines for the education of English language learners: Research-based recommendations for serving adolescent newcomers.* Portsmouth, NH: RMC Research Corporation, Center on Instruction.

Frasco, R. D. (2008). Effectiveness of *Reading First* for English language learners: Comparison of two programs (Doctoral dissertation, Walden University). *Dissertation Abstracts International, 69*(03A), 141–879.

Fu, D. (2004). Teaching ELL students in regular classrooms at the secondary level. *Voices from the Middle, 11*(4), 8–15.

Fuchs, D., & Deshler, D. D. (2007). What we need to know about responsiveness to intervention (and shouldn't be afraid to ask). *Learning Disabilities Research and Practice, 22,* 129–136.

Fuchs, D., & Fuchs, L. (2005, May). *Operationalizing Response-to-Intervention (RTI) as a method of LD identification.* Retrieved from *www.state.tn.us/education/speced/doc/sefuopertifaq.pdf.*

Fuchs, D., Morgan, P. L., Young, C. L., & Rise, T. (2003). Responsiveness-to-intervention: Definitions, evidence, and implications for the learning disabilities construct. *Learning Disabilities Research and Practice, 18*(3), 157–171.

Fuchs, L., & Fuchs, D. (2006). A framework for building capacity for responsiveness to intervention. *School Psychology Review, 35,* 621–626.

Fuchs, L. S., Fuchs, D., Hamlett, C. L., Walz, L. & Germann, G. (1993). Formative evaluation of academic progress: How much growth can we expect? *School Psychology Review, 22,* 27–48.

Furrer, C., & Skinner, E. (2003). Sense of relatedness as a factor in children's academic engagement and performance. *Journal of Educational Psychology, 95,* 148–162.

Gay, G. (2010). *Culturally responsive teaching* (2nd ed.). New York: Teachers College Press.

Genesee, F., Lindholm-Leary, K., Saunders, W. M., & Christian, D. (Eds.). (2006). *Educating English language learners: A synthesis of research evidence.* New York: Cambridge University Press.

Gersten, R., Baker, S. K., Shanahan, T., Linan-Thompson, S., Collins, P., & Scarcella, R. (2007). *Effective literacy and English language instruction for English learners in the elementary grades.* Washington, DC: National Center for Education Evaluation and Regional Assistance, Institute of Education Sciences, U.S. Department of Education.

Gersten, R., Beckmann, S., Clarke, B., Foegen, A., Marsh, L., Star, J. R., et al. (2009). *Assisting students struggling with mathematics: Response to intervention (RtI) for elementary and middle schools* (NCEE 2009-4060). Washington, DC: National Center for Education Evaluation and Regional Assistance, Institute of Education Sciences, U.S. Department of Education.

Gersten, R., Compton, D., Connor, C. M., Dimino, J., Santoro, L., Linan-Thompson, S., et al. (2008). *Assisting students struggling with reading: Response to intervention and multi-tier intervention for reading in the primary grades: A practice guide* (NCEE 2009-4045). Washington, DC: U.S. Department of Education, Institute of Education Sciences, National Center for Education Evaluation and Regional Assistance.

Gersten, R., Woodward, J., & Darch, C. (1986). Direct instruction: A research-based approach to curriculum design and teaching. *Exceptional Children, 53*(1), 17–31.

Gibbs, J. T., & Huang, L. N. (1998). A conceptual framework for assessing and treating minority youth. In J. T. Gibbs & L. N. Huang (Eds.), *Children of color: Psychological interventions with minority youth* (2nd ed., pp. 1–29). San Francisco: Jossey-Bass.

Glover, T. A., & Albers, C. A. (2007). Considerations for evaluating universal screening assessments. *Journal of School Psychology, 45*, 117–135.

Goldenberg, C. (2008). Teaching English language learners: What the research does—and does not—say. *American Educator 32*(2), 8–11, 14–19, 22–23, 42–43.

Goldenberg, C. (2010). Improving achievement for English learners: Conclusions from recent reviews and emerging research. In G. Li & P. A. Edwards (Eds.), *Best practices in ELL instruction* (pp. 15–43). New York: Guilford Press.

Good, R. H., Kame'enui, E. J., Simmons, D. S., & Chard, D. J. (2002). *Focus and nature of primary, secondary, and tertiary prevention: The CIRCUITS model* (Technical Report No. 1). Eugene: University of Oregon, College of Education, Institute for the Development of Educational Achievement.

Gopaul-McNicol, S., & Thomas-Presswood, T. (1998). *Working with linguistically and culturally different children: Innovative clinical and educational approaches.* Boston: Allyn & Bacon.

Gravois, T. A., & Nelson, D. (2014). Best practices in instructional assessment of writing. In P. Harrison & A. Thomas (Eds.), *Best practices in school psychology: Data-based and collaborative decision making* (pp. 203–217). Bethesda, MD: National Association of School Psychologists.

Griffin, A. J., Parsons, L., Burns, M. K., & VanDerHeyden, A. (2007). *Response to intervention research to practice.* Washington, DC: National Association of State Directors of Special Education.

Gutierrez, G., & Vanderwood, M. L. (2013). A growth curve analysis of literacy performance among second-grade, Spanish-speaking English-language learners. *School Psychology Review, 42*, 3–21.

Hamilton, L., Halverson, R., Jackson, S., Mandinach, E., Supovitz, J., & Wayman, J. (2009). *Using student achievement data to support instructional decision making* (NCEE 2009-4067). Washington, DC: National Center for Education Evaluation and Regional Assistance, Institute of Education Sciences, U.S. Department of Education.

Hamilton, C., & Shinn, M. R. (2003). Characteristics of word callers: An investigation of the accuracy or teachers' judgments of reading comprehension and oral reading skills. *School Psychology Review, 32*, 228–240.

Hamre, B., & Pianta, R. (2005). Can instructional and emotional support in the first grade classroom make a difference for children at risk of school failure? *Development, 76*(5), 3–16.

Harlow, C. (2003). *Education and correctional populations.* Washington, DC: U.S. Department of Justice, Bureau of Justice Statistics.

Harris, J. D., Gray, B. A., Davis, J. E., Zaremba, E. T., & Argulewicz, E. N. (1988). The exclusionary clause and the disadvantaged: Do we try to comply with the law? *Journal of Learning Disabilities, 21*, 581–583.

Hasbrouck, J., & Tindal, G. A. (2006). Oral reading fluency norms: A valuable assessment tool for reading teachers. *The Reading Teacher, 59*, 636–644.

Heartland Area Education Agency 11. (2002). *Improving children's educational results through data-based decision-making.* Johnston, IA: Author.

Hopf, A., & Martínez, R. S. (2006). Implementation of Instructional Level Assessment (ILA) within a Response to Intervention (RTI) model of service delivery. *School Psychologist, 60*(2), 75–78.

Hosp, M. K., Hosp, J. L., & Howell, K. W. (2007). *The ABCs of CBM: A practical guide to curriculum-based measurement.* New York: Guilford Press.

Ikeda, M. J., Neessen, E., & Witt, J. C. (2008). Best practices in universal screening. In A. Thomas & J. Grimes (Eds.), *Best practices in school psychology* (5th ed., pp. 103–114). Bethesda, MD: National Association of School Psychologists.

Ikeda, M. J., Tilly, W. D., Stumme, J., Volmer, L., & Allison, R. (1996). Agency-wide implementation of problem solving consultation: Foundation, current implementation, and future directions. *School Psychology Quarterly, 11*, 228–243.

Individuals with Disabilities Education Improvement Act of 2004, Public Law 108–446, 118 Stat. 2647 (codified at 20 U.S.C. § 1400 *et seq.*).

Jacob, S., & Hartshorne, T. S. (2003). *Ethics and law for school psychologists* (4th ed.). Hoboken, NJ: Wiley.

Jankowski, E. A., & Heartland Area Education Agency 11. (2003). Heartland Area Education Agency's problem solving model: An outcomes-driven special education program. *Rural Special Education Quarterly, 22*, 29–36.

Jiménez, R. T., García, G. E., & Pearson, P. D. (1996). The reading strategies of bilingual Latina/o students who are successful English readers: Opportunities and obstacles. *Reading Research Quarterly, 31*, 90–112.

Jimerson, S. R., Burns, M. K., & VanDerHeyden, A. M. (2007). Response to intervention at school: The science and practice of assessment and intervention. In S. R. Jimerson, M. K. Burns, & A. M. VanDerHeyden (Eds.), *Handbook of response to intervention: The science and practice of assessment and intervention* (pp. 3–9). New York: Springer.

Johnson, E., Semmelroth, C., Allison, J., & Fritsch, T. (2013). The technical properties of science content maze passages for middle school students. *Assessment for Effective Intervention, 38*, 214–223.

Joseph, L. M. (2006). Incremental rehearsal: A flashcard drill technique for increasing retention of reading words. *The Reading Teacher, 59*, 803–807.

Jung, L. A., & Grisham-Brown, J. L. (2006). Moving from assessment information to IFSPs: Guidelines for a family-centered process. *Young Exceptional Children, 9*(2), 2–11.

Kame'enui, E. J., & Simmons, D. C. (1999). *Toward successful inclusion of students with disabilities: The architecture of instruction: Vol. 1. An overview of materials adaptations*. Reston, VA: Council for Exceptional Children.

Kamil, M. L., Borman, G. D., Dole, J., Kral, C. C., Salinger, T., & Torgesen, J. (2008). *Improving adolescent literacy: Effective classroom and intervention practices: A Practice Guide* (NCEE 2008-4027). Washington, DC: National Center for Education Evaluation and Regional Assistance, Institute of Education Sciences, U.S. Department of Education.

Katsiyannis, A. (1990). Provision of related services: State practices and the issue of eligibility criteria. *Journal of Special Education, 24*, 246–252.

Kavale, K. A. (2005). Identifying specific learning disability: Is responsiveness to intervention the answer? *Journal of Learning Disabilities, 38*, 553–562.

Kazdin, A. E. (2010). *Single-case research designs: Methods for clinical and applied settings*. New York: Oxford University Press.

Keller-Allen, C. (2006). *English language learners with disabilities: Identification and other state policies and issues*. Alexandria, VA: Project Forum.

Kettler, R. J., Glover, T. A., Albers, C. A., & Feeney-Kettler, K. A. (Eds.). (2014). *Universal screening in educational settings: Evidence-based decision making for schools*. Washington, DC: American Psychological Association.

Kieffer, M. J. (2008). Catching up or falling behind?: Initial English proficiency, concentrated poverty, and the reading growth of language minority learners in the United States. *Journal of Educational Psychology, 100*, 851–868.

Klingner, J. K., Artiles, A. J., & Barletta, L. M. (2006). English language learners who struggle with reading: Language acquisition or LD? *Journal of Learning Disabilities, 39*, 108–128.

Klingner, J. K., & Geisler, D. (2008). Helping classroom reading teachers distinguish between language acquisition and learning disabilities. In J. K. Klingner, J. J. Hoover, & L. M. Baca (Eds.), *Why do English language learners struggle with reading?: Distinguishing language acquisition from learning disabilities* (pp. 57–73). Thousand Oaks, CA: Corwin Press.

Knight-Teague, K., Vanderwood, M. L., & Knight, E. (2014). Empirical investigation of word callers who are English learners. *School Psychology Review, 43*, 3–18.

Kopriva, R., & Albers, C. A. (2013). Considerations for testing students with special needs. In K. F. Geisinger (Ed.), *APA handbook of testing and assessment in psychology: Vol. 3. Testing and assessment in school psychology and education* (pp. 369–390). Washington, DC: American Psychological Association.

Kovaleski, J. F., Tucker, J. A., & Stevens, L. J. (1996). Bridging special and regular education: The Pennsylvania initiative. *Educational Leadership, 53,* 44–47.

Leafstedt, J. M., & Gerber, M. M. (2005). Crossover of phonological processing skills: A study of Spanish-speaking students in two instructional settings. *Remedial and Special Education, 26,* 226–235.

Lee, O., Quinn, H., & Valdes, G. (2013). Science and language for English language learners in relation to Next Generation Science Standards and with implications for Common Core State Standards for English language arts and mathematics. *Educational Researcher, 42,* 223–233.

Limbos, M., & Geva, E. (2002). Accuracy of teacher assessments of second-language students at risk for reading disability. *Journal of Learning Disabilities, 34,* 137–151.

Linan-Thompson, S., Vaughn, S., Prater, K., & Cirino, P. T. (2006). The response to intervention of English language learners at risk for reading problems. *Journal of Learning Disabilities, 39,* 390–398.

Lindholm-Leary, K., & Borsato, G. (2006). Academic achievement. In F. G. Genesee, K. Lindholm-Leary, W. M. Saunders, & D. Christian (Eds.), *Educating English language learners: A synthesis of research evidence* (pp. 176–222). New York: Cambridge University Press.

Lindholm-Leary, K., & Hernandez, A. (2011). Achievement and language proficiency of Latino students in dual language programs: Native English speakers, fluent English/previous ELLs, and current ELLs. *Journal of Multilingual and Multicultural Development, 32,* 531–545.

Linn, D., & Hemmer, L. (2011). English language learner disproportionality in special education: Implications for the scholar-practitioner. *Journal of Educational Research and Practice, 1*(1), 70–80.

Lopez, M. G., & Tashakkori, A. (2006). Differential outcomes of two bilingual education programs on English language learners. *Bilingual Research Journal, 30,* 123–145.

Lyon, G. R. (2005). Why scientific research must guide educational policy and instructional practices in learning disabilities. *Learning Disability Quarterly, 28,* 140–143.

Machek, G. R., & Nelson, J. M. (2007). How should reading disabilities be operationalized?: A survey of practicing school psychologists. *Learning Disabilities Research and Practice, 22,* 147–157.

Malecki, C. K. (2014). Best practices in written language assessment and intervention. In P. Harrison & A. Thomas (Eds.), *Best practices in school psychology: Data-based and collaborative decision making* (pp. 187–202). Bethesda, MD: National Association of School Psychologists.

Markham, P. L., & Gordon, K. E. (2007). Challenges and instructional approaches impacting the literacy performance of English language learners. *Multiple Voices for Ethnically Diverse Exceptional Learners, 10*(1/2), 73–81.

Marston, D., Muyskens, P., Lau, M., & Canter, A. (2003). Problem-solving model for decision making with high-incidence disabilities: The Minneapolis experience. *Learning Disabilities Research and Practice, 18*(3), 187–200.

Martinez, R. S. (2014). Best practices in instructional strategies for reading in general education. In P. Harrison & A. Thomas (Eds.), *Best practices in school psychology: Student level services* (pp. 9–17). Bethesda, MD: National Association of School Psychologists.

Martinez, R. S., Harris, B., & McClain, M. (2014). Practices that promote English reading for English learners (EL). *Journal of Educational and Psychological Consultation, 24,* 128–148.

Mathes, P. G., Pollard-Durodola, S. D., Cárdenas-Hagan, E., Linan-Thompson, S., & Vaughn, S. (2007). Teaching struggling readers who are native Spanish speakers: What do we know? *Language, Speech, and Hearing Services in Schools, 38,* 260–271.

Matson, S. C., & Haglund, K. (2000). Relationship between scholastic and health behaviors and reading level in adolescent females. *Clinical Pediatrics, 39*, 275–280.

McCardle, P., Mele-McCarthy, J., Cutting, L., Leos, K., & D'Emilio, T. (2005). Learning disabilities in English language learners: Identifying the issues. *Learning Disabilities Research and Practice, 20*, 1–5.

McCardle, P., Mele-McCarthy, J., & Leos, K. (2005). English language learners and learning disabilities: Research agenda and implications for practice. *Learning Disabilities Research and Practice, 20*, 68–78.

McConnell, S., Bradfield, T., & Wackerle-Hollman, A. (2014). Early childhood literacy screening. In R. J. Kettler, T. A. Glover, C. A. Albers, & K. A. Feeney-Kettler (Eds.). *Universal screening in educational settings: Evidence-based decision making for schools* (pp. 141–170). Washington, DC: American Psychological Association.

McCook, J. E. (2006). *The RTI guide: Developing and implementing a model in your schools.* Horsham, PA: LRP Publications.

McCurdy, M. M., Coutts, M. J., Sheridan, S. M., & Campbell, L. M. (2013). Ecological variables in school-based assessment and intervention planning. In R. Brown-Chidsey & K. J. Andren (Eds.), *Assessment for intervention: A problem-solving approach* (2nd ed., pp. 39–61). New York: Guilford Press.

McLoyd, V. (1998). Socioeconomic disadvantage and child development. *American Psychologist, 53*, 185–204.

Meisinger, E. B., Bradley, B. A., Schwanenflugel, P. J., Kuhn, M. R., & Morris, R. D. (2009). Myth and reality of the word caller: The relation between teacher nominations and prevalence among elementary school children. *School Psychology Quarterly, 24*, 147–159.

Meltzer, J., & Hamann, E. T. (2005). *Meeting the literacy development needs of adolescent English language learners through content area learning: II. Focus on classroom teaching and learning strategies.* Providence, RI: Education Alliance at Brown University.

Moats, L. C. (n.d.). *Whole-language high-jinks: How to tell when "scientifically-based reading instruction" isn't.* Washington, DC: Thomas B. Fordham Institute.

Moughamian, A. C., Rivera, M. O., & Francis, D. J. (2009). *Instructional models and strategies for teaching English language learners.* Portsmouth, NH: RMC Research Corporation, Center on Instruction.

Nakamoto, J., Lindsey, K. A., & Manis, F. R. (2007). A longitudinal analysis of English language learners' word decoding and reading comprehension. *Reading and Writing, 20*, 691–719.

National Clearinghouse for English Language Acquisition. (2011). *Orange County Department of Education: District Focus: California, School Year 2009–10.* Washington, DC: Author.

National High School Center. (2009). *Educating English language learners at the high school level: A coherent approach to district- and school-level support.* Washington, DC: American Institute for Research.

National Institute for Direct Instruction. (2011). About DI. Retrieved from *www.nifdi.org/what-is-di/basic-philosophy.*

National Institute of Child Health and Human Development (NICHD). (2000). *Report of the National Reading Panel: Teaching children to read: An evidence-based assessment of the scientific research literature on reading and its implications for reading instruction* (NIH Publication No. 00-4769). Washington, DC: U.S. Government Printing Office.

National Reading Panel. (2000). *Report of the National Reading Panel: Teaching children to read: An evidence-based assessment of the scientific research literature on reading and its implications for reading instruction: Reports of the subgroups.* Rockville, MD: NICHD Clearinghouse.

No Child Left Behind Act of 2001 [NCLB], Public Law No. 107-110, 115 Stat. 1425 (2002).

Office of English Language Acquisition, Language Enhancement, and Academic Achievement for

Limited English Proficient Students. (2013). *The Biennial Report to Congress on the Implementation of the Title III State Formula Grant Program: School Years 2008–10.* Washington, DC: Author.

Olson, R. K. (2004). SSR, environment, and genes. *Scientific Studies of Reading, 8,* 111–124.

Olvera, P., & Gómez-Cerrillo, L. (2014). Integrated intellectual assessment of the bilingual student. In A. B. Clinton (Ed.), *Assessing bilingual children in context: An integrated approach* (pp. 109–135). Washington, DC: American Psychological Association.

O'Neal, D. D., Ringler, M., & Rodriguez, D. (2008). Teachers' perceptions of their preparation for teaching linguistically and culturally diverse learners in rural eastern North Carolina. *Rural Educator, 30*(1), 5–13.

Orosoco, M. J., & Klinger, J. (2010). One school's implementation of RTI with English language learners: "Referring into RTI." *Journal of Learning Disabilities, 43,* 269–288.

Páez, D. (2004). *Culturally competent assessment of English language learners: Strategies for school personnel* (Helping Children at Home and School II: Handouts for Families and Educators). Bethesda, MD: National Association of School Psychologists.

Parisi, D. M., Ihlo, T., & Glover, T. A. (2014). Screening within a multitiered early prevention model: Using assessment to inform instruction and promote students' response to intervention. In R. J. Kettler, T. A. Glover, C. A. Albers, & K. A. Feeney-Kettler (Eds.), *Universal screening in educational settings: Evidence-based decision making for schools* (pp. 19–45). Washington, DC: American Psychological Association.

Peterson, D. W., Prasse, D. P., Shinn, M. R., & Swerdlik, M. E. (2007). The Illinois flexible service delivery model: A problem-solving model initiative. In S. R. Jimerson, M. K. Burns, & A. M. VanDerHeyden (Eds.), *Handbook of response to intervention: The science and practice of assessment and intervention* (pp. 300–318). New York: Springer.

Proctor, C. P., Carlo, M., August, D., & Snow, C. (2005). Native Spanish-speaking children reading in English: Toward a model of comprehension. *Journal of Educational Psychology, 97,* 246–256.

Quay, L. (2010). *Higher standards for all: Implications of the Common Core for Equity in Education.* Berkeley: The Chief Justice Earl Warren Institute on Race, Ethnicity, and Diversity.

Razfar, A. (2010). Repair with confianza: Rethinking the context of corrective feedback for English learners. *English Teaching: Practice and Critique, 9*(2), 11–31.

Reschly, D. J., & Bergstrom, M. K. (2009). Response to intervention. In T. B. Gutkin & C. R. Reynolds (Eds.), *The handbook of school psychology* (4th ed., pp. 434–460). Hoboken, NJ: Wiley.

Reschly, A. L., Busch, T. W., Betts, J., Deno, S. L., & Long, J. D. (2009). Curriculum-based measurement oral reading as an indicator of reading achievement: A meta-analysis of the correlational evidence. *Journal of School Psychology, 47,* 427–469.

Reschly, D. J., & Hosp, J. L. (2004). State SLD identification policies and practices. *Learning Disability Quarterly, 27,* 197–213.

Rhodes, R., Ochoa, S. H., & Ortiz, S. O. (2005). *Assessing culturally and linguistically diverse students: A practical guide* New York: Guilford Press.

Riley-Tillman, T. C., & Burns, M. K. (2009). *Evaluating educational interventions: Single-case design for measuring response to intervention.* New York: Guilford Press.

Roberts, B. (1998). "I No evrethENGe": What skills are essential in early literacy? In S. Neuman & K. Roskos (Eds.), *Children achieving: Best practices in early literacy* (pp. 38–55). Newark, DE: International Reading Association.

Rodriguez, J., & Carrasquillo, A. L. (1997). Hispanic limited English-proficient students with disabilities: A case study example. *Learning Disabilities, 8,* 167–174.

Roseberry-McKibbin, C., & O'Hanlon, L. (2005). Nonbiased assessment of English language learners: A tutorial. *Communication Disorders Quarterly, 26*(3), 178–185.

Rosenfield, S. (1987). *Instructional consultation.* Hillsdale, NJ: Erlbaum.

Rueda, R., & Windmueller, M. P. (2006). English language learners, LD, and overrepresentation: A multilevel analysis. *Journal of Learning Disabilities, 39*, 99–107.

Sáenz, L. M., Fuchs, L. S., & Fuchs, D. (2005). Peer-assisted learning strategies for English language learners with learning disabilities. *Exceptional Children, 71*, 231–247.

Salend, S. J., Garric Duhaney, L. M., & Montgomery, W. (2002). A comprehensive approach to identifying and addressing issues of disproportionate representation. *Remedial and Special Education, 23*, 289–299.

Sanetti, L. M., & Kratochwill, T. R. (2013). Treatment integrity assessment within a problem-solving model. In R. Brown-Chidsey & K. J. Andren (Eds.), *Assessment for intervention: A problem-solving approach* (2nd ed., pp. 297–320). New York: Guilford Press.

Sanetti, L. M., & Kratochwill, T. R. (Eds.). (2014). *Treatment integrity: A foundation for evidence-based practice in applied psychology*. Washington, DC: American Psychological Association.

Saunders, W. M. (1999). Improving literacy achievement for English learners in transitional bilingual programs. *Educational Research and Evaluation, 5*, 345–381.

Saunders, W. M., & Goldenberg, C. (1999). Effects of instructional conversations and literature logs on limited- and fluent-English-proficient students' story comprehension and thematic understanding. *Elementary School Journal, 99*, 277–301.

Shanahan, T., Callison, K., Carriere, C., Duke, N. K., Pearson, P. D., Schatschneider, C., et al. (2010). *Improving reading comprehension in kindergarten through 3rd grade: A practice guide* (NCEE 2010-4038). Washington, DC: National Center for Education Evaluation and Regional Assistance, Institute of Education Sciences, U.S. Department of Education.

Shanahan, T., & Shanahan, C. (2008). Teaching disciplinary literacy to adolescents: Rethinking content area literacy. *Harvard Educational Review, 78*, 40–59.

Shapiro, E. S. (2011). *Academic skills problems: Direct assessment and intervention* (4th ed.). New York: Guilford Press.

Shinn, M. (Ed.). (1998). *Advanced applications of curriculum-based measurement*. New York: Guilford Press.

Shinn, M. R. (2008). Best practices in using curriculum-based measurement in a problem-solving model. In A. Thomas & J. Grimes (Eds.), *Best practices in school psychology* (5th ed., pp. 243–261). Bethesda, MD: National Association of School Psychologists.

Siegler, R., Carpenter, T., Fennell, F., Geary, D., Lewis, J., Okamoto, Y., et al. (2010). *Developing effective fractions instruction for kindergarten through 8th grade: A practice guide* (NCEE 2010-4039). Washington, DC: National Center for Education Evaluation and Regional Assistance, Institute of Education Sciences, U.S. Department of Education.

Simmons, D. C., & Kame'enui, K. J. (2003). *A consumer's guide to evaluating a core reading program Grades K–3: A critical elements analysis*. Denver, CO: Education Commission of the States.

Sirin, S. R. (2005). Socioeconomic status and academic achievement: A meta-analytic review of research. *Review of Educational Research, 75*, 417–453.

Skiba, R. J., Poloni-Staudinger, L., Simmons, A. B., Feggins-Azziz, L. R., & Chung, C. (2005). Unproven links: Can poverty explain ethnic disproportionality in special education? *Journal of Special Education, 39*, 130–144.

Slavin, R. E., Chamberlain, A., & Daniels, C. (2007). Preventing reading failure. *Educational Leadership, 65*(2), 22–27.

Snow, C. E., Burns, M. S., & Griffin, P. (Eds.). (1998). *Preventing reading difficulties in young children*. Washington, DC: National Academy Press.

Snyder, T. D., & Dillow, S. A. (2013). *Digest of education statistics 2012*. (NCES 2014-015). Washington, DC: National Center for Education Statistics, Institute of Education Sciences, U.S. Department of Education.

Spaulding, S, Carolino, B., & Amen, K. (2004). *Immigrant students and secondary school reform: Compendium of best practices*. Washington, DC: Council of Chief State School Officers.

Speece, D., & Case, L. (2001). Classification in context: An alternative approach to identifying early reading disability. *Journal of Educational Psychology, 93*, 735–749.

Stanovich, K. E. (1986). Matthew effects in reading: Some consequences of individual differences in the acquisition of literacy. *Reading Research Quarterly, 21*, 360–407.

Stevens, F. (1993). *Opportunity to learn: Issues of equity for poor and minority students.* Washington, DC: National Center for Education Statistics.

Stewart, L. H. (2014). Best practices in developing academic local norms. In P. Harrison & A. Thomas (Eds.), *Best practices in school psychology: Foundations* (pp. 301–314). Bethesda, MD: National Association of School Psychologists.

Stormont, M., Reinke, W. M., Herman, K. C., & Lembke, E. S. (2012). *Academic and behavior supports for at-risk students: Tier 2 interventions.* New York: Guilford Press.

Strom, K. J. (2000). *Profile of state prisoners under age 18* (Bureau of Justice Statistics, NCJ 176989). Washington, DC: U.S. Department of Justice.

Telzrow, C. F., McNamara, K., & Hollinger, C. L. (2000). Fidelity of problem-solving implementation and relationship to student performance. *School Psychology Review, 29*, 443–461.

Thomas, W. P., & Collier, V. P. (1997). *School effectiveness for language minority students.* Washington, DC: National Clearinghouse for Bilingual Education.

Tilly, W. D. (2003, December). *Heartland Area Education Agency's evolution from four to three tiers: Our journey—our results.* Paper presented at the National Research Center on Learning Disabilities Responsiveness-to-Intervention Symposium, Kansas City, MO.

Tomlinson, C. A. (1999). *The differentiated classroom: Responding to the needs of all learners.* Alexandria, VA: Association for Supervision and Curriculum Development.

Torgesen, J. K., Houston, D. D., Rissman, L. M., Decker, S. M., Roberts, G., Vaughn, S., et al. (2007). *Academic literacy instruction for adolescents: A guidance document from the Center on Instruction.* Portsmouth, NH: RMC Research Corporation, Center on Instruction.

Tran, L., Sanchez, T., Arellano, B., & Swanson, H. L. (2011). A meta-analysis of the RTI literature for children at risk for reading disabilities. *Journal of Learning Disabilities, 44*, 283–295.

Uchikoshi, Y. (2005). Narrative development in bilingual kindergartners: Can Arthur help? *Developmental Psychology, 41*, 464–478.

U.S. Department of Education. (2006a). *WWC intervention report: Reading mastery.* Washington, DC: Institution of Education Sciences.

U.S. Department of Education. (2006b). *WWC intervention report: Instructional conversations and literature logs.* Washington, DC: Institution of Education Sciences.

U.S. Department of Education. (2006c). *WWC intervention report: The Vocabulary Improvement Program for English Language Learners and Their Classmates.* Washington, DC: Institution of Education Sciences.

U.S. Department of Education. (2007a). *WWC intervention report: Direct Instruction, DISTAR, and Language for Learning.* Washington, DC: Institution of Education Sciences.

U.S. Department of Education. (2007b). *WWC intervention report: Bilingual cooperative integrated reading and composition.* Washington, DC: Institution of Education Sciences.

U.S. Department of Education. (2009). *Schools and staffing survey: Public school, BIE school, and private school data files, 2007–08.* Washington, DC: National Center for Education Statistics.

U.S. Department of Education. (2010a). *WWC intervention report: Arthur.* Washington, DC: Institution of Education Sciences.

U.S. Department of Education. (2010b). *WWC intervention report: Peer assisted learning strategies.* Washington, DC: Institution of Education Sciences.

U.S. Department of Education. (2010c). *WWC intervention report: Read Well.* Washington, DC: Institution of Education Sciences.

U.S. Department of Education. (2011a). *The condition of education 2011* (NCES 2011-033). Washington, DC: Institute of Education Sciences, National Center for Education Statistics.

U.S. Department of Education. (2011b). *National assessment of educational progress.* Washington, DC: Institute of Education Sciences, National Center for Education Statistics.

U.S. Department of Education. (2012a). *Common Core of Data "Local Education Agency Universe Survey," 2002–03 through 2010–11.* Washington, DC: National Center for Education Statistics.

U.S. Department of Education. (2012b). *Common Core of Data "State Nonfiscal Survey of Public Elementary/Secondary Education" 1990–91 through 2010–11 and projections of education statistics to 2021.* Washington, DC: National Center for Education Statistics.

U.S. Department of Education. (2012c). *National evaluation of Title III implementation—report on state and local implementation.* Washington, DC: Office of Planning, Evaluation and Policy Development, Policy and Program Studies Service.

U.S. Department of Education. (2013, March). *Teacher shortage areas nationwide listing 1990–1991 through 2013–2014.* Washington, DC: U.S. Department of Education, Office of Postsecondary Education.

U.S. Department of Health and Human Services. (2001). *Mental health: Culture, race, and ethnicity—A supplement to Mental Health: A report of the Surgeon General.* Rockville, MD: Author.

VanDerHeyden, A. M., & Burns, M. K. (2010). *Essentials of response to intervention.* Hoboken, NJ: Wiley.

VanDerHeyden, A. M., Witt, J. C., & Gilbertson, D. (2007). A multi-year evaluation of the effects of a Response to Intervention (RTI) model on identification of children for special education. *Journal of School Psychology, 45,* 225–256.

Vaughn, S., & Fuchs, L. S. (2003). Redefining learning disabilities as inadequate response to instruction: The promise and potential problems. *Learning Disabilities Research and Practice, 18,* 137–146.

Vaughn, S., Linan-Thompson, S., & Hickman, P. (2003). Response to intervention as a means of identifying students with reading/learning disabilities. *Exceptional Children, 69,* 391–409.

Vaughn, S., Linan-Thompson, S., Mathes, P. G., Cirino, P. T., Carlson, C. D., Pollard-Durodola, S. D., et al. (2006). Effectiveness of Spanish intervention for first grade English language learners at risk for reading difficulties. *Journal of Learning Disabilities, 39,* 56–73.

Vaughn, S., Mathes, P. G., Linan-Thompson, S., & Francis, D. J. (2005). Teaching English language learners at risk for reading disabilities to read: Putting research into practice. *Learning Disabilities Research and Practice, 20,* 58–67.

Wagner, R. K., Francis, D. J., & Morris, R. D. (2005). Identifying English language learners with learning disabilities: Key challenges and possible approaches. *Learning Disabilities Research and Practice, 20,* 6–15.

Walker, A., Shafer, J., & Iams, M. (2004). Not in my classroom: Teacher attitudes toward English language learners in the mainstream classroom. *NABE Journal of Research and Practice, 2*(1), 130–160.

Walker, C. L., & Stone, K. (2011). Preparing teachers to reach English language learners: Pre-service and in-service initiatives. In T. Lucas (Ed.), *Teacher preparation for linguistically diverse classrooms* (pp. 127–142). New York: Taylor & Francis.

Walker, H. M., & Shinn, M. R. (2002). Structuring school-based interventions to achieve integrated primary, secondary, and tertiary prevention goals for safe and effective schools. In M. R. Shinn, H. M. Walker, & G. Stoner (Eds.), *Interventions for academic and behavior problems II: Preventative and remedial approaches* (pp. 1–25). Bethesda, MD: National Association of School Psychologists.

Wentzel, K., Battle, A., Russell, S., & Looney, L. (2010). Social supports from teachers and peers as predictors of academic and social motivation. *Contemporary Educational Psychology, 35,* 193–202.

Wiley, H. I., & Deno, S. L. (2005). Predictors of success for English language learners on a state standards assessment. *Remedial and Special Education, 26,* 207–214.

Wisconsin Department of Public Instruction. (2005). *Final report: Special education eligibility criteria study.* Madison, WI: Author.

Woodward, J., Beckmann, S., Driscoll, M., Franke, M., Herzig, P., Jitendra, A., et al. (2012). *Improving mathematical problem solving in grades 4 through 8: A practice guide* (NCEE 2012-4055). Washington, DC: National Center for Education Evaluation and Regional Assistance, Institute of Education Sciences, U.S. Department of Education.

World-Class Instruction Design and Assessment. (2007a). *English language proficiency standards—prekindergarten through grade 5.* Madison: University of Wisconsin–Madison.

World-Class Instruction Design and Assessment. (2007b). *English language proficiency standards—grade 6 through grade 12.* Madison: University of Wisconsin–Madison.

World-Class Instruction Design and Assessment. (2012a). *2012 amplification of the English language development standards, kindergarten–grade 12.* Madison: University of Wisconsin–Madison.

World-Class Instruction Design and Assessment. (2012b). *The English language learner can do booklet.* Madison: University of Wisconsin–Madison.

World-Class Instruction Design and Assessment. (2012c). *ACCESS for ELLs: Interpretive guide for score reports.* Madison: University of Wisconsin–Madison.

Xu, Y., & Drame, E. (2008). Culturally appropriate context: Unlocking the potential of response to intervention for English language learners. *Early Childhood Education Journal, 35,* 305–311.

Zannou, Y., Ketterlin-Geller, L. R., & Shivraj, P. (2014). Best practices in mathematics instruction and assessment in secondary settings. In P. Harrison & A. Thomas (Eds.), *Best practices in school psychology: Data-based and collaborative decision making* (pp. 233–246). Bethesda, MD: National Association of School Psychologists.

Zehler, A. M., Fleischman, H. L., Hopstock, P. J., Stephenson, T. G., Pendzick, M. L., & Sapru, S. (2003). *Descriptive study of services to LEP students and LEP students with disabilities* (Policy Report: Summary of Findings Related to LEP and SPED-LEP Students). Arlington, VA: Development Associates, Inc.

Zhang, D., & Katsiyannis, A. (2002). Minority representation in special education. *Remedial and Special Education, 23,* 180–188.

Index

Page numbers in italics indicate tables or figures.